Programming the Brain:
Educational Neuroscience
Perspective

Programming the Brain: Educational Neuroscience Perspective

PEDAGOGICAL PRACTICES AND STUDY SKILLS FOR ENHANCED LEARNING AND METACOGNITION

• • •

Chandana Watagodakumbura, PhD

ISBN: 1541040139
ISBN 13: 9781541040137
Library of Congress Control Number: 2016920788
CreateSpace Independent Publishing Platform
North Charleston, South Carolina

To
my parents,
Uncle Sudu and Aunt Stella,
my wife, Inoka, and our two daughters, Manushika and Methshika:
thank you for being inspirational
at different stages of my life.

Contents

Preface · xxi

Part I   Introduction to Neuroscience Facts and
            Concepts Related to Learning · 1

Chapter 1   Basic Facts, Structure, and Features of
            the Human Brain · 3
            Human Brain Facts · 3
            Physical Layers of the Human Brain · · · · · · · · · · · · · · 4
               Three Layers Based on the Time of Evolution · · · · · · · · 4
               Neocortex and Its Lobes · 5
               Limbic System · 9
               Anterior Cingulate Cortex (ACC) · · · · · · · · · · · · · · · 10
            Brain Lateralisation · 11
               Lateralisation versus Specialisation · · · · · · · · · · · · · · · 11
               The Need for a Balanced Use of Different
               Functions of Two Cerebral Hemispheres · · · · · · · · · · · 12
               Internal Physical Differences between Left and Right
               Hemispheres · 13
               Contemporary Education Systems' Bias towards
               Left-Hemispheric Orientation · · · · · · · · · · · · · · · · · · 14
            Brain Cells: Neurones · 15
            Memory and Related Structures in the Brain · · · · 17

Basic Types of Memory · 17
Short-Term Memory · 17
Long-Term Memory · 18
Procedural Memory and Automaticity · · · · · · · · · · · · 19
Some Other Interesting Brain Features · · · · · · · · 20
Neural Darwinism · 20
Novelty Seeking · 20
Storing Patterns · 21
Hierarchical Response · 22

**Chapter 2   Some Neuroscience Concepts That Explain
Learning Processes** · 25
Further Categorisation of Memory · · · · · · · · · · · · 26
Explicit and Implicit Memories · · · · · · · · · · · · · · · · 26
Episodic and Semantic Memories · · · · · · · · · · · · · · · 27
Working Memory and Its Impact on Learning · · · · · · 28
Defining Types of Learning · · · · · · · · · · · · · · · · · 29
Learning as Acquisition of Lasting Representations · · · 29
Explicit and Implicit Learning · · · · · · · · · · · · · · · · · 30
Phases of Learning · 30
Learning Voluntary Actions to the Level of Automaticity 32
Incidental or Implicit Learning · · · · · · · · · · · · · · · · 33
*Associative Recall and Recognition Tests as Means of
Evaluating Learning* · 34
Emotions and Learning · 35
Hebbian Learning · 36
Attention · 37
Attention as Directing Cognitive Resources · · · · · · · · 37
Selective Attention and Binocular Rivalry · · · · · · · · · 38
Consciousness · 39
Consciousness as a Traceable, Scientific Problem · · · · · 39
*Consciousness and Its Relationship to the Prefrontal
Cortex (PFC)* · 39

Consciousness and Its Association with a
Range of Contents · 40
The Integrated Theory of Consciousness · · · · · · · · · · · 40
Metacognition · 42
Metacognition as Thinking about Thinking or
Beyond Thinking · 42
Metacognition and an Analogy from the
Contemporary Business World · · · · · · · · · · · · · · · · · · 43
Metacognition and How It relates to Consciousness · · · · 43
Metacognition and How It Helps to Achieve
Neural Efficiency · 45
Metacognition and How It Relates to Mindfulness
Meditation · 45

Part II   **Commonly Used Learning-Related Concepts and**
Measures from the Viewpoint of Neuroscience · · · · · 49

Chapter 3   **Mostly Learning-Related Concepts from the**
Viewpoint of Educational Neuroscience · · · · · · · · · · · 51
Chunking · 52
Sense and Meaning · 53
Enabling Lasting Memories by Making
Sense and Meaning · 53
Processing Information in the Working Memory to
Make Sense and Meaning · 54
The Outcome When Sense and Meaning Are Not Made 54
Transfer · 55
Transfer as the Key to Problem Solving and
Creative Thinking · 55
Integrated Thematic Units to Enable Transfer · · · · · · · 56
Rehearsal · 57
Initial and Secondary Rehearsal · · · · · · · · · · · · · · · · · 57
Massed and Distributed Rehearsal · · · · · · · · · · · · · · · · 58

Rote and Elaborative Rehearsal · 59

Developing Metacognition as Part of Rehearsal · · · · · · 60

Wait Times · 61

Learner Motivation and Attention · · · · · · · · · · · · 62

Higher Level of Motivation Leading to Better Attention 62

Intrinsic and Extrinsic Motivation · · · · · · · · · · · · · · 63

Additional Motivational Factors · · · · · · · · · · · · · · · · 64

Enabling Positive Emotions as Motivators · · · · · · · · · · 65

Enabling Creative Thoughts as Motivators · · · · · · · · · 66

**Understanding the Focus on Concepts/Details
and Implicit Memories Created through
Incidental Learning** · 67

*Abstract/Generalised Concepts as Lasting
Semantic Memories* · 67

*Assessing High-Level Concepts Retained as Implicit
Memories through Incidental Learning* · · · · · · · · · · · 68

Types of Problem Solving or Decision Making · · · 69

Veridical and Adaptive Decision Making · · · · · · · · · · 69

*Contribution of Properties of the Situation and
Individuals in Decision Making* · · · · · · · · · · · · · · · · · 71

*Decision Making or Problem Solving in Science
Streams as a Creative Process* · · · · · · · · · · · · · · · · · · 72

**Differentiating Machines and Human Brains in
Regards to Learning** · 73

Selectionist and Instructionist Operations · · · · · · · · · · 73

*Machines as Mindless Devices Lacking
Metacognitive Abilities* · 74

*The Role of Prefrontal Cortex (PFC) in
Human/Creative Decision Making* · · · · · · · · · · · · · · 74

**Chapter 4   Some Learning-Related Measures: Intelligence,
Emotions, and Creativity from the Viewpoint of
Educational Neuroscience** · 77

Intelligence · 77
  What Is Intelligence? · 77
  Multiple Facets of Intelligence · · · · · · · · · · · · · · · · · 79
  Multiple Types of Intelligence and Brain Lateralisation/
  Specialisation · 80
  Developing Multiple Types of Intelligence and Human
  Development · 82
  Intelligence and Neural Efficiency · · · · · · · · · · · · · · · 82
  Intelligence and Dynamic Properties of the Cortex · · · · 83
Emotions · 84
  What Are Emotions? · 84
  Role of Emotions · 85
  Positive Emotions and Frontal Lobe Activation · · · · · · 86
  Emotions, Higher-Order Processing, and Long-Term
  Memory Formation · 87
  Empathy as an Important Emotion · · · · · · · · · · · · · · · 87
  Empathising and the Function of Mirror Neurones · · · 88
Creativity · 88
  What Is Creativity? · 88
  Differentiating "Big C" Creativity and
  "little c" creativity · 89
  Differentiating Creativity and Wisdom · · · · · · · · · · · · 90
  Creative Activities and Frontal Lobe Activation · · · · · · 91
  Creative Activities, Individuality and
  Self-Expression, and Minimisation of Inhibition or
  Self-Regulation · 92
  Teaching Creativity · 93

Chapter 5   Popular Learning Theories from the Viewpoint
             of Educational Neuroscience · · · · · · · · · · · · · · · · · · 95
  Kolb's Experiential Learning Cycle · · · · · · · · · · · · · 95
  Deep, Surface, and Strategic Learning · · · · · · · · · · 97
  Constructivist Theory of Learning · · · · · · · · · · · · · 99

Gifted Learner Characteristics/
Overexcitabilities · 100
What Does It Mean to Be Gifted? · · · · · · · · · · · · · · 100
Vulnerabilities of Gifted Individuals · · · · · · · · · · · · · 101
Auditory-Sequential and Visual-Spatial Learning
Preferences · 102
Left- and Right-Hemispheric Orientation of
Auditory-Sequential and Visual-Spatial Learners
Respectively · 102
Inclination of Visual-Spatial Learners to
Engage in Higher-Order Learning · · · · · · · · · · · · · 104
Bloom's Taxonomy and Its Applications from the
Viewpoint of Educational Neuroscience · · · · · · · · 104
Complexity Levels of Bloom's Taxonomy · · · · · · · · · · 104
Deductive and Inductive Reasoning and Brain
Lateralisation · 106
Convergent/Lower-Order and Divergent/
Higher-Order Thinking · 107
Bloom's Taxonomy in General from the Viewpoint of
Educational Neuroscience · · · · · · · · · · · · · · · · · · · 108
Higher-Order Learning and Frontal Lobe Activation 109
Use of the Constructivist Theory of Learning and
Targeting Upper Levels of Bloom's Taxonomy · · · · · · 110
Differentiating between Complexity and Difficulty
Levels of Bloom's Taxonomy · · · · · · · · · · · · · · · · · 111
Higher-Order Right-Brain Activities and Lower-
Order Left-Brain Activities · · · · · · · · · · · · · · · · · 112

Chapter 6 **Reflecting on the Goals of Education, Taking**
the Concepts of Educational Neuroscience into
Consideration · 116
Producing Better Problem Solvers and Decision
Makers as a Goal of Education · · · · · · · · · · · · · · · 116

What Does Better Decision Making or
Problem Solving Mean? · 116
Enhanced Consciousness and Better Decision Making
or Problem Solving · 117
Transfer of Learning and Better Decision Making or
Problem Solving · 118
Role of Metacognition in Decision Making or
Problem Solving · 119
Pursuing Human Development as a Goal of
Education · 120
Human Development to Higher Levels as a Lifelong
Learning Process · 120
Human Development and Physiological Changes in
Cerebral Cortex · 121
Human Development as Defined in Dabrowski's
Theory of Positive Disintegration (TPD) · · · · · · · · · · 121
Primary Integration as Defined by Dabrowski as a
Barrier to Human Development to Higher Levels · · · 122
Human Development as Defined in Maslow's
Theory of Self-Actualisation · · · · · · · · · · · · · · · · · 123
Self-Actualisation and Healthy and Sick Societies as
Presented by Maslow · 125
Human Development as Defined in Jung's Theory of
Analytical Psychology (Jungian Psychology) · · · · · · · 126
The Process of Individuation by Becoming Conscious
of the Shadow as Described in Jung's Theory of
Analytical Psychology · 128
Human Development as a Holistic Process as
Opposed to a One-Sided One · · · · · · · · · · · · · · · · 129
Transferring Explicit Learning to Implicit
Memories as a Goal of Education · · · · · · · · · · · · · 129
Transferring Implicit Learning to Explicit
Memories as a Goal of Education · · · · · · · · · · · · · 131

Becoming Fair to All Learners of a Neurodiverse
Society as a Goal of Education · · · · · · · · · · · · · · · · · 133

Part III   Useful Pedagogical Practices and Study
Skills from the Viewpoint of Neuroscience · · · · · · · · 137

Chapter 7   Delivering Learning Content Following the
Concepts of Educational Neuroscience · · · · · · · · · · · 139
Highlighting High-Level Concepts Ahead of
More Specific Details During a Teaching-Learning
Session · 139
*Highlighting High-Level Concepts to Make Use of
Limited-Capacity Working Memory Efficiently* · · · · · 140
*High-Level Concepts as Knowledge Crossing Multiple
Domains* · 141
*Relating High-Level Concepts to Individualised
Knowledge in Unique Ways* · · · · · · · · · · · · · · · · · · · 142
*Managing Session Time Effectively Only Highlighting
High-Level Concepts While Giving Details on
Need Basis* · 143
Asking Questions as a Means of Presenting
Following the Constructivist Theory of Learning · 144
Controlling the Pace of Presentation
Appropriately for Enabling Learners to
Construct Knowledge · 145
*Deciding the Pace of Presentation Considering the
Relative Slowness in Engaging the Frontal Lobes* · · · · 145
*Higher Wait Times as a Means of Ensuring
Higher-Order Learning* · 147
*Appropriate Pace of Delivery for Creating
Lasting Memories* · 147
Motivating Learners to Engage in Deeper Learning
by Giving Facts from Educational Neuroscience · 148

Intrinsic Motivation as a Means of Achieving a
Higher Level of Engagement · · · · · · · · · · · · · · · · · 148
Lasting Value of Learning to Develop a Higher Level of
Consciousness as the Motivator · · · · · · · · · · · · · · · · 149
Creating Positive Emotions as Means of Motivating · · 151
Getting Learner Attention Entirely on the
Teaching-Learning Process or Discussion · · · · · · · 151
Binocular Rivalry and the Need to Focus on
One Thing at a Time · 152
Minimising Harmful Anxiety and Divided Attention 152
Raising Helpful Anxiety to Get Learner Attention · · · 153

Chapter 8 **Assessing Learners Following the Concepts of**
Educational Neuroscience · 155
Forming Open-Ended Conceptual Questions
Minimising the Need for Rote Rehearsal and
Associative Recall · 156
To Direct and Encourage Learners to Provide Unique,
Individualised Answers · 156
Encouraging Learners to Provide Creative or
Higher-Order Answers, Even in Science Education · · 157
Deciding an Appropriate Time Duration with
Diligence for Assessments · · · · · · · · · · · · · · · · · · · 158
Assessing Higher-Order Learning and How
It Helps Form Lasting Semantic Memories · · · · · 159
Assessment Focusing the High End of Bloom's
Taxonomy · 159
Assessment Guiding Learners in Forming
Lasting Semantic Memories · · · · · · · · · · · · · · · · · 160
Designing Assessment Taking Constructivism and
Implicit Learning into Consideration · · · · · · · · · · 161
Taking into Consideration the Subjective Nature of
Knowledge in Assessment · · · · · · · · · · · · · · · · · · · 161

Taking into Consideration Implicit Learning in Assessment · 161

Accommodating Inclusiveness in Assessment · · · · · · · · 162

Designing Assessment Encouraging Adaptive Decision Making/Recognition Tests ahead of Veridical Decision Making/Associative Recall · · 163

Negative Implications of Multiple-Choice Questions Mostly Focusing on Testing Associative Recall · 165

Rethinking on the Time Factor in Assessments when Individualised, Unique Answers are Expected Utilising the Frontal Cortex Essentially Instead of Succumbing to Automaticity · 166

Constructing Assessments That Help Enhancing Learner Consciousness and Wisdom into a Higher Level of Human Development · · · · · · · · · · · · · · · · 168

Chapter 9   Curriculum Construction Following the Concepts of Educational Neuroscience · · · · · · · · · · · 171

Expectations of a Curriculum Based on Inputs from Educational Neuroscience · · · · · · · · · · · · · · · 171

Deciding the Contents or Topics to Be Included within a Curriculum · · · · · · · · · · · · · · · 173

What Contents or Topics Need to Be Included and Where to Find Them? · 173

Giving Consideration to the Limited Time Duration Available for Carrying out the Curriculum · · · · · · · 174

A Curriculum as a Means of Generating Positive Reminiscences towards a Path of Lifelong Learning · 175

Deciding and Designing the Learning Material or Documents That Are Made Available to Learners · 176

*What Should We Include in Teaching-Learning
Materials or Aids We Provide, and What Is the
Purpose of It, Per Se?* · 176
*Structure and Organisation of Teaching-
Learning Materials or Aids Provided* · · · · · · · · · · · 177
**Deciding and Designing Diverse Assessment
Components of a Curriculum** · · · · · · · · · · · · · · · · 178
Deciding on the Type of Assessment · · · · · · · · · · · · · 178
Deciding on the Number of Assessments in a Curriculum 178
Deciding on the Coverage of Assessment · · · · · · · · · · · 179
**Deciding on Having a Balance Between the Theory
and Practical Components (if Applicable) of a
Curriculum** · 180
**Provision of Additional Learning Activities to
Support Enhanced Learning** · · · · · · · · · · · · · · · · 181

**Chapter 10 Advising Learners on Study Skills Following the
Concepts of Educational Neuroscience** · · · · · · · · · · · 183
**General Educational Neuroscience Facts That
Motivate and Enhance Learning** · · · · · · · · · · · · · 183
Value of Learning and in Pursuit of Lifelong Learning ·183
*Getting Motivated to Learn Contents That
Appear to Be Difficult* · 184
*Be Open-Minded and Unafraid of the Large Volumes
of Data, Information, and Knowledge We Receive* · · · 185
*Develop an Understanding of Personality Traits
Based on Our Neurological Bias, and Be Bold in
Accepting Who You Are* · 186
*Understand and Appreciate That We Are Better
at Adaptive Decision Making as Human Beings
(as Opposed to Veridical Decision Making); Be
Prepared to Face Ambiguity and Complexity* · · · · · · 187

Be Willing to Accept the Status Quo That Achieving
Human Development Does Not Always Translate
into Achieving Economic Development · · · · · · · · · · · 189
**Encourage Learners to Develop a Clear
Understanding of What Learning and Education
Are All About and Engage in Metacognitive
Practices Regularly** · 190
**Useful Facts Related to Enhancing
Learning in a Formal Learning or Education
Environment** · 191
Before a Teaching-Learning Session · · · · · · · · · · · · 191
During a Teaching-Learning Session · · · · · · · · · · · · 191
After a Teaching-Learning Session · · · · · · · · · · · · 193

Final Words · 197
**Comprehending Learning and Education in a
Deeper Sense** · **197**
**The Essential Need to Focus on Higher-Order
Learning** · 198
**Fostering Creative and Novelty-Seeking
Instincts of the Human Brain** · · · · · · · · · · · · · · · 198
**Emphasising Human Development as a Main
Goal of Education and Learning** · · · · · · · · · · · · · 199
**Lifelong Learning as an Essential
Component of Individual Well-Being** · · · · · · · · · 200
**The Importance of Balancing Economic
Development and Human Development** · · · · · · · 201
**Meaningful Learning Essentially as an
Interdisciplinary Phenomenon** · · · · · · · · · · · · · 204
**The Essential Need to Develop Reflective and
Metacognitive Capacities** · · · · · · · · · · · · · · · · · 204
**The Need to Develop Inclusive and Fairer
Educational Systems** · 205

Consciousness and an Analogy from the
Technology Space—Big Data · · · · · · · · · · · · · · · 206
Developing Empathy, Tolerance, Resilience,
and Humility through Human Development
as Essential Qualities of Interpersonal and
Intrapersonal Intelligence · · · · · · · · · · · · · · · · · 207
Identifying Limitations of Current Learning,
Education, and Social Systems with the
Intention of Overcoming Them · · · · · · · · · · · · · 208
References · 211
Index · 235

Preface

• • •

LEARNERS AND EDUCATORS WHO REFLECT beyond the ordinary level we succumb to are constantly intrigued by the contemplation of the purpose of education or learning. Some will have no hesitation in concluding, though in a conventional manner, that it is all about finding employment, especially a more lucrative one. Some others may look beyond this constrained view in search of a more meaningful, lasting value. This latter group has come to a realisation that finding employment—no matter how lucrative—does not necessarily bring satisfaction, contentment, or mental and physical well-being. They pursue extended learning or education to develop a healthy lifestyle, enhance their mental well-being, and be content. What benefits would a healthy lifestyle, including mental well-being, bring us? The purpose of this book is to investigate the complex question of the purpose of education or learning from the emerging and critical viewpoint of educational neuroscience. The target audience of the book is mainly educators, adult learners, and other curious individuals who seek to know what learning and education are all about in a deeper sense or evidence-based manner.

The term *neuroscience* is perhaps not new to many of us; it is the area of study in which we learn how the brain and neural system are structured and work. As you may know, the human brain is a wondrous organ that controls our operations, including thinking. As expected, in the emerging field of educational neuroscience, we attempt to understand human learning from the new viewpoint of neuroscience. We get to clarify how learning is related to brain structures and its growth and enhancement. Yes, we see a physical growth of brain structures or neural networks taking place due to learning; learning is not merely a logical phenomenon as we may have assumed in the past. Educational neuroscience brings some interesting revelations in understanding learning in a deeper sense. In fact, the evolution of the human species is a direct consequence of how the brain and neural system evolved over the years. Scientists have put forth the idea that the enhanced consciousness that results in the development of the brain (or more specifically, to the growth of the frontal lobes) is the pinnacle of human evolution. Now that neuroscientists have revealed some important facts about our brains and neural systems, isn't it time we consider them seriously—and rely on them to engage in enhanced learning to direct us to the next spiral of human evolution?

This book is a product of my grappling with contemporary educational systems for nearly thirty years as both a learner and an educator. As a highly reflective learner and education practitioner since my teenage years, I have continuously looked for answers to some deep-seated questions. What does education truly mean? Has it a lasting meaning beyond passing examinations? Is education leading us only to find employment and develop lucrative careers, or does it also seek to develop good citizenship skills as well? More specifically, is it all about finding work in an industrial and technological world, playing second fiddle to machines, and disregarding the fact that we are primarily human beings with states of mind? How do you reliably measure academic success or achievement? Is it intrinsic or extrinsic by nature, or is it dependent on the environment in which it is measured? Is learning defined as the ability to reproduce what the teacher said in its exact form in the examination, or is it about generating your own valid and useful ideas? If learners are to produce accurate creative or idiosyncratic answers, how should we compare and judge that one is better than the other? What is the basis to do that? Do the outcomes of assessments or examinations always reflect a learner's real potential as a human being? If not, is it a fault of the learner for nonconformance or the system for being narrow in scope? What do the numeric percentage values we award (commonly as part of evaluations for various assessments) truly indicate? Can we be so precise to the level of one percentage point and get a real meaning? Do assessments have to be time constrained? Does producing a quick answer demonstrate a higher ability, or is it better to take a more time to produce a more optimal solution? What does *intelligence* mean? Is speed an essential part of the measure of intelligence? What does *creativity* mean, and should it be part of any learner's assessment? Further, can an inappropriate assessment demoralise a learner, possibly for the rest of his or her life, to the point that he or she adopts a self-image of being useless? Is competition among learners essential for motivating them to engage in learning appropriately? Are emotions and sensitivities of individuals related to learning? If so, how? What does giftedness mean, and in what common ways are gifted learners deemed vulnerable? How do learning and abilities relate to mental illness, as in the famous case of American Nobel Prize-winning mathematician John Nash? How do we compare and evaluate two teaching-learning environments meaningfully in an evidence-based or scientific manner? Do we have a reference system of education to get guided?

If you take a deep breath to reflect without being robotic, the list will go on; you may even be better off by not reflecting and getting yourself confused. However, remember that metacognitive practices of developing self-awareness through reflection help us to embark on a path of self-improvement and growth, and that can lead to sustainable societies.

I would like to put forth the following caveat for readers: *We do not blindly expect all learners or educators to embrace the findings or evidence reaching us from the field of educational neuroscience.* For some individuals and groups, there is a high level of resistance to rely on the findings of neuroscience for the purpose of getting guided on learning and education. For them, it may be that neuroscience is still an emerging field; as such, the results may not be convincing enough to be applied to a primarily and conventionally social-science discipline of learning or education. My point is that we are not going to find solutions to all of our existing problems in learning or education overnight by magically embracing educational neuroscience. However, this work seeks to emphasise important additional perspectives through which we might view learning or education. In fact, it is too important to neglect the useful concepts and notions that have emerged over the last few decades, especially from a field that describes human features, nature, and evolution so compellingly. The concepts or notions that have emerged are not always entirely foreign to us; rather, they validate (or at times, invalidate) some of our previously held beliefs. At other times, they have presented notions in a more confirming way. Some relevant examples can be found within the work done by Abraham Maslow, Kazimierz Dabrowski, John Dewey, and Carl Jung; their prophetic ideas are reaffirmed through the current work of neuroscience. After all, as human beings, shouldn't we first pursue the practices that are sustainable for human evolution, so that we may progress to the next level above? Aren't we tired of the status quo, one that mostly lacks hope for the survival of the human species?

I would like to add a word about how the title of the book—*Programming the Brain: Educational Neuroscience Perspective: Pedagogical Practices and Study Skills for Enhanced Learning and Metacognition*—came to be. I have a background in computer programming and have completed a couple of related postgraduate degrees including a PhD. I have observed how we can get certain things done from conventional computers by giving written instructions to them. We have to provide these instructions to computers in a very strict manner, so as not to confuse the machine. Once correctly instructed, they perform the specified tasks precisely and in a straightforward way. After nearly twenty years as a teacher in higher education, I was compelled to investigate how learning occurs. It occurred to me that we do a kind of "programming" of the brains of our learners, essentially with their help, similar to the methods we use to program computers. We use the term *programming* to describe the process of performing sequential activities in a methodical way. Even though programming a human brain is a complex task, we can identify important measures that can be followed in a methodical way, as opposed to doing things in a haphazard manner. The effort to properly program a human brain can take a lifetime, and a good knowledge of educational neuroscience would help this endeavour immensely. Further, this programming exercise can be undertaken by learners on their own, or they may get some assistance from time to time. The desired outcome of this programming task is the development of human mind, as you would agree.

This book is organised into three main parts.

The first part introduces learners to basic facts and concepts of neuroscience as they are related to learning, presenting the structure and functions of the human brain and neural system. Once the appropriate background knowledge has been introduced, readers will be better equipped to follow the other two parts of the book more comfortably.

In part two, we look at learning-related concepts from the viewpoint of educational neuroscience. For example, in one chapter in this section, we elaborate on some widely used learning theories by going through them from the perspective of educational neuroscience. In another, we dive into some learning-related measures, namely intelligence, emotions, and creativity.

Finally, in part three, we discuss some widely used pedagogical practices and study skills from an educational neuroscience viewpoint. These pedagogical practices include facilitating teaching-learning sessions, constructing assessment, and curriculum design.

Readers may note that references were mainly provided for the extensive fundamental knowledge provided in parts one and two. In part three, we discuss how the theoretical knowledge introduced previously can be applied in more practical teaching-learning environments by both teachers as well as learners. Consequently, readers may find some summarised fundamental knowledge being repetitively highlighted while presenting practical applications in part three.

Chandana Watagodakumbura
Melbourne, Australia
December 2016

PART I

Introduction to Neuroscience Facts and Concepts Related to Learning

• • •

CHAPTER 1

Basic Facts, Structure, and Features of the Human Brain

• • •

To HELP READERS TO BETTER understand subsequent chapters, we start by introducing them to some basic information about the physical structure and distinctive features of the human brain. In its current form, the human brain is the outcome of millions of years of evolution. As such, it is interesting to find out how those highly evolved structures and features help us in learning en route to higher levels of human development or self-actualisation. In this chapter, we first pay attention to how physical layers of the brain were developed at different time periods of human evolution, as well as the interesting functional differences in externally symmetric cerebral hemispheres and the building blocks of the brain or neural system. One of the essential functions of forming memories as lasting representations and memory-related supporting structures are presented next, before highlighting some exciting features such as neural Darwinism and the novelty-seeking nature of the brain in the end.

HUMAN BRAIN FACTS

The human brain is an amazing structure with infinite capabilities; some scientists even refer to it as the most powerful force on Earth (Sousa 2011). An adult human brain is a walnut-shaped organ of about 1,100 to 1,300 cubic centimetres of volume, with a weight of around 1,300 to 1,440 grams. In other words, it is about the size of a small grapefruit and can fit in your palm. Even though the brain is only about 2 percent of the body weight, it consumes about 20 percent of our energy, giving an indication of its power. It is located at the top of the spinal cord and cradled in the skull by surrounding protective membranes.

PHYSICAL LAYERS OF THE HUMAN BRAIN

THREE LAYERS BASED ON THE TIME OF EVOLUTION

Based on the time of development, there are three layers of the brain: the *reptilian brain*, the *mammalian brain*, and the *neocortex* (MacLean 1967; Baars and Gage 2010).

The reptilian brain, situated at the bottom, is the oldest layer of the brain; it is composed of the brain stem, the structures that dominate in the brains of snakes and lizards. This part of the brain controls survival activities such as breathing, heart rate, and balance.

The mammalian brain is layered over the reptilian brain and consists of a system of brain parts referred to as the limbic system. On the whole, the limbic system plays a significant role in human emotions and is informally referred to as the "emotional brain."

The third layer of the brain is the neocortex or primate brain. Located at the top, it is the most recent addition to our brain (evolutionarily). It consists of the wrinkled covering of cerebral hemispheres (the left and the right). The neocortex plays a significant role in cognitive, linguistic, motor, sensory, and social abilities. It gives considerable flexibility in creativity via adaptation to changing environments. We can see that through evolution, the human brain moved from only having initial survival capabilities (breathing and heart rate) in the reptilian brain to have more human features (linguistic, social, and creative abilities) supported by the neocortex. The mammalian brain or the limbic system, the second central layer to evolve, signifies the role emotions such as fear and pleasure play in human operations. The neocortex is densely interconnected with the limbic system and gives human beings the capacity to control the expression of emotions. Making use of the connectivity in the opposite direction, sensations such as pleasure, motivation, and fear are used to guide human cognitive actions and behaviour. Throughout this book, we highlight this structural interconnectivity of brain organs and regions that support its holistic operation as an integral unit, as opposed to the functioning of a disconnected and individual set of organs.

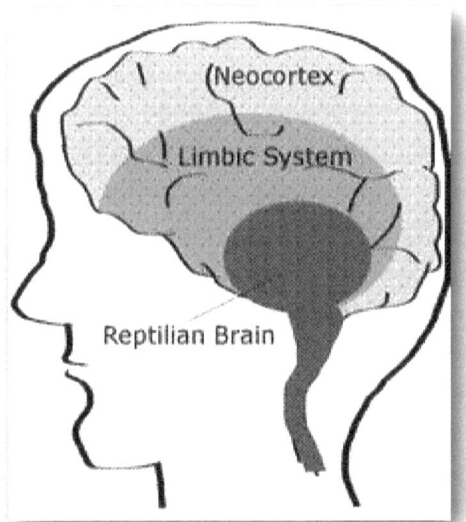

Three Layers of the Brain Based on the Time of Evolution

NEOCORTEX AND ITS LOBES

The neocortex, the outer layer of the brain, has four major lobes: the frontal lobe, parietal lobe, temporal lobe, and occipital lobe (Baars and Gage 2010). One significant feature of the brain structure is its functional localisation. That is, the brain is composed of a vast number of functionally specialised regions (Luria 1976; Geschwind 1979; Edelman and

Mountcastle 1978). There are about one hundred Brodmann areas, so to speak, now recognised in the neocortex. For example, the speech-related region found in the left hemisphere is called Broca's area; it helps language production. It is located in the left frontal lobe that is known as the language region (Aminoff and Daroff 2003). Another example is Wernicke's area, which is specialised for processing receptive language and is located in the left upper part of the temporal lobe. (However, it is interesting to note that the right side of the brain is believed to be sensitive to emotional content of language—such as humour and irony—that have more complex and integrated meaning.)

Further, the sensory or input regions of the neocortex (visual cortex, auditory cortex, and somatosensory cortex) are located in the posterior lobes (the parietal, temporal, and occipital lobes). This back-of-the-brain large region encompassing three cortical lobes is also the part of the neocortex for associative processes where information from various senses is integrated together for higher-order processing. More specifically, the parietal lobe does multisensory integration and has also evolved much larger in humans than other primates, similar to the prefrontal cortex (PFC). The temporal lobe is not only the sound- and language-processing region, it also contains conceptual representations for semantic knowledge. (We'll discuss semantic memory later in chapter 2.) We see a significant function of the human brain—the development of the capacity to integrate information that enables more meaningful, deeper understanding of information. In effect, we may infer that, through evolution, human beings developed the capacity to be wiser by seeing things in integrated, multi-dimensional perspectives. We will discuss further how the phenomena of wisdom and consciousness relate to the integration of information from multiple brain regions later.

The motor or output regions of the neocortex are located in the frontal lobe. The motor cortex works with the cerebellum to coordinate learning of motor skills. The PFC is the nonmotor part of the frontal cortex, and it is perhaps the most distinctively cognitive part of the brain. The PFC is specifically needed for functions such as initiating activities, planning, working memory, changing one's mental set from one line of thinking to another, monitoring the effectiveness of one's actions, detecting and resolving conflicting plans for action, inhibiting plans and actions that are ineffective or self-defeating, social cognition (how to behave), verbal expression of language, and regulating excesses of emotional systems. Considering these higher-order capabilities of the PFC, we will highlight later how significant it is for educators to stimulate the PFC of learners in the pursuit of enhanced learning. For achieving this objective, educators are required to use appropriate instructional techniques, as we will explore later.

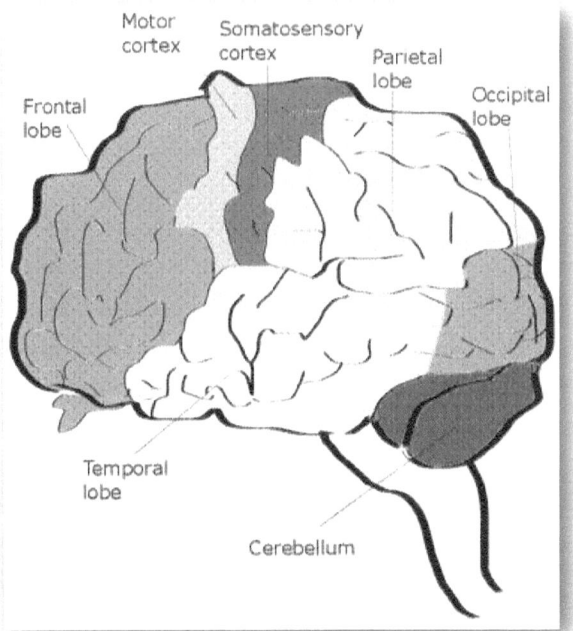

Four Major Lobes and Other Parts of the Neocortex plus the Cerebellum

It is of particular interest to understand that the frontal lobe is referred to as the "organ of civilisation." The role the frontal lobes play in cognition is uniquely human, and without their development, civilisation could never have arisen (Fuster 1997; Goldberg 2001; Ingvar 1985; Luria 1966). A correlation has also been identified between frontal activation and longer reaction time and a sense of subjective or unique effort. In summary, the frontal lobe (or more specifically the PFC) is used for human activities such as language, thought, and executive control of higher-order processes. It connects directly with every distinct functional unit of the brain (Nauta 1972). This connectivity allows the PFC to coordinate and integrate the functions of other brain structures. We get to see again the significance of the role played by integration of the neural networks of knowledge that provide deeper understanding and representation for developing human evolution and civilisation. Further, the PFC matures slowly into early adulthood, indicating possible significant improvements and changes individuals can have in attitudes and decision making up until the age of twenty years or so. Consequently, it is imperative that children and teenagers are given proper attention, guidance, and supervision by mature adults in their decision-making activities.

It is worth noticing that while the posterior half of the neocortex deals with the perceptual present, the anterior half tries to predict and control the future. However, all four lobes of the neocortex and their processes are intricately intertwined with each other. As a result, educators have to get our learners to relate the perceived senses/information to other stored information in the other parts of the brain. This task necessarily requires making use of the anterior half so that this integrated information will be useful in future. To reiterate: getting learners to reproduce the sensed information as is ("rote learning") is not sufficient. Further, the neocortex, which is vital for cognitive functions, interacts constantly with major so-called satellite organs of the subcortex such as the thalamus, basal ganglia, cerebellum, hippocampus, and whole limbic region in the massively interconnected brain. The use of the term "satellite organs" indicates that these organs act as communication hubs that exchange neural signals across various brain regions. In fact, thalami (the plural of thalamus) are great traffic hubs of the brain. They connect different cortical areas, and there are significant cortico-thalamo-cortical circuits that have been shown to play a role in attentional processing and other higher-order cognitive functions. What is interesting to note is that brain's ability to integrate diverse information received from different regions into a more meaningful whole. We will introduce later the phenomenon referred to as consciousness essentially as an integrative process, one that neuroscientists describe as the expression of the highest level of human evolution.

LIMBIC SYSTEM

It is worth noting that the limbic system (the "emotional brain") evolved before the neocortex, which supports higher-order operations. If we go by the stage or time of evolution of the emotional brain, we can understand the important role emotions play as drivers of behaviour as an essential need in human operations. Contrary to the understanding held years ago that emotions play a subordinate role to cognition, we now have evidence that emotions, in fact, *guide* our cognitive operations; emotions motivate us to engage in certain cognitive tasks while guiding us to refrain from some others (Sylwester 1998). Further, extensive structural connectivity between the limbic system and the neocortex enables them to operate as a united whole, integrating their different functions (Zull 2002, 2011). The main constituents of the limbic system include the amygdala, hippocampus, and hypothalamus. The hippocampus plays a significant role in consolidating learning by converting information from short-term memory to long-term storage; this may take days to months (Baars and Gage 2010). The amygdala is believed to encode emotional messages for long-term storage. We see here again the important role emotions and the limbic system play in learning or forming lasting memories on this occasion. While we as a society generally dislike seeing its members reacting emotionally (and especially excessively), it is worth understanding the potential benefits of properly guided emotions and learning how to use them appropriately. (We will explore this later in the section on metacognition.) On the whole, especially at workplaces, we prefer to interact with emotionless robots rather than with highly sensitive, overreacting individuals, to achieve naively defined production or profit targets. Later, and on a similar note, we will discuss how individuals identified as gifted learners can be directed to manage and benefit from their higher emotional vulnerability through metacognitive practices.

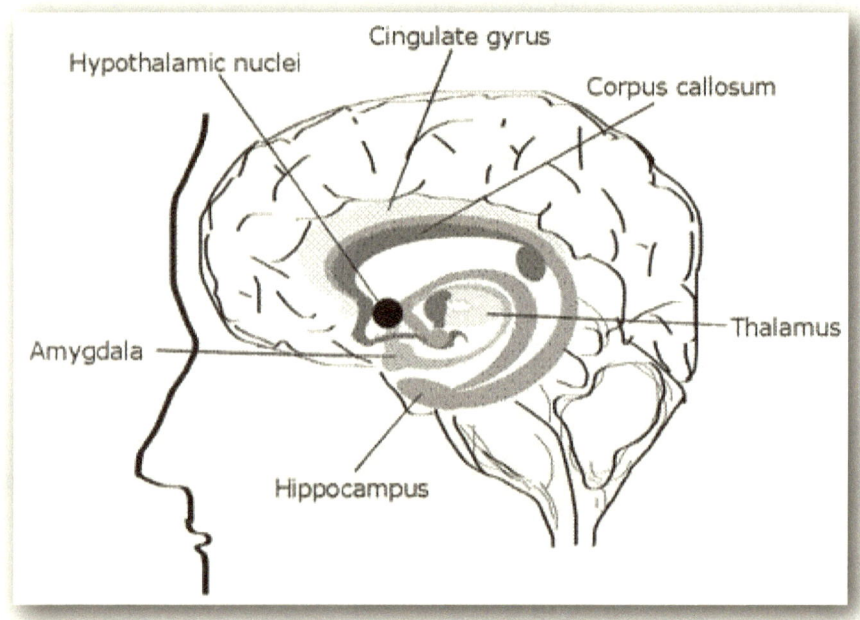

Limbic System (cross section)

ANTERIOR CINGULATE CORTEX (ACC)

The ACC is an evolutionarily new specialisation of the neocortex and is located at the boundary of the limbic cortex and the frontal lobe. It is specifically highlighted here because of the significant role it plays in establishing the bridge between the cognitive and emotion parts of the brain. The functions it performs include emotional self-control, focused problem solving, error recognition, and adaptive responses to changing conditions. The ACC contains special spindle-shaped neurones that are only found in human beings and great apes. These cells, which are relatively longer than other neurones, appear to connect to diverse parts of the brain, including the emotion parts. As a result, they perform an essential coordination or integration role in solving different problems. Further, spindle cells emerge postnatally, and their survival may be enhanced or reduced by environmental conditions of enrichment or stress. Consequently, these environmental conditions may influence adult competence or dysfunction in self-control and problem solving (Zull 2011; Allman 2001). In other words, the ACC is considered as the area of metacognition in the brain, as the linkage of emotions to cognition itself is a powerful, integrative aspect of the metacognitive process, which we will elaborate upon later in the text.

Brain Lateralisation

Lateralisation versus Specialisation

The ability of certain areas of the brain to perform unique functions is known as cerebral specialisation, as we have discussed under brain localisation previously. If the specialised activity is mainly limited to one whole hemisphere, it is called *cerebral lateralisation* (Sousa 2011). Naturally, we tend to think that any two symmetrical organs (such as eyes) would operate identically by providing redundant services and compensating if one becomes weaker. However, research studies show that the right and left hemispheres of the brain have distinctly different functions that are not readily interchangeable (Sperry 1966). The left-hemisphere processes input in a sequential and analytical manner; is time sensitive; generates spoken language; does arithmetic operations (repetitive ones, not mathematical operations or modelling); recognises words and numbers (as words); is active in constructing false memories; and is better at arousing attention to deal with outside stimuli.

The right hemisphere processes input more holistically and abstractly; is space sensitive; interprets language through gestures, facial movements, emotions, and body language; does relational and mathematical operations; recognises faces, places, objects, and music; is more truthful in recall; puts events in spatial patterns; is better in internal processing; gathers information more from images than from words; and looks for visual patterns (Gazzaniga 1998a, 1998b; Gazzaniga, Ivry, and Mangun 2002; Semenza et al. 2006; Sweeney 2009). If you go through these sets of functions performed by each of the hemispheres, we can make some useful meanings or inferences. The left hemisphere plays emphasis on sequential operations by possibly processing a limited set of relatively new information.

For example, in analytical operations, we may go into more detail in a convergent manner within the existing context or framework itself. We may become active in false memories because we do not access and integrate more confirming diverse information adequately. We may seek outside stimuli more specifically as we do not access adequate information internally and integrate them. On the other hand, the right hemisphere is inclined to perform parallel operations by possibly processing relatively a large quantity of new information. For example, information can be processed holistically and abstractly when we have access to large volumes of new data/information simultaneously or in parallel; this large amount of new data/information/knowledge can then be generalised to form abstract concepts. We may interpret language through gestures, facial movements, emotions, and body language as we get to access and process relatively large volumes of new information/data in a parallel or simultaneous manner. We can be more truthful in recall, as we have processed and stored large quantities of related information and can access them in parallel and simultaneous manner when required.

The Need for a Balanced Use of Different Functions of Two Cerebral Hemispheres

We have two cerebral hemispheres that perform two significantly different but useful sets of functions, depending on the situations we are experiencing.

The left hemisphere is sensitive to time and sequencing and may help to produce less complex outputs by processing relatively small volumes of new data/information in a time-sensitive manner. The right hemisphere, on the other hand, will endeavour to produce more optimal and comprehensive outputs by processing larger volumes of new data/information while disregarding the timing factor. The challenge then for educational designers is to develop a curriculum to encourage learners to have a balanced use of the two hemispheres so that they may produce relatively comprehensive and complete outputs in a time-sensitive manner as well.

Further, it is important for learners to be aware of the existence of two such significantly different approaches or outputs depending on a more preferred hemispheric use, as well as the need to have a trade-off in many real-life situations. In effect, individuals should learn to avoid any bias towards one extreme set of activities, disregarding the existence of another perspective altogether. The most important question, however, is not about the existence of two significantly different set of functions for the two hemispheres. Instead, it is what if an arbitrary individual—for some reason or through a natural bias—*prefers* to use the functionality of one hemisphere ahead of the other on a regular basis in a comprehensive manner? Will this define two significantly different personality characteristics for an individual, depending on which hemisphere he or she prefers to use predominantly (Silverman 2002)? Will such personality characteristics have a significant impact on an individual's operational efficiency as a member of society? More importantly, from the perspective of this text, will the predominant use of one cerebral hemisphere over the other have an impact on the way an individual learns? We will extend this discussion further from diverse viewpoints throughout this text.

INTERNAL PHYSICAL DIFFERENCES BETWEEN LEFT AND RIGHT HEMISPHERES

As we would expect, the left and right hemispheres are found to be physically different internally, even though they appear to be identical externally. The left hemisphere is found to have more grey matter, so to speak, while the right hemisphere has more white matter (Sousa 2011). The grey matter is comprised of relatively shorter branches of a neurone, known as dendrites, that connect to other neurones; the white matter represents relatively longer branches of neurones, known as axons, that connect to the dendrites of other neurones. The more tightly packed neurones of the left hemisphere are better able to handle intensely detailed work by connecting to the neurones in the close-by regions, while the right hemisphere's white matter containing neurones with longer axons connects with brain regions farther away. Going by our previous inference that the right-hemispheric processing involves a relatively larger volume of data/information compared to the left-hemispheric processing, we can infer that the right-hemisphere processes more diverse or seemingly unrelated data/information accessed from different regions of the brain. The long-range connections help the right hemisphere come up with broad but rather vague concepts, explaining its association with human creativity. However, despite the specialisation of different brain regions we observe, either in the form of localisation or lateralisation, one of the most exciting features of the human brain is its ability to integrate the different activities taking place in specialised areas into a unifying whole. In fact, a structural confirmation to this effect is provided by the connection made between the two cerebral hemispheres through the largest fibre bundle in the brain, the corpus callosum.

CONTEMPORARY EDUCATION SYSTEMS' BIAS TOWARDS LEFT-HEMISPHERIC ORIENTATION

Despite this significant revelation of the need and desire of the brain to operate as a unifying whole, it is widely observed and accepted that educational institutes are predominantly left-hemispheric oriented. They emphasise structured environments that run to specific time schedules; favour facts, details, and rules ahead of patterns, integration, and creativity; and predominantly follow verbal instructions (Sousa 2011). We extend our discussions in later chapters on the implications of brain lateralisation and how mostly right-hemispheric-oriented visual-spatial or gifted learners suffer in a system that is predominately left-hemispheric oriented, sometimes to the extent of getting alienated.

Brain Cells: Neurones

The building blocks of the neural system are the brain cells called neurones. Neurones are similar to the other cells of the body, but they are highly specialised for electrochemical signalling across cells and systems (Baars and Gage 2010; Sousa 2011). Tens of billions of neurones in the human brain are connected by trillions of transmission points known as synapses, which can be excitatory or inhibitory regarding passing a signal. An average neurone may have ten thousand input branches (dendrites) and one or two output fibres (axons). Synapses are known to grow throughout the adult lifetime; small dendrite spines can grow in minutes to support new synapses. The growth of synapses is directly related to human creativity and learning, as we will elaborate upon later. Interestingly, and to highlight a slightly different matter, nerve cells or neurones fire their spikes much more slowly than the electronic arrays that run conventional computers. Consequently, we will see later how human brains and conventional computers are better at doing significantly different sets of tasks, regarding the speed of operation.

From another point of view, a neurone can be considered as a switch, a biological version of the electronic switches in computers. The input branches of each nerve, the dendrites, can be viewed as integrators, adding up the voltage inputs from tens of thousands of incoming signals over a very brief period. Since the brain has about a hundred billion nerve cells and trillions of synapses, it can be thought of as an extensive collection of information processors, somewhat like the World Wide Web (WWW). In fact, when we learn new contents, the learned information is stored as connected neuronal networks. As we see throughout this book, the challenge we face as educators is to enable creating more integrated and useful neural networks of knowledge within our learners. The more integrated the knowledge networks, the more lasting and useful they become, as we see later on.

Recent studies of neurones of people of different occupations show that the more complex the skills demanded, the greater the number of dendrites that were found on the neurones. This increase in dendrites allows for more connections between neurones, resulting in more sites in which to store learned information/concepts.

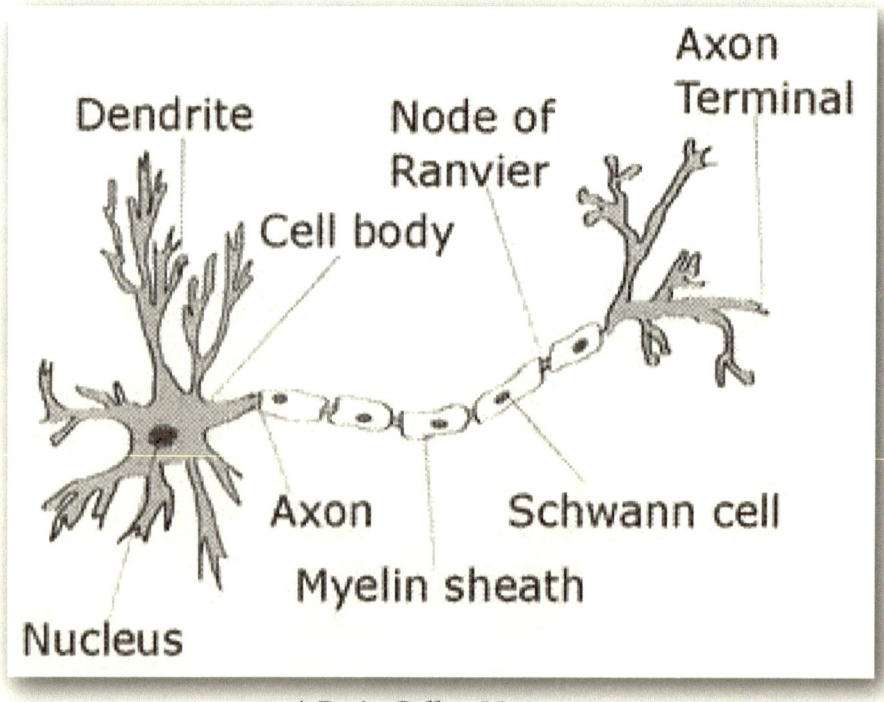

A Brain Cell or Neurone

Memory and Related Structures in the Brain

Basic Types of Memory

An important function supported by the brain structure is memory, which is defined as a lasting representation that is reflected in thought, experience, or behaviour (Baars and Gage 2010; Sousa 2011). Human memory is commonly studied in two forms: short-term memory and long-term memory. Short-term memory is referred to by cognitive neuroscientists to include all the early steps of temporary memory that will later be transformed into more stable long-term memory. Short-term memory primarily includes immediate memory and working memory (Cowan 2009; Gazzaniga, Ivry, and Mangun 2002; Squire and Kandel 1999).

Short-Term Memory

The type of short-term memory referred to as *immediate memory* operates subconsciously or consciously, and as the name implies, it holds data for a short period of up to about thirty seconds. The other category of short-term memory, termed as *working memory* (Baddeley 2000; Baddeley and Hitch 1974; Cowan, et al. 2005), is defined as a set of mental processes holding limited information in a temporarily accessible state in service of cognition. It is the place where conscious processing or connection of available information meaningfully occurs. Information in working memory can come from the sensory/immediate memories or be retrieved from long-term memory. Brain-imaging studies show that most working-memory activities occur in the frontal lobes. The functioning of working memory can be explained by a three-part system containing an executive, central control mechanism and two subordinate components—phonological loop (auditory signals) and visuospatial sketchpad (visual/spatial signals)—involved in rehearsal (Baddeley 2003; Gazzaniga, et al. 2002). Consequently, in a teaching/learning environment, both verbal and visual information together allow students to become involved more effectively in the learning process; it also increases retention. This increased retention occurs because working memory has both verbal and visual components, and each selects, organises, and processes its respective information before sending it to the frontal lobe for further integration and interpretation. In essence, the learner creates both a verbally based model and a visually based model of new learning before integrating it. We will highlight the significance of presenting information in both verbal and visual modes further when we discuss the two prominent learning styles referred to as auditory-sequential and visual-spatial. The central control mechanism, located in the prefrontal cortex, manages the interaction between the two subordinate systems and long-term memory. Working storage, which is dynamic and hence more vulnerable to disruptions than permanent memories, is located in temporal cortex and prefrontal regions.

LONG-TERM MEMORY

As the name implies, long-term memory is the process where large quantities of information are stored on a permanent or longer-duration basis (Dudai 2004; LeDoux 1996; Lees et al. 2000; McGaugh 2000). Long-term memory may be located in many places, including the entire neocortex and subcortical structures, such as basal ganglia and cerebellum. The neocortex is believed to encode long-term memories by altering dynamic synaptic connections among billions of neurones. There are trillions of such synapses in the cortex and its satellite organs, as mentioned before. It is interesting to note the vast number of memory traces our brain can hold through a diverse and a large number of synaptic connections. This greater number of possible different synaptic connections/memory traces gives an indication of the extent to which a human brain can become creative through holding and accessing a large volume of information. Memories are believed to be unstable and vulnerable to interference in the early hours after they are formed or learned; after about a day, they appear to be consolidated or made more enduring (Hobson and Stickgold 1995). It signifies the need of an emotionally stable environment for learners, especially the ones who are emotionally vulnerable, to thrive through the process of memory consolidation. This process of memory consolidation is thought to require a process known as protein synthesis, and RNA and sleep and dreaming seem to support this process. It is important to note the need for a good night's sleep for completing the task of enhanced learning. The commonly known slogan for memory consolidation into long-term memory is "Neurones that fire together wire together." It emphasises the need to engage in an elaborate rehearsal of the contents studied, as we highlight in detail later.

PROCEDURAL MEMORY AND AUTOMATICITY

We have the experience of performing some tasks quite spontaneously or automatically without paying much attention to them or using much of our cognitive resources. Some examples are a driver's ability to navigate a familiar route or an expert typing on a keyboard. Initially, these automatic skills start out under cortical control, but after some sufficient practice, they tend to come under subcortical control (Chein and Schneider 2005). When a task we perform is under cortical control, we utilise cognitive resources, using neural networks found in the neocortex to carry out the work. After a reasonable amount of practice with the task, our neural system is capable of transferring the execution of the work to subcortical organs, releasing cognitive resources for other possible tasks. The cerebellum, one such subcortical organ, is connected to the regions of the brain that perform mental and sensory functions. As a result, it can perform the above-mentioned practised tasks automatically, without conscious attention to detail. The release of resources in this manner allows the conscious part of the brain (such as the neocortex) the freedom to attend to other mental activities, thus enlarging the cognitive scope. Once a skill is mastered, brain activity shifts to the cerebellum, which organises and coordinates the movements and timing to perform the task. This mechanism is known as "forming procedural memory," and the brain no longer needs to use its higher-order processes and related resources; the performance of the skill becomes automatic (Hatakenaka, Miyani et al. 2007; Penhune and Doyon 2005; Press, Casement et al. 2005; Walker, Stickgold et al. 2005). We will revisit the topic of procedural memory and automaticity more specifically when we discuss assessment-related concepts in detail. We should focus on evaluating the learner's ability to use cognitive resources effectively, instead of procedural memory or automaticity.

SOME OTHER INTERESTING BRAIN FEATURES

NEURAL DARWINISM

A brain feature known as Neural Darwinism (Baars and Gage 2010) suggests that brain development and brain dynamics are selectionist in nature, not instructionist (as in the case of digital computers that can only carry out a limited set of explicit symbolic instructions). In effect, neurones in the brain (or more specifically, dendrites) can select new connections among themselves and outgrow the existing number of connections, whereas a digital computer's understanding is restricted to pre-existing symbols or instructions. This feature of the human brain that relates to its creative operation is referred to as *neuroplasticity*; it continually reorganises itself by inputs received, possibly throughout the lifespan. The term Neural Darwinism is related to Darwin's theory of evolution - concept of survival of the fittest; neural connections that regularly fire are more likely to survive than those that do not (which will die out). We will relate this useful feature of Neural Darwinism as a possible lifelong learning ability of human beings to achieve a higher level of human development into creative individuals with wisdom, later in the text.

NOVELTY SEEKING

Researchers have revealed how creative instincts of human beings are supported by brain structures and operations. For example, part of our success as a species can be attributed to the brain's persistent interest in novelty; human beings expect changes—or more specifically, improvements—to occur in the environment (Sousa 2011). Conversely, an environment that contains mainly predictable or repeated stimuli lowers the brain's interest in the outside world, tempting it to turn within for novel sensation. It is understood that some may even turn to drugs and alcohol to seek the satisfaction of experiencing novelty. Further, new research reveals that students are more likely to gain a greater understanding of and derive greater pleasure from learning when they are allowed to transform the learning process with creative thoughts and products. As educators, we have to encourage learners to explore without being hampered by inappropriate assessment or failure, as we elaborate later. We will also discuss how we can support novelty seeking or creative instincts of learners by encouraging open-minded thinking and appropriate minimisation of self-regulation. Then we will be able to direct natural novelty-seeking instincts of human beings to something more positive (the achievement of a higher level of human development) instead of something negative (drug or alcohol use).

STORING PATTERNS

It is understood that the brain retains memories by storing sequences of patterns, and recalling just one piece related to the pattern can activate the whole. That is, we can also recall or identify the same thing in different forms, such as recognising our best friend from behind or by her walk or voice. Typically, computers do not deal well with such variations (Hawkins and Blakeslee 2004). In other words, it implies that we retain information or memories as connected sets of neural networks or in a more abstractly generalised manner rather than individual pieces. As a result, to achieve enhanced learning, we have to relate the contents we learn to as many other concepts of knowledge as possible. This process of forming relations allows learned contents to be retrieved more efficiently using some different priming clues.

Hierarchical Response

Researchers have observed a pattern in the way we respond to sensory inputs: it is organised hierarchically. Any input that is of a higher priority diminishes the processing of information of a lower priority (Baars and Gage 2010; Sousa 2011). The brain's primary job is to help its owner survive. Thus, any data interpreted as a threat to the survival of the individual will be processed immediately and with a higher focus. This response is reflexive, indicating neither much thinking is involved nor an extensive time is taken. Other emotional data/information (other than life-threatening ones) make the next level of priority. When an individual responds emotionally to a situation, the limbic system, stimulated by the amygdala, plays a major role, and more complex cerebral processes are suspended. This response is also a reflexive one. However, under certain conditions, emotions can enhance memory by causing the release of some hormones that stimulate the amygdala to signal brain regions to strengthen memory. In the absence of both life-threatening and highly emotional inputs, the brain is free to pay attention to other input data and respond in a more reflective manner. Based on the above hierarchical responding paradigm, when it comes to learning, it is important that learners are emotionally stable so they can pay attention and focus entirely on learning. In other words, it is imperative that the basic needs of learners are satisfied *before* any effective and lasting learning takes place.

To Sum Up

Isn't it amazing to see how an organ weighing only 2 percent of our total body weight manages our operations utilising 20 percent of the energy generated in our body? Even more amazing, the brain is composed of billions of functional cells (neurones) that are linked through trillions of connection points (synapses) that accommodate its integrated operations as a whole. When the evolution of the human brain over millions of years is carefully analysed, we see that a layer supporting life through breathing and heartbeat was the first to evolve, followed by a layer yielding emotions or the drive for survival. Finally, there was the third layer, the one that allowed human beings to perform cognitive operations or to think and modify their environment and possibly even improve their quality and purpose of life. On a related note, in the theory of hierarchical needs of self-actualisation presented by Abraham Maslow, it is essential that basic human needs (food, shelter, and security) are satisfied before individuals can move on to higher levels of self-actualisation, as we will elaborate upon later. Interestingly, the brain demonstrates both specialisation and lateralisation. In the former, some modular units or regions perform unique specialised functions; in the latter, externally symmetrical cerebral hemispheres engage in functions that complement each other for more efficient and meaningful human operation. It is not difficult to understand that one of the essential duties of the human brain is the formation of and storage of memories. We make use of existing memories along with information being perceived to form new memories, by combining the pieces of information in diverse and individualised ways. Once these new memories are formed, they will have to be transformed to more lasting memories or representations so that we can make use of them later, when the appropriate circumstances arise. Further, through procedural memories, brain resources are utilised more efficiently by releasing cognitive resources from widely practised tasks to more demanding different tasks. Following Darwin's theory of evolution, the human brain has the capacity known as Neural Darwinism to retain memories or neural connections we use most while removing the ones we use least. Neural Darwinism is a very useful feature that we can make use of to train our brain for what most interests us. The human brain's natural feature of novelty-seeking behaviour helps us to continue our evolution as a species, further improving the quality and purpose of our lives. With the capacity to deal with large volumes of information in an efficient manner, our brains possess the ability to recognise and store patterns, while a demonstrated hierarchical responding feature allows our neural system to direct brain resources for tasks that make us survive first ahead of other tasks that make our operations more efficient and meaningful.

CHAPTER 2

Some Neuroscience Concepts That Explain Learning Processes

• • •

THIS CHAPTER IS INTENDED TO provide readers with some prominent neuroscience concepts that explain learning processes, mainly the phenomenon of *human memory* and how it relates to learning. In this regard, we identify different types of memories and definitions of learning, and we highlight how these various representations either complement or provide a more comprehensive understanding of the other. Human memory is mainly differentiated here as *implicit* or *explicit* and *episodic* or *semantic*. Learning is presented in relation to *implicit* or *explicit, automaticity, incidental learning, Hebbian learning, emotions and learning,* and *associative recall/ recognition* tests as measures of learning evaluations. *Attention* is highlighted as the starting point of any learning that could occur in a pervasive manner, rather than what happens merely in a classroom environment. Then we present one of the most important phenomena being researched currently: *consciousness*. It is considered significant because when learning is properly continued in a lifelong manner, enhanced consciousness into higher levels of human development is identified to be the outcome. Finally, we introduce the term *metacognition*, which has attracted the intense attention of educational practitioners as the means of raising self-awareness in learners.

FURTHER CATEGORISATION OF MEMORY

EXPLICIT AND IMPLICIT MEMORIES

Human memory (Squire 2004, 2009; Baars and Gage 2010) in general can be defined as a lasting representation that is reflected in thought, experience, or behaviour. In one categorisation, it is divided into two main types: *explicit* and *implicit* memories. Explicit memory refers to a memory with conscious awareness; the individual possessing it can declare its existence and comment on its content either verbally or nonverbally (Cohen and Squire 1980; Ryle 1949). Consequently, such memories are known as *declarative memories.* On the other hand, implicit memory (*nondeclarative memory*) is not accompanied by the conscious awareness that one has such a memory; the existence of implicit memory is inferred only from the effects it has on behaviour. Further, implicit memories may be retained without an intention to remember and accessed commonly by priming tasks (Banaji and Greenwald 1995; Curran 2001; Knowlton, et al. 1996). Another type of nondeclarative memory is referred to as *procedural memory*; some examples of procedural memory are learning of some motor (driving) and cognitive (reading) skills. Procedural memories are formed through extensive practice, when the brain process shifts from reflective to reflexive in a phenomenon referred to as *automaticity.* Procedural and declarative memories seem to be stored in different regions of the brain, and declarative memory can be lost under some circumstances, while procedural memory is spared (Rose 2005).

In one of the goals of learning, we should be able to convert our explicit memories to implicit memories, as is the case when forming procedural memories. During the learning process, we initially use our cognitive processes and resources, and once the learned activity is practised to a sufficient level, the practised activity is transformed to procedural memory, releasing the cognitive processes and resources that were held. The freed cognitive resources allow them to be reused for additional learning tasks. The transformation of explicit memories to implicit (or procedural) memories and the subsequent release of cognitive resources at the end allows the brain to function more efficiently, accommodating us to continue learning in a nonrestrictive manner. This process of efficient brain resource utilisation, supported biologically by the brain structures, enables us with a continuous path of learning, forming more and more neural networks of knowledge yielding individuals of wisdom and enhanced consciousness, as we see in detail later. Conversely, when we form implicit memories unconsciously as we are exposed to daily experiences, we should be able to convert them to explicit memories through the process of learning. To help learners transform their implicit memories to explicit ones, educators need to relate the concepts or abstract theories learned in the classroom environment to as many real-life scenarios (possibly held implicitly) as possible. In this way, learners become conscious of their implicit memories, which enable them to use or relate them more usefully. If educators are unable to help or guide learners to transform their implicit memories to explicit ones, we may end up in a situation in which the learners will possess some tools or knowledge that they cannot use or do not know how to take advantage.

EPISODIC AND SEMANTIC MEMORIES

Explicit or declarative memory can further be divided into two types: episodic (autobiographical) memory and semantic memory (Tulving 1972, 1985). Episodic memory refers to memories that have a particular source in time, space, and life circumstances. In contrast, semantic memories involve facts (high-level concepts and generalisations) about ourselves, the world, and other knowledge that we share within a community; they are independent of the spatial and temporal contexts in which they were acquired. Further, episodic memories are remembered consciously and are susceptible to being forgotten; semantic memories give a feeling of knowing, rather than a fully conscious recollection, and are less vulnerable to being forgotten. Initially, memories are episodic and context dependent, and over time, they are transformed into semantic memories (Penfield and Milner 1958).

As we can see, episodic memories carry more detailed information, especially in relation to time, space. and life circumstances. On the other hand, semantic memories contain more abstract, high-level, or generalised or summarised information. Usually, abstract or generalised information can be connected to many other similar sets of information more easily. A couple of justifications we can rationalise for this possibility is that this abstract or generalised information tends to cross the boundaries of disciplinary domains or subject areas. They also last longer in memory. To reiterate, the quality of being independent of the contexts of time, space, and life circumstances makes semantic memories essentially more general, abstract, and devoid of associated specific details. Consequently, as we will elaborate later, in an ideal teaching-learning environment, it is important that educators put the emphasis on abstract or generalised concepts and information, including whilst doing assessments. Not doing this more specifically would result in not only less useful and somewhat futile learning experiences, it also disadvantages visual-spatial or gifted learners who are more right-hemispheric oriented and tend to think abstractly, as we elaborate throughout this text.

WORKING MEMORY AND ITS IMPACT ON LEARNING

In the last chapter, we discussed how contents are first processed in the working memory before they are transferred to long-term memories. To understand the impact of working memory on learning, we use the studies conducted by Miller in 1956. He discovered that working memory could handle only a few items at once, as it has a limited capacity. This functional capacity changes with age; children have a smaller capacity than adolescents and adults (Cowan, et al. 2010; Gilchrist, Cowan, et al. 2009). The working memory time span for preadolescents is about five to ten minutes, while it is about ten to twenty minutes for adolescents and adults

(Russel 1979; Medina 2008; Portrat, Barrouillet et al. 2008). For the focus to continue, there must be some change in the way an individual is dealing with the item. When the survival and unrelated emotional elements are minimal or absent, the act of transferring information from short-term memory to long-term memory requires other factors (such as sense and meaning) to be addressed, as we discuss in detail later. In general, if an individual is motivated or curious to learn about the thing or matter being presented, we can expect that he or she would process related information in the working memory for a longer period. The implication of the limit in working memory is that there is a need to use the limited capacity efficiently; only the most important and related contents of the matter being rehearsed need to be taken into working memory for processing. Being able to stop unrelated information from getting in the way of learning also allows the brain to avoid becoming cluttered. Further, the processing needs to be done thoroughly, making as many valuable connections as possible, so as to put the contents on a path to long-term memory before any further materials are taken into working memory for processing.

DEFINING TYPES OF LEARNING

LEARNING AS ACQUISITION OF LASTING REPRESENTATIONS

Learning can be defined as the acquisition of enduring representations or images involving a broad range of brain areas and activities (Baars and Gage 2010). Very often, the unstated goal of learning is to turn explicit problem solving into the implicit kind. In explicit problem solving, you pay attention to the tasks you are involved in consciously, and with enough quality practice, you would develop the ability to do the same tasks implicitly or relatively unconsciously. In effect, we have internalised what we have learned to the degree that we can respond to similar situations in a somewhat spontaneous or automatic way. We mentioned this phenomenon of internalising earlier in the text as automaticity and forming procedural memory. If we do not practise long enough to achieve this required degree of internalisation, we may not respond to similar (but different in some ways) situations in the way we learned and wanted. Instead, we may react in the way we were used to before learning, possibly in a nonideal, nonoptimal, or biased way. We will refer to a notion called transfer later in the text as the goal of learning, similar to what we discussed here as internalising or transforming explicit memories to implicit ones.

Explicit and Implicit Learning

Analogous to the way we discussed explicit and implicit memories, learning can also be explicit or implicit. Explicit or declarative learning involves conscious learning, while implicit (unconscious) learning (Berry and Dienes 1993; Cleeremans 1993) results in as a side effect of conscious input. In effect, even for implicit learning, conscious events guide the learning process. In other words, one has to pay attention and be conscious, at least at the initiating stage, for learning to take place, either explicitly or implicitly. But there is no exclusively conscious learning, as both conscious and unconscious processes always take place together. In the event of implicit learning, we are more likely to create implicit memories, and we may not be aware of their existence. Consequently, to make these implicit memories more useful or readily usable in real-life situations, we will have to transform them to explicit memories through some means, as mentioned earlier.

Phases of Learning

In a complete learning cycle, three phases can be identified: learning, retention, and retrieval. Retention is viewed as unconscious, although it is shaped by conscious experiences. Explicit learning occurs when we pay attention to new information until it becomes conscious. In implicit learning—which is the most common form of learning, interestingly—the brain begins learning as soon as it is placed in any new environment, ideally in the absence of threatening or highly emotional stimuli. In these situations, simple novelty is enough to trigger attention and learning, including significantly evoked potentials that sweep through the entire cortex. Naturally, the novelty-seeking human brain will benefit from learning when helpful anxiety levels are maintained by exposure to new information, as we elaborate later. It implies that when individuals can keep a positive frame of mind about learning, they can engage in constant learning, mostly implicitly from their daily experiences. In other words, if one is rightly motivated, learning does not have to take place necessarily in a classroom or formal teaching-learning environment. As soon as we experience or understand new information with enough clarity, our brains can store it (Seitz and Watanabe 2005). Sometimes it may require repeated attention to new or complicated information for us to get a sense of clarity. To improve clarity, the new information we are introduced to can be connected to as many other related pieces of information as possible. In other words, new information presented can be viewed from as many other perspectives as possible.

Any new material may seem vague or hard to understand at first; however, when we spend time thinking about it or paying attention to it, a clearer sense of meaning tends to appear. Lack of persistence towards improving the clarity of what we learn by providing adequate time for rehearsal or processing can be a major contributory factor for lacklustre learning. The key challenge we face as individuals in learning is maintaining an appropriate level of motivation, especially of an intrinsic nature, to continue in the process of learning by clarifying things, even difficult ones. This high degree of motivation will have to be maintained all the time, even outside formal teaching-learning environments, to be benefited from our regular experiences. For us to be motivated, we will have to be conscious of the lasting benefits of learning, whatever is learned and whenever it is done—making more and more useful neural networks of knowledge that leads to seeing reality better or comprehending our environment, world, or universe better.

LEARNING VOLUNTARY ACTIONS TO THE LEVEL OF AUTOMATICITY

In general, the more predictable a sensorimotor skill becomes, the less it will become conscious (Baars and Gage 2010). The fading of conscious access to habitual skills is commonly called automaticity, and it goes along with a loss of precise voluntary control over habitual details. In effect, the brain takes more time to solve novel problems, and voluntary actions performed solving those problems become automatic with practice. As they become automatic, we tend to lose executive control over them, and associated cortical activity reduces (Chein and Schneider 2005; Coulthard, et al. 2008; Langer and Imber 1979; Raaijmakers and Shiffrin 1992; Schneider 2009; Shiffrin and Schneider 1977). Once even very complex processes are learned, they seem to require less cortical activity. Effortful tasks show a wider spread of brain activity; the brain takes more time to solve novel problems, and switching from one task to another seems to require additional mental resources beyond those involved in routine and automatic actions. It appears to indicate the recruitment of neuronal resources that are needed to work together to perform a task that is new or unpredictable. In other words, repetitive events tend to fade from consciousness unless they have special significance or at least some differences from previous occurrence of the events.

Earlier, we discussed how automaticity relates to the phenomenon of procedural memory, in which memories are held in subcortical organs. While automaticity can bring efficiency through quicker responses and more efficient use of cortical resources, there can be some limitations we experience in the measure. We may get into a situation of performing certain tasks habitually without reflection or executive control. Even if we can improve the way we are used to attending to a particular task (due to exposure to new information or data), we may continue to perform it habitually, possibly through lack of motivation to change. For example, we may continue to engage in our pedagogical practices in the way we were used to for years, despite the availability of more convincing new information or data to perform them differently and more effectively. In these situations, we will have to have a good judgement on when we need to be reflective and when we can give in to our habitual practices. The significance of the human brain's automaticity needs to be viewed from the perspective of continuous or lifelong learning. Once something is learned to the level of automaticity or expertise, we need to identify new areas into which to extend our learning or to engage our released brain (cortical) resources. When this continuous learning process takes place, connecting newly learned knowledge networks to the older ones, it leads to developing enhanced consciousness into an evolving human being, as discussed earlier. As a general rule, whenever we get exposed to new, related knowledge or learn new content, we should review our habits or longstanding practices for possible improvements, using cortical resources and executive control. Such an approach and attitude essentially leads us to a path of lifelong learning and self-improvement.

INCIDENTAL OR IMPLICIT LEARNING

Most of our learning is identified to be incidental (Baars and Gage 2010; Eide and Eide 2004), meaning that it occurs as a result of paying attention and becoming conscious of the incidents that take place in the environment. In effect, we do not deliberately memorise things all the time; explicitly attempting to memorise is only one way to make learning happen. In other words, we do not have to be in formal learning environments all the time to achieve learning. We learn through the day-to-day life experiences or incidents we encounter. In most of these situations, it is possible that we retain traces of implicit memories. With our current practices, academic learning is mostly explicit, with teachers pointing out the things to be learned and students doing their best to commit them to memory. However, it is revealed that most ordinary human learning is implicit (Bowers, et al. 1990; James 1890; Metcalfe 1986; Yzerbyt, et al. 1998). For example, social habits and languages are mostly learnt implicitly. Looking from another perspective, most of our knowledge is tacit knowledge, and most of our learning takes place implicitly before it can be stated explicitly.

As highlighted before, one of the goals of learning is to transform learners' vast amount of tacit or implicit knowledge into more clarified, explicit knowledge that can be made use of when circumstances require. In this regard, educators should be able to get our learners to express their tacit or implicit knowledge through appropriate assessment tasks, as we will discuss later in more detail.

It is worth noting that decades ago—before the emergence of the vast amount of neuroscience knowledge—the famous American education philosopher John Dewey identified the significance of experience in education (Dewey 1957, 1963). He raised the issue of having an undesirable split between the formal and informal or incidental and intentional modes of education. Especially in science education, he highlighted the need to explain the concepts with real-life experiences.

ASSOCIATIVE RECALL AND RECOGNITION TESTS AS MEANS OF EVALUATING LEARNING

When it comes to assessment, academic exams usually test associative recall ("What is the capital of Australia?") rather than a recognition test ("How would you compare capital cities of Australia and France?"). Associative recall tests give much lower estimates for accurate memories than recognition tests (Baars and Gage 2010). That is, in the associative recall, we expect more exact answers than in recognition tests. Interestingly, these exact answers are the ones that are likely to be forgotten soon (Tulving 1972, 1985), as they are usually retained as episodic memories. We may question the validity of assessing a learner's capacity to recall a fact or procedure that is likely to be forgotten within hours or days. As a longstanding practice, we rely heavily on associative-recall tests as we strictly stick to a specific curriculum within a specified period. We do so because we can manage the teaching-learning environment more easily and rigidly by fulfilling the accountability requirement by asking questions with definite answers that were also presented within a specified period. Learners can neither confront the assessor on the level of accuracy of the answer nor on the scope of the question, as there is only one definite answer that had been discussed within the set curriculum. We inadvertently presume that learners only learn what we introduce in a teaching-learning environment within a particular curriculum. We want them to reproduce what they learnt within this set curriculum during the specific period, in the exact form in response to assessments. We may ask ourselves if we are *indoctrinating* instead of *educating*. Are we making learners robotic? We impede the ability of human creativity—a biological, specieswide feature well supported by brain structures—to blossom. We completely disregard the implicit or incidental learning they carry with them to the class. With these approaches, we create passive, unhappy learners. In contrast to associative recall tests, recognition tests (or open-minded questions) can be used effectively to test implicit learning, as we will elaborate upon later. In recognition tests, we can give learners clues for them to express and elaborate on subjectively. They will scan their brains to access related memories to produce individualised, unique answers to the questions where there can be many acceptable and equally valid answers. Also note that in recognition tests, we want learners to have a feeling of *knowing* (as is the case with semantic memories) rather than being able to recall exact, detailed descriptions with references to time and space contexts (as is the case with episodic memories). Further, those semantic memories will last longer in memory, making them more useful than easily forgotten episodic memories.

EMOTIONS AND LEARNING

It is widely accepted now that emotions help to enhance learning, contrary to some beliefs held otherwise years ago. In the event of emotional stimuli, there is evidence that some unconscious learning takes place. It gives much stronger evidence for implicit learning in which some inferential processes take conscious input and encode unconscious results. In other words, emotional learning results in implicit emotional memory that retains classically conditioned emotional relationships that cannot be voluntarily recollected or reported (Phelps and LeDoux 2005; Panksepp 1998). We may question the value of emotional memories that cannot be voluntarily recalled or reported. However, similar to other implicit memories, they are likely to be retrieved involuntarily through priming in appropriate circumstances. Further, psychological evidence shows that moderate levels of emotional arousal at the time of an event lead to better retention of explicit memories (Sylwester 1998). That is, explicit memories are better consolidated by the reception of emotional stimuli by the amygdala. Also, we highlighted earlier how the limbic system (the emotional brain) is structurally well connected to the neocortex (the cognitive part of the brain) and plays a significant role in the consolidation of short-term memories to long-term ones (Baars and Gage 2010). Further, the hippocampus—as an essential structure in the emotional brain—plays a significant role in consolidating learning by converting information from short-term memory to long-term storage. On a related matter, the emotional sensitivity of visual-spatial or gifted learners, who are markedly right-hemispheric oriented, provides an explanation for their higher ability of learning, provided that conducive environments are present, as we will discuss in detail later.

Hebbian Learning

Hebbian learning, named after the neuropsychologist Donald Hebb, is summarised as "neurones that fire together, wire together" (Hebb 1949). It indicates that the more frequently individual synaptic connections that are realised, the more likely they are to form lasting neural networks. In other words, synaptic connections that are rarely used will eventually die out (Diamond 1996, 2001). This notion is a very simple idea about how we can explain the way learning takes place. If we are keen to create lasting memories of particular contents learnt, it is required to engage in elaborative rehearsal for extended periods, creating more neural networks of knowledge, as we will highlight later. In fact, it is observed that forming new synaptic connections, a process known as *synaptogenesis* (Huttenlocher, et al. 1982; Huttenlocher 1994) takes place throughout one's lifespan, enabling a lifelong learning process for human beings that is well supported by the brain's structures. Put differently, cortical plasticity or neuroplasticity lasts throughout the lifetime of a human being. However, in a changing, dynamic world, unlearning also has a significant role to play. That is, we will have to let misconceptions or inaccurate knowledge we may have held die out from our neural system. Consequently, we see value in losing memories in some situations, as it enables us to relearn more accurately. A similar concept, known as Neural Darwinism—"survival of the fittest" cells and synapses—was presented by Edelman in 1989. In fact, human brains are identified to be *selectionist* rather than being *instructionist*, meaning that synaptic connections can grow by selecting new connection points, not merely being restricted by a pre-existing limited set of instructions, as is the case in conventional computers. In other words, human brains can be creative by learning newly formed knowledge that is represented in the form of new synaptic connections that did not exist before.

ATTENTION

ATTENTION AS DIRECTING COGNITIVE RESOURCES
When we walk along a street, if our senses are fully functional, we are able to see and hear many things. But at a certain point in time, how many things can we pay attention to simultaneously? What does neuroscience reveal about our capacity for attention? The word *attention* seems to imply the ability to direct cognitive resources to some event (Anderson et al. 2000; Baars and Gage 2010; Fletcher et al. 1995; Seitz and Watanabe 2005), as we would expect. It has a kind of pointing or directive sense. Human beings usually perform a phenomenon known as *selective attention*, which implies making a choice amongst possible events. Consciousness, as we discuss in detail later, seems to be the experience of an event after

it has been selected by paying attention. In effect, if we do not select an item or event as worthy of our attention, we would not become conscious of it. In fact, we can decide what to become aware of in some situations voluntarily, or the selection can also be automatic if some intense, dynamic, or biologically or personally relevant stimuli are received. In the real world, voluntary and involuntary attentions are mixed. In summary, attention is defined as the ability to select information for cognitive purposes. This selection may be shaped by emotions (Zull 2002), motivation, and salience, and is at least partly under executive control. For example, in a teaching-learning session, we can pay attention to what the facilitator says in the absence of other threatening and highly emotional stimuli. If such threatening or highly emotional stimuli are present, learners need to attend to those issues before effective learning can take place on another matter.

SELECTIVE ATTENTION AND BINOCULAR RIVALRY

The term *binocular rivalry* is used to describe the process of selective attention further in neuroscience (Logothetis 1998; Tong, et al. 1998). When two items are looked at the same time using one eye on each item, using a pair of binoculars at an instance of time, we can only see one item properly or consciously. In other words, we cannot concentrate well on two things at the same time, even though we see them both simultaneously. That is, when a person is given a task that requires in-depth, meaningful analysis of some given material, memory under divided attention is much worse than memory under full attention. Deeper processing requires time to complete, and divided attention limits the time allotted for encoding (Anderson, et al. 2000; Fletcher, et al. 1995). For example, in a teaching-learning session, if a learner is emotionally upset for some reason while attempting to listen to the facilitator, he or she may not be able to pay attention fully to the learning contents introduced. In learning, what we usually do is just pay attention to new material, even if it seems hard to understand. The biggest challenge is to pay continued attention to new and difficult-to-understand information and to be patient enough to allow our brains to do the wonder, ask the questions, and ultimately comprehend any new material (Seitz and Watanabe 2005).

CONSCIOUSNESS

CONSCIOUSNESS AS A TRACEABLE, SCIENTIFIC PROBLEM

The phenomenon referred to as consciousness is less familiar to us than the notions of intelligence, emotions, and creativity we discuss in detail later in the text. However, in recent years, researchers and scientists have shown increasing interest in the study of consciousness. Perhaps the greatest change over the last twenty-five years or so within cognitive science has been the acceptance of consciousness as a legitimate and traceable scientific problem, contrary to the beliefs previously held otherwise (Baars, et al. 2003; Edelman 1989, 1993, 2005, and 2007; Edelman and Tononi 2001; Koch 1996; Palmer 1999; Tononi and Edelman 1998; Tulving 2002). So, what does consciousness mean—scientifically? Let's try to shed some light on the topic.

CONSCIOUSNESS AND ITS RELATIONSHIP TO THE PREFRONTAL CORTEX (PFC)

Consciousness is understood to be the result of the neuronal interaction between thalamocortical systems; while the neocortex is the primary organ associated with consciousness, some subcortical regions may also be involved. The evolution of consciousness is understood to be the highest expression of the developed brain that parallels developments in the PFC. In effect, an individual can evolve as a human being through enhancing consciousness. Because the PFC acts as an organ connecting many other brain regions, we can infer that consciousness indicates the ability of our brain to function in a highly connected and integrated manner. Put differently, the ultimate goal of our brain development is to get it to function in as integrated and connected a way as possible.

What it means is that various knowledge networks we hold in our brain—possibly from diverse disciplinary areas or domains—are well and meaningfully connected, enabling us to experience a deeper and broader understanding of the environment, world, universe, or reality. As we elaborate later, achieving a higher level of human development is indicative of reaching a higher level of consciousness. Synonyms used for *consciousness* are *awareness, explicit cognition,* and *focal attention.* Consciousness can be identified mainly in two levels: *primary* and *higher-order consciousness.* The former is concerned with the perceptual world, whilst the latter is related to abstractions and thought. The higher-order consciousness represents more human specific features, necessarily making use of the PFC to form abstractions and thoughts that are more of human activities, compared to sensing, such as seeing and hearing that other species are capable of as well.

Consciousness and Its Association with a Range of Contents

One significant property of consciousness is its use of an extraordinary range of contents: sensory perception, visual imagery, emotional feelings, inner speech, abstract concepts, and action-related ideas and the like (Baars and Gage 2010). Involvement of a wide variety of contents reflects the fact that consciousness is associated with multiple brain regions. An integrative view of consciousness suggests interactions occur amongst brain regions involved in a conscious recall, conscious control of motor skills, and the like.

The Integrated Theory of Consciousness

Of particular interest to the phenomenon of consciousness is Giulio Tononi's Integrated Theory of Consciousness (Balduzzi and Tononi

2008; Koch and Tononi 2008; Tononi 2008). It provides a way to study consciousness using a rigorous scientific approach. The integrated theory of consciousness is a framework that is built on the notion that consciousness is a consequence of systems that have a large amount of differentiated information that is also highly integrated. In other words, to accomplish a higher level of consciousness, the brain must balance the degree of pacing and coordination against the need for local neurones and their neighbours to work on local functions. That is, there must be a balance between integration (of information in diverse regions) and differentiation (of information in local neural networks) of information.

To summarise the idea, a computer may have a large quantity of memory (say 16 GB), but since these memory pieces are not integrated, computers do not have consciousness. Scientists have also been able to quantify the level of consciousness with a measure called *neural complexity* (C) (Edelman and Tononi 2001). High values of C characterise conscious events and reflect the extent to which the dynamics of a neural system are both integrated and differentiated. Consciousness in humans can also be understood with the cognitive architecture known as the Global Workspace Theory (GWT) (Baars 1988, 2002). The GWT proposes that momentarily dominant information is widely distributed in the brain. That is, the nervous system can be viewed as a massively distributed set of special-purpose networks. Consequently, coordination, control, and novel problem solving could take place by way of central information exchange. Conscious involvement of brain resources is particularly useful when novel information needs to be combined and integrated. Looking at learning from the perspective of consciousness, we can infer that learners need to connect everything they learn to the best possible level—ideally from diverse domains or disciplinary areas—to a unified whole. In other words, to enhance consciousness, individuals need to be encouraged to learn in multiple domain areas, explicitly as well as implicitly, whenever possible. They also need to work to identify the relationships or connectivity among those knowledge networks formed, so they see an integrated and unified knowledge base that helps in their decision making.

METACOGNITION

METACOGNITION AS THINKING ABOUT THINKING OR BEYOND THINKING
In simple terms, metacognition is thinking about thinking, learning about learning, or cognition about cognition. It is raising self-awareness essentially or becoming conscious of self-knowledge. The term *meta* is a Greek word meaning *beyond*. When we comprehend beyond our cognition or thinking, it necessarily raises our consciousness on how we feel about our thinking. That is, we can link the cognitive and emotion parts. With metacognition, we become aware of our thinking and how we feel about it; inversely, we become aware of what we feel, and we get to think about it (Allman 2001; Zull 2011). For example, we may get to know whether we enjoy our learning or if it is a complicated matter to us. We may become conscious of our states of mind and realise, for example, that if we feel anger, we can think about possible actions to alleviate that anger. A couple of important features about metacognition are that it is a function performed by an individual for himself or herself; based on the self-knowledge developed, the individual can take an executive action or make decisions to regulate and improve the condition or situation in which he or she is involved. That is, an individual cannot develop metacognition for some other person or make a decision accordingly for that other person. Since we develop self-awareness through metacognition, we also become conscious of our strengths as well as our weaknesses. When we become aware of our weaknesses or limitations, we develop the important quality of humility that guides us to unlearn, as well as relearn, skills needed in the pursuit of personal improvement (Smyre 2006). As mentioned before in the text, the anterior cingulate cortex (ACC) is the region of the brain that is involved mostly in metacognitive activities. The ACC is well positioned between

the limbic system and the frontal lobe to perform the necessary function of linking cognitive and emotional activities of the mind. Further, relatively longer cells referred to as spindle neurones in the ACC are capable of connecting and integrating many parts of the brain outside the region of the ACC.

METACOGNITION AND AN ANALOGY FROM THE CONTEMPORARY BUSINESS WORLD

We can bring up some analogies from the real world to elaborate on the phenomenon of metacognition. In the business world, we have business projects or processes that organisations or teams carry out. In a typical project or process, there can be different phases that are performed by various members of the project or process team, possibly in different time periods. In addition to team members who directly take part in these activities, we usually have an individual referred to as a project or process manager to oversee the progress of the project or process in order to direct it in the right direction to achieve the the project or process goals. This resembles the function of metacognitive activities, in which we monitor the progress of our own thinking or learning. The purpose of this self-monitoring task is to identify any weakness in our thinking or learning processes so that we can self-control or self-regulate to improve the processes. However, a significant difference between the above two examples is that in metacognition, the same individual monitors and controls (self-regulates) the thinking or learning process while the project manager—an outsider—does the function of monitoring and controlling of the project in a business project.

METACOGNITION AND HOW IT RELATES TO CONSCIOUSNESS

It is important to observe the relationship between consciousness (the phenomenon we discussed in the previous section) and metacognition (as described in the two previous paragraphs). It appears that we emphasise the integration of a vast number of neural networks of knowledge in consciousness, possibly focusing on multiple domain areas that are spread across the neocortex. In metacognition, we highlight a similar process of integration, but mainly between the cognitive and emotion parts of the brain. As a result, we can be metacognitive even concerning a single domain of knowledge, as contemporary social and economic trends push individuals on a silos-based development path of a single discipline. In other words, by definition, we may be able to develop metacognitive skills in a constrained manner, directing our thoughts along a single domain path. Considering the significance of consciousness as a means of integrating diverse neural networks of knowledge across the borders of domains, the challenge is now for enhancing consciousness while at the same time being metacognitive.

This ultimate goal of unifying the brain functions in an entirely holistic manner is the path to higher levels of human development and or self-actualisation. That is, we endeavour to develop and integrate cognitive knowledge across the whole neocortex, crossing the borders of multiple disciplines while at the same time using that knowledge to monitor and self-control emotions and vice versa. In other words, when we become highly knowledgeable, penetrating artificial domain boundaries, that awareness is likely to help us control our emotions better or become more emotionally intelligent. As we can see, there is no short cut to developing emotional intelligence other than developing enhanced consciousness. Further, when we develop a higher level of emotional intelligence, we are likely to develop positive emotions such as empathy and resilience in the face of challenges. Conversely, we become capable of using our thoughtfully self-regulated emotional drives for achieving purposeful cognitive tasks or engaging in significant problem-solving activities. When we develop metacognitive abilities and use them in the lifelong learning process, we essentially get involved in a continuous personal-improvement process that leads to higher levels of self-actualisation. In other words, we have to practice metacognition using a reference of the highest possible level of human development or learning, making sure not to use any reference level below, in a never-ending pursuit of personal excellence. In fact, the development of metacognitive abilities can be seen as the formation of an additional neural network of knowledge that controls or regulates our thinking in a unified, holistic manner. In doing so, we introduce an extra dimension to our existing level of consciousness for the purpose of improving it.

METACOGNITION AND HOW IT HELPS TO ACHIEVE NEURAL EFFICIENCY

As discussed in the previous paragraphs, when consciousness is enhanced through learning, we form denser neural networks of knowledge. Through metacognitive practices, we appear to have the opportunity to make the above denser neural networks more efficiently connected (Zull 2011). When clarity of what is learnt is improved through self-awareness and reflection, we have the opportunity to simplify knowledge by getting rid of unnecessary or least-used neural networks. Consequently, in doing so, we make our clearly established, essential neural networks more efficient. Another possible way to achieve this higher efficiency is the phenomenon of automaticity, as we discussed before. In the phenomenon of automaticity, the control of highly practised cognitive tasks is transferred to sub-cortical structures of the brain, releasing cortical resources for carrying out new cognitive tasks. As we can see, when we achieve higher levels of human development by enhancing consciousness using metacognitive practices, we essentially make our neural operations more efficient.

METACOGNITION AND HOW IT RELATES TO MINDFULNESS MEDITATION

Mindfulness is a practice that gives something intentional focus or holds something in attentional awareness. In meditation, the goal is to achieve a relaxed state where the mind is still and the body is in a state of low physiological arousal. In regards to neuroscience, this state occurs when the parasympathetic nervous system is activated while the body is at rest.

A relaxed or meditative state of mind helps mindfulness. That is, when our brain is not troubled by the stress response, we can think clearly. The term *mindfulness* is commonly associated with focused-attention meditation. There are three aspects to focused attention: paying attention to the body, feelings, and inner emotional world and mind. By paying attention to the mind, we monitor our thoughts. As we can see, these are metacognitive practices that enable raising self-awareness through thinking about our thoughts and feelings. In fact, practices in mindfulness are used increasingly as psychological approaches to improving mental health (Gates 2016).

Investigations into the brains of religious individuals, who have thousands of hours of meditation under their belts, have revealed that these individuals have positive alterations in their brains. These changes were identified to be similar to the changes that occur because of new learning and experiences, a feature of neuroplasticity. Research conducted into integrative body-mind training (IBMT), which is similar to the focused-attention meditation, has revealed an improved blood flow in the left anterior cingulate cortex (ACC) and insula. In fact, these are the areas crucial for self-regulation, as we highlighted before. The most profound benefits of meditative mindfulness practices were identified to be as improved attentional and emotional regulation (Gates 2016).

To Sum Up

In this chapter, we introduced some important neuroscience concepts related to learning processes. Considering the large number of new experiences we encounter on a daily basis, we shouldn't be surprised to come to know that most of our learning is implicit and takes place as it incidentally creates implicit memories at times. By making a point to simply pay attention to these experiences and relate them to our existing memories by processing adequately in the working memory, we are in a position to learn in a lifelong manner enhancing our metacognition and consciousness.

Metacognition refers mainly to the linkage of cognitive and emotional functions of the brain for a more holistic operation through raising self-awareness to engage in self-regulation.

Consciousness is a phenomenon that scientists have paid significant interest in the recent past, because of its significance in human evolution. It is essentially the phenomenon of integration of a vast number of differentiated neural networks of knowledge across many regions of the brain, possibly belonging to multiple areas of domains. Consequently, it is time we focus on enhancing learner consciousness as an important goal of education or any learning. Our lifelong-learning process is made efficient by the brain feature known as automaticity, in which cortical resources and executive control are released for new learning when a sensorimotor action is practised to a high level. Highlighting the need for holistic brain operations, both cognitive and emotional, we got to see the important role played by emotions in learning, especially creating lasting memories. Further, as part of evaluating learning, we got to see the importance of recognition tests, as opposed to commonly but inappropriately used associative recall tests in academic environments. Following the principle of Hebbian learning, we have the opportunity to program our brains in the right directions to get them to perform what is sustainable for social and human evolution. According to Hebbian learning, if we continue learning what we need to learn the most and disregard what we don't need, our brains may retain the neural networks of memory that are most useful to us while removing the less-wanted ones.

Commonly Used Learning-Related Concepts and Measures from the Viewpoint of Neuroscience

• • •

CHAPTER 3

Mostly Learning-Related Concepts from the Viewpoint of Educational Neuroscience

• • •

SOME MOSTLY LEARNING-RELATED CONCEPTS ARE presented in this chapter by elaborating on them from the standpoint of educational neuroscience. We start by highlighting the human feature of learning by grouping information into chunks or identifying patterns by abstracting or generalising. The need for linking the perceived or sensed information to a learner's existing knowledge bases and determine a value in learning a particular content are presented for making sense and meaning. The transfer of learning is portrayed as one of the prime goals of learning, in which learners become capable of using a learned concept or idea in a related but different application or scenario. For enhanced learning, the need to process information in the working memory, by linking it to knowledge in the long-term memory for an adequate amount of time as well as a number of occasions, is highlighted as rehearsal. The need for longer wait times when presenting information to learners by asking questions, as is the case in constructivist approach, is brought to the reader's attention next. The significance of the learner motivation level in accomplishing active learning and its role in getting learner attention is emphasised before raising the value of focusing on high-level or abstract concepts, as they are retained as implicit memories through incidental learning more commonly. Different problem-solving and decision-making processes are presented as end uses of learning, followed by a discussion on differentiating between the types of solutions human brains and machines are more capable of undertaking.

CHUNKING

The term *chunking* refers to the process in which working memory perceives or compresses a set of data as a single item, similar to the way we understand a set of letters as one word (Sousa 2011). It appears to be related to the innate human characteristic and survival ability to seek patterns in the environment (Feigenson and Halberda 2004; Brady, Konkle, and Alvarez 2009). In other words, the human brain is highly capable of dealing with abstract or high-level concepts containing a vast amount of knowledge in a concise manner, as opposed to dealing with a high degree of details. Chunking occurs in two ways: in one situation, it is a deliberate and goal-oriented process initiated by the learner, such as learning a poem one line at a time. In other cases, it is subtle, automatic, and linked to perceptual processes, as when we learn to read by increasing the number of words from a single word to two words, to a phrase, and so on (Bor, Duncan, et al. 2003). Since chunking allows us to deal with a few blocks of rich information rather than a large number of small fragments, it gives us the ability to solve problems by accessing a large amount of relevant knowledge from long-term memory to be used in working memory.

Further, chunking is more of an ability to organise our knowledge base for the better use of limited working memory. In that, we can arrange information in a hierarchical manner—information-rich abstract or high-level concepts at the top and more detailed, specific information at lower levels. Then we can take information at higher and more abstract levels as much as possible into limited working memory to manage its capacity efficiently when solving problems. We as educators can rely on this information-organisation feature when introducing new contents to our learners by enabling utilisation of their working memories more efficiently. In effect, we need to minimise unnecessary or less-useful details entering a learner's working memory and cluttering his or her understanding. Further, we need to make learners mindful of the difference between high-level concepts and detailed information, for them to pay more emphasis to the former. Once a limited number of high-level concepts are processed in the working memory, following the principles of chunking and hierarchical organisation of contents while minimising any clattering that would occur due to introducing unnecessary detail at the same time, learners will be able to transfer new learning into long-term memory more efficiently.

SENSE AND MEANING

ENABLING LASTING MEMORIES BY MAKING SENSE AND MEANING
When survival and other emotional elements are not present, transferring information from short-term memory to long-term memory requires other factors that need to be addressed. One such important factor is whether sense and meaning are attached to the new learning from the perspective of the learner (Sousa 2011). When we say "the content or new learning makes sense to the learner," we mean that he or she can then connect prior knowledge to the new learning. In other words, the learner can comprehend new knowledge based on what he or she knows about the world or how it operates. Even if educators introduce entirely new contents or concepts to learners, we should be able to relate them to some previous experiences of the learners for them to make sense. Learners would feel that they are extending their existing knowledge base and get to understand the world better rather than something entirely foreign to them landing on their heads. Further, they will be forming an integrated or connected network of knowledge—a prime requirement of enhancing consciousness—instead of getting introduced to an isolated piece of information. Turning to the second point, when meaning is attached to new learning, it becomes relevant to the learner in a foreseeable manner, and there is a purpose or motivation for the learner to pay attention to it. That is, the new information introduced needs to be meaningful and useful to the learner somehow in the context of his or her understanding or operation. If both sense and meaning are present, the likelihood of transferring from the short-term to long-term storage is very high. Then

it is understood to have substantially more cerebral activity followed by dramatically improved retention (Maquire et al. 1999; Poppenk et al. 2010; Rittle-Johnson and Kmicikewycz 2008). Of the two criteria, meaning has a greater impact on the probability that information will be stored in long-term memory. One way to attach meaning to new learning is to help students to make connections between subject areas by integrating curricula; it increases meaning and retention, especially when students recognise a future use of the new learning.

PROCESSING INFORMATION IN THE WORKING MEMORY TO MAKE SENSE AND MEANING

When the introduction of new content is detected from the sensory organs and sensory parts of the cerebral hemispheres, it will be processed in the working memory while sense and meaning are being made. To make sense, previously learnt and related contents would need to be retrieved from long-term memory and fed into the working memory alongside the newly sensed information. For this to happen, learners will be made to essentially use the frontal lobes that connect almost all the other regions of the brain. Consequently, the degree of making sense is dependent on the learner's existing neural networks of knowledge and is dependent on individual learner characteristics. Similarly, making meaning is a subjective process, depending on different aspirations of the learners. Following the theory of constructivism—in which learners construct knowledge on an individual basis—we see the subjectivity of learning, even when the same contents are presented to a diverse set of learners.

THE OUTCOME WHEN SENSE AND MEANING ARE NOT MADE

It is also interesting to note the possible outcomes if learners do not find sense and meaning in what they get introduced to in a session. The newly introduced content will become standalone pieces of information, without having a firm structure to get them connected to explicitly. The frontal lobes, an important organ in regards to engaging in higher-order learning, will not be utilised to connect this newly introduced information to the existing neural networks of knowledge. Consequently, such pieces of information introduced will disappear after being in short-term memory for a few hours (or days, at most). They are unlikely to get transferred to long-term memory, as proper connections with the other neural networks of knowledge are not made. It implies a lacklustre attitude towards learning in which learners are reluctant to invest a reasonable amount of time to create lasting memories, possibly due to lack of some dispensable time or in fear of new information that would contradict one's existing framework of knowledge.

For example, if a certain learner starts preparing for an examination at the last moment, he or she will try to cram as much information as possible into short-term memory in a brief period. Some researchers refer to such attempts of learning as *surface* or *strategic learning*, aimed mainly at getting through the examination rather than learning deeply per se. Further, such a learner will see meaning in what he or she learns in a very limited sense, lacking in intrinsic motivation.

Transfer

Transfer as the Key to Problem Solving and Creative Thinking

The phenomenon known as the transfer is one of the ultimate goals of teaching and learning. It encompasses the ability to learn in one situation and then use that knowledge, possibly in a modified or generalised form, in other circumstances (Sousa 2011). The transfer is the key process involved in problem solving, creative thinking, and all other higher mental processes involved in the creation of inventions and artistic products. As you may see, the degree or quality of the transfer is dependent on two things: how well a learner can generalise the contents learned, so that they can be readily reused in as many future situations as possible, and how well they can be transferred from short-term to long-term memory.

The transfer can be described as a two-part process: transfer during learning and transfer of learning. In the former, the effects past learning have on the acquisition and processing of new learning are highlighted; in the latter, the degree to which the learner becomes capable of applying new learning to future situations is presented. Further, the transfer can be categorised as positive and negative transfers; in the positive transfer, prior learning helps the learner with new learning; prior learning interferes with the learner's understanding of new learning in the negative transfer. We can see here a close relationship between the concepts of making sense and meaning highlighted in the previous paragraph and transfer; the more the learner makes sense and meaning, thereby enhancing the level of understanding and interest in the content, the more efficiently the function of transfer can takes place.

INTEGRATED THEMATIC UNITS TO ENABLE TRANSFER

One way educators achieve successful transfer is by introducing integrated thematic units, in which a series of lessons derived from multiple domain or disciplinary areas are conducted on a specific theme. Factors that affect the transfer process include the context and degree of original learning (through making sense and meaning) and highlighted critical attributes of a concept (Hunter 2004). In regards to the first factor, it is important to understand that if something is worth teaching, it needs to be explained well; that is, high-level or abstract concepts need to be highlighted in the most generic forms possible. A generic form can be used in many specific situations or applications with appropriate modifications. To enhance clarity when a high-level concept is presented, specific applications related to it should be demonstrated (while still maintaining the significance of the generic form as the one that can be reused in different situations, most likely with some modifications). The second factor highlights the need to emphasise the unique characteristics of the concepts learned. With these unique features, the highlighted concept will be differentiated clearly with other concepts so that it can be readily used in appropriate situations or applications. Further, it is understood that significant and efficient transfer occurs if we only teach to achieve it (Hunter 2004; Mestre 2002; Perkins and Saloman 1988). The proper and frequent use of methodologies enabling transfer enhances the constructivist approach substantially (Brooks and Brooks 1999) to learning, and vice versa.

As highlighted in the previous section of making sense and meaning, if a learner does not achieve the transfer of knowledge, new information will be retained in short-term memory for a limited period. At the same time, it would make them useful only in a very narrow sense, as that would happen in a surface or strategic-learning exercise.

REHEARSAL

INITIAL AND SECONDARY REHEARSAL

In the context of learning, the term *rehearsal* is used principally to refer to the processing of information in working memory to make meaningful connections or inferences (Sousa 2011). It is a critical component that helps efficient transference of information from the working memory to long-term memory. There are two major factors associated with the process of rehearsal: the amount of time devoted to rehearsal and the type of rehearsal. The amount of time spent for rehearsal applies to two stages, either the initial or secondary stage. Initial rehearsal occurs when information first enters the working memory (the time when sense and meaning are attached). Several studies showed that during longer rehearsals, which may even take place at a secondary stage, the amount of activity in the frontal lobe determined whether items were stored or forgotten (Buckner, Kelley, and Petersen 1999; Wagner, et al. 1998).

As discussed before, the frontal lobe is the place where working memory is located and the most cognitive part of the brain that connects with almost all the other functional units of the brain. Consequently, we can rationalise that through rehearsing, we process pieces of information entering working memory by meaningfully connecting them with the other information retrieved from the other parts of the brain to make valid and useful inferences. The longer we engage in the process of rehearsing, the clearer our inferences become, and this enables the transfer of knowledge from working memory to long-term memory. Imagine the familiar situation again where learners prepare for a test or examination hurriedly and at the last moment; their only goal is to cram as much information as possible into their short-term memory. The learners will not spend enough time rehearsing this information in the working memory, making new connections in an idiosyncratic manner so that created inferences can be transferred into long-term memory; instead, the information will be crammed into short-term memory and will be forgotten within a few days at the most.

MASSED AND DISTRIBUTED REHEARSAL

Another categorisation of the task of practising or rehearsal is whether it is a *massed practise* or a *distributed practise*. Practising new learning during time periods that are very close together is called massed practise; immediate memory (a type of short-term memory) is involved here substantially. Some example situations are mentally rehearsing a new phone number, cramming for an exam, and trying a different example of applying new learning within a short period. In distributed practise, a more sustained practise over time is done, or a spacing effect is introduced. It is the key to retention in long-term memory, as is the case of secondary rehearsal (Seabrook, Brown, and Solity 2005; Metcalfe, Kornell, and Son 2007; Carpenter, Pashler, and Cepeda 2009; Hunter 2004). In distributive rehearsal, we first recall related information from our long-term memory—a critical phase of the complete learning cycle—before processing further in working memory by improving clarity and making more connections amongst the sets of information accessible. Distributive practice is usually something done by learners on their own following a formal teaching-learning session with the help of a facilitator. However, a spiral curriculum in which key concepts are revised at regular intervals is a useful method we can undertake to engage learners in distributed practice with the help of a facilitator.

ROTE AND ELABORATIVE REHEARSAL

We also differentiate between the types of rehearsal which can be either rote rehearsal or elaborative rehearsal (Sousa 2011). When a learner has to remember information exactly the way it entered working memory, it is termed as rote rehearsal. As you would expect, the frontal lobe activation is minimal (if it occurs at all) in rote rehearsal activities. Some examples are when a poem, telephone number, or multiplication table is remembered. Elaborative rehearsal, on the other hand, takes place when new learning is associated with prior learning to form new connections. Contents of prior learning could be stored in many parts of the brain as long-term memory, and they can be retrieved via the prefrontal cortex (PFC) in the frontal lobes that connect many brain regions together. As mentioned before, since there is a correlation between frontal lobe activation and longer reaction time, elaborative rehearsal is likely to take more time; however, it leads to better retention in long-term memory, as the clarity of the information processed is improved through elaborative rehearsal.

In contrast, rote rehearsal is a quicker process that is likely to retain information in short-term memory, as is the case when cramming information for a test or examination. The attachment of sense and meaning to new learning, as discussed before, can only occur if learners get an adequate time to process (rehearse) it in working memory. When learners do not get enough time for elaborative rehearsal, they have no option but to resort more frequently to rote rehearsal. Consequently, when presenting new information to learners in a teaching-learning session, it is important to manage the pace of delivery of information so that learners get enough time for elaborative rehearsal. In a similar vein, when learners engage in distributive or secondary rehearsal—for example, when preparing for a test or examination, it is important that they allow adequate time to engage in elaborative rehearsal, instead of trying to rush through, resulting a futile exercise of rote rehearsal. Further, when we set assessments as educators, we should endeavour to discourage learners from engaging in rote rehearsal (or rote memorisation, as it is commonly known) by giving due care on the designing aspect of assessment tasks. If we expect learners to reproduce what we described during the teaching-learning session or what was provided in the teaching-learning material in the exact form they were presented, then learners would resort quickly to rote rehearsal practices, merely for the purpose of scoring high on the respective assessments, despite no real learning being achieved. Instead, we should set assessment in a manner that requires learners to provide well-constructed and individualised answers essentially by engaging in elaborative rehearsal processes.

DEVELOPING METACOGNITION AS PART OF REHEARSAL

Learners should be explicitly encouraged to engage in metacognitive practices as part of rehearsal they carry out at various times. That is, they should develop an awareness of how they linked newly introduced information to their existing knowledge bases, how successful they were in doing so, how long they did it, how enjoyable the experience was, etc. When done at regular intervals, such self-reflective practices will help learners to be aware of their learning process as well as to take control of it. This additional layer of self-awareness or consciousness as part of regular rehearsal exercises—because it oversees the overall learning process—is very useful for learners to develop, as it will guide them to be independent lifelong learners.

Wait Times

As an educator, have you thought seriously about the pace of delivery in a teaching-learning session? We introduce the term "wait time" as a related measure in this context. The wait time described here is the period of teacher silence that follows posing a question to the learner cohort before the first student is called upon for a response (Sousa 2011). Studies reveal that higher wait times (about five seconds) showed improved learning outcomes (Rowe 1974), providing an increased number of higher-order responses. These questions that require longer wait times will essentially have to be thought-provoking ones, requiring learners to engage in more elaborative rehearsal using the frontal lobes before responding. In other words, they would not be questions that require mere recall (or rote memorisation) of factual information, as they can be answered relatively quickly if the answers are known to the learners.

Instead, these questions will be more open ended, requiring inductive or divergent thinking or generalisations and can have multiple acceptable answers. Further, the same researcher also noted that constant longer wait times resulted in positive changes in the behaviour of teachers by giving them an inclination to use an increased number of higher-order questions. We can rationalise here that educators who see the value of allowing an adequate or longer wait time for learners to answer are not afraid of taking a longer time to ask the right question; they can see the significance of the same efforts to get the learners engaged. Further, the educator will not be in a hurry to rush through as much information as possible during the limited time duration; instead, he or she will be more relaxed in his or her interaction with the learners. With higher-order questioning and longer wait times, the teaching-learning process essentially becomes a discussion of a dialectic nature, as opposed to a didactic one.

LEARNER MOTIVATION AND ATTENTION

HIGHER LEVEL OF MOTIVATION LEADING TO BETTER ATTENTION

In a teaching-learning process, getting the full attention of learners is of immense significance. As described by the phenomenon known as the binocular rivalry (Baars and Gage 2010) as a human limitation, in a way, a learner cannot pay his or her full attention to more than one thing at a time (Logothetis 1998; Tong, et al. 1998). When full attention is paid to the contents being introduced or the teaching-learning process, a learner's entire brain resources are focused on it, and this results in a very high level of engagement. A learner has to have a high degree of motivation towards the task or area being learned to pay full attention.

In some cases, learners can be motivated to learn a particular area or task if they are emotionally attached to it. In other words, emotions can play a significant role motivating learners to pay attention (Damasio 2005; Goleman 2005; Zull 2002, 2011; Panksepp 1998). In some other situations, learners see some lasting value in what they learn because the contents learned are likely to be highly useful in the future; this aspect we discussed earlier as having a meaning in what they learn. As educators, we have the responsibility of motivating learners on the subject matter so that they pay full attention. One general way of motivating learners during a teaching-learning process is to present high-level, abstract concepts or generalisations instead of more specific details. Since high-level concepts often cross the boundaries of domains, we can engage a higher number of learners in the teaching-learning process, based on their preferred domain of knowledge. Since high-level concepts represent inter-domain knowledge, they can be more useful in a wide range of day-to-day life applications as well. Also, since these high-level concepts are usually stored as semantic memory, as discussed before, they last longer in learner memory (Tulving 1972, 1985). These lasting memories can further be linked to other concepts learned in future as well. Further, educators can provide exclusive time for learners to take notes, if required, as divided attention (Anderson, et al. 2000; Fletcher, et al. 1995) on listening and note-taking at the same time can hamper the level of attention and deep engagement. Disturbed attention and engagement would negatively impact understanding achieved through the formation of new neural networks.

Intrinsic and Extrinsic Motivation
The longer an item being learnt is processed (or rehearsed) in the working memory, the greater the probability that sense and meaning are attached, and therefore the greater level of retention in long-term memory (Sousa 2011) can be achieved. Recent research studies have validated the longstanding belief that motivation is the key to the amount of attention and time devoted to a learning activity. Focus and learning take place at the highest possible level when the learner is intrinsically motivated to learn the contents being presented (Walker, Greene, and Mansell 2006; Wigfield and Eccles 2002). A learner will get intrinsically motivated on learning an item or some contents if the outcome of that learning will have a long-lasting value to the learner, while an extrinsic motivation will lead a learner to achieve a relatively short-term goal.

Enhancing wisdom or consciousness that leads to a higher level of human development through learning is a long-lasting, broadly understood motivation of intrinsic nature, whereas in many cases, obtaining a higher grade at the forthcoming examination or test can be a short-term, more narrowly perceived motivation of an extrinsic nature. Extrinsic motivators can only be of value to get students started on a learning topic before they can move towards more intrinsic rewards, following better comprehension. However, extrinsic motivators do not always align well with long-lasting, intrinsic motivators. For example, if an assessment component is focused on testing merely the ability of rote memorisation, getting a higher grade for that evaluation will not lead learners towards a higher level of human development through enhanced wisdom or consciousness. Consequently, it is important that educators always align well any short-term, extrinsic motivators we define and use to more sustainable, intrinsic, and purposeful motivators so that the engagement of learners is increased.

ADDITIONAL MOTIVATIONAL FACTORS

Researchers have identified some other practices that can be used to motivate learners (Diamond and Hopson, 1998; Hunter 2004; Moore 2005). Teachers can relate the new item being learnt to as many past neural networks of learning as possible, including as many real-world examples. When learners improve clarity on what they have learnt before—by viewing them from different perspectives or get to understand and explain real-world phenomena better, they become motivated to engage in the process of learning. Researchers have noticed significant student disengagement resulting from facilitators not being able to connect classroom studies to real-world applications (Larkin 2016). Giving timely feedback on learner thinking during a teaching-learning session is another such practice we can use to motivate learners to continue processing and make corrective actions until the completion of successful learning.

An additional measure that educators can adjust for motivating learners is referred to as *the level of concern* (Sousa 2011). We can try to introduce and maintain an appropriate level of concern for the learners to have an anxiety level that is helpful for learning, rather than crossing the boundary to a higher anxiety level that is harmful. When a helpful anxiety level is maintained, it develops a desire for learners to do well; a harmful anxiety level will threaten learners to keep away from engagement. For example, if educators mention that the contents being introduced are not hard to master if an appropriate learning methodology is followed, it would develop a helpful anxiety level within learners, thanks to an excitement level due to the newness of the content that is presented at an acceptable level as it can be mastered. On the other hand, if we signify the level of difficulty (possibly based on previous learner responses or conventional perception of the subject area), learners would develop a harmful anxiety level towards the contents being learnt, resulting in disengagement from the learning process.

ENABLING POSITIVE EMOTIONS AS MOTIVATORS
Another way of looking at the level of concern contributing towards learner motivation is the emotional status of the learner. Recent studies reaffirm that as learners generate positive emotions, their scope of attention broadens and critical-thinking skills are enhanced (Sousa 2011). With a higher level of attention, brain resources, especially cortical resources, are more focused on the process of learning. That is, they are in a better state to associate sense to what they learn by connecting them with their previous learning and looking at them more objectively or critically. In contrast, neutral and negative emotions narrow the scope of attention and thinking (Fredrickson and Branigan 2005; Zenasni and Lubart 2011). Emotions affect learning in two distinct ways: the emotional status of the environment in which learning occurs (implicit memory) and the degree to which emotions are associated with the learning content (explicit memory). When students feel positive about their learning environment, such as the presence of a nonauthoritative, friendly facilitator, a biochemical called endorphins is released in the brain. Endorphins produce a feeling of euphoria and stimulate the frontal lobes.

To recall, as frontal lobes connect to almost all the other functional units of the brain, contents being learnt can be readily associated with related previous learning. Consequently, the learning experience is made more pleasurable and fruitful. Conversely, if students are stressed and have a negative feeling about the learning environment, a hormone called cortisol is released. Cortisol travels throughout the brain and body and activates defence behaviours, such as fight or flight. As a result, the frontal lobe activity is reduced, possibly disconnecting with many other regions of the brain, in order to focus on the more urgent matter of identifying the cause of stress and how to deal with it (Kuhlmann, Kirschbaumm, and Woolf 2005; Tollenaar et al. 2009).

ENABLING CREATIVE THOUGHTS AS MOTIVATORS

Recent research reveals that students are more likely to gain greater understanding and pleasure from learning when they are allowed to transform the learning experience through creative ideas and products (Sousa 2011). That is, we can infer that learners, naturally as creative human beings, dislike rote rehearsal or memorisation in which they have to reproduce what they gather in the exact form it is collected. They would engage in rote rehearsal only if accommodations and encouragements are present for them, mainly through inappropriately set assessment. Instead, they gain pleasure in connecting what they gather with their previous learning or their other existing neural networks of knowledge in numerous ways.

It is understood that our success as a species can, to a certain extent, be attributed to the brain's persistent interest in novelty; that is, as human beings, we like to see changes occurring within ourselves (more specifically, the neural networks we possess) and in our environment. Conversely, if an environment contains mainly predictable or repeated stimuli, the brain's interest and attention on the task at hand is lowered, and attempts are made within for novel sensation. As a result, we can make learners pay more attention by enabling and encouraging them and giving them enough freedom to make new connections between new knowledge introduced and past learning or experience. When we facilitate the process of transfer appropriately by allowing learners to make sense and meaning of the new knowledge, learners will be more motivated to engage in the learning process.

UNDERSTANDING THE FOCUS ON CONCEPTS/DETAILS AND IMPLICIT MEMORIES CREATED THROUGH INCIDENTAL LEARNING

ABSTRACT/GENERALISED CONCEPTS AS LASTING SEMANTIC MEMORIES
As we have highlighted before, learning abstract concepts is a higher-order learning process associated with enhancing human consciousness. These abstract concepts are often generalisations (Penfield and Milner 1958) across multiple domains, and as a result, they can be presented from or connected to multiple perspectives. In this way, by highlighting broader concepts, we can reach out to learners from diverse backgrounds possessing various neural networks of knowledge. Consequently, the ability to present abstract concepts in a generalised manner viewing from multiple domains is a very potent tool for educators to possess. Also, compared to detailed, more specific procedures stored as episodic or autobiographical memory (Baars and Gage 2010; Tulving 1972, 1985), abstract concepts learned are stored as semantic memories for a longer period. Usually, only some conceptual parts of the episodic memories we absorb will be retained in the longer run as semantic memories. Consequently, in academic learning environments, which are explicit in nature, it is important that we highlight relatively a small number of high-level concepts or generalisations rather than a higher number of more precise, detailed descriptions. By emphasising a limited number of abstract concepts instead of a larger number of detailed descriptions, we can make use of a learner's limited-capacity working memory more efficiently to enable him or her to engage in elaborative rehearsal to form new and useful neural networks of knowledge. Filling the working memory of a learner with large volumes of specific detail will not help him or her to connect them to existing knowledge bases or, as we highlighted before, to make sense and meaning of them. More specifically, in assessments, we need to test the learner's ability to understand and retain high-level concepts instead of specific details,

which will be kept in his or her memory for a very short duration of time. If we focus on specific details instead of high-level concepts, learners tend to engage in rote rehearsal activities to reproduce the crammed contents in short-term memory.

ASSESSING HIGH-LEVEL CONCEPTS RETAINED AS IMPLICIT MEMORIES THROUGH INCIDENTAL LEARNING

In a related note, it has been observed that most of our learning is identified to be implicit (Baars and Gage 2010). That is, we retain some knowledge unconsciously as a by-product of a conscious input. We can infer here that if a learner is capable of keeping some knowledge unconsciously for a longer period, it is stored in as semantic memory. In effect, through incidental learning, some vague high-level concepts are likely to be retained as implicit memories. Consequently, in our assessments, it is important that we evaluate learners' implicit learning components as well by giving them an opportunity to formulate answers amalgamating their implicit memories as well. To assess implicit learning components, one possible approach we can take would be to include open-ended questions and observe the accurate, relevant, and useful inference they can make. Open-ended questions can perform a priming function to stimulate learners' brains and retrieve implicit memories (Roediger and McDermott 1993). In other words, we will not be able to assess a learner's implicit learning component by asking associative-recall or objective-type questions with only one correct answer. Instead, we should test the learner's ability to make a comparative judgement on a more open-ended matter. Our assessments here can be recognition tests, rather than associative recall. When an associative recall is pursued, the learner will scan his or her brain in search of an exact answer to a given question, possibly from short-term memory, while in a recognition pursuit, he or she will scan the brain for any related content that can be presented as a possible answer.

As you may recognise, the latter is a more creative approach to problem solving, while the former can be the norm when only explicit learning is pursued. This can occur when educators expect the learners to reproduce information as memorised in its exact form, resulting in a rote rehearsal engagement. Further, in this approach, we support the constructivist theory of learning, in which learners make meaning individually within themselves using the priming contents they get introduced. By doing this, we make our assessment fairer and more valid, as far as active and lasting learning has taken place. Further, gifted learners are observed to be highly capable in incidental learning (Eide and Eide 2004); hence we give them a fairer chance to demonstrate their learning when more open-ended questions are used, promoting inclusive practices.

TYPES OF PROBLEM SOLVING OR DECISION MAKING

VERIDICAL AND ADAPTIVE DECISION MAKING
Individuals need to become better decision makers and problem solvers through education. When we refer to decision making and problem solving, it is implied that there are many possible decisions we can make in a given scenario and possible solutions to the problems we attempt to solve, as opposed to having one fixed decision or solution that can be achieved procedurally. Some of these possible decisions and solutions we consider as appropriate can be very close to other similar possible decisions and solutions. As a result, differentiating these decisions and solutions from some other similar possibilities can be tough; their differences can be very subtle. To make the optimal decision or to find the optimal solution, taking into consideration as many or all the related facets, it requires well-developed and highly structured thinking. This practice is significantly different from another commonly used approach of routinely following one small step at a time until we find a specific or deterministic answer.

Usually, machines or computers are better suited for carrying out such routine procedures a significant number of times more accurately without getting bored or some kind of disruption. However, in schools or colleges, we are usually given a problem or question, and we must find or write the correct answer. Usually, only one right answer exists to these questions or problems. For example, balancing a chequebook by carrying out some repetitive tasks, remembering the capital city of a country, or a deterministic value are similar tasks. By finding the correct answer, we say that we engage in veridical decision making (Baars and Gage 2010). However, apart from high school exams, college tests, and factual and computational trivia, most decisions we make in our everyday lives do not have intrinsically correct solutions we can obtain by following routine steps. That is, the decisions we make as individuals are not always objective; rather, in most cases, they are subjective. What career path to take and what location to visit on vacation are examples of decisions we make in ambiguous situations. Even though there are no deterministic answers to such questions, we can optimise our decisions by taking into consideration as many related dimensions or perspectives as possible for the decision-making process.

What dimensions or perspectives we take into account would essentially depend on individual experiences and characteristics, such as existing neural networks of knowledge, resulting in highly subjective outcomes in some instances. By making a decision or choice in this way, we engage in adaptive decision making. The decision-making process referred to here is adaptive, because different subjective outcomes are reached depending on what factors or dimensions are taken into consideration. Further, these factors and dimensions, as well as their degree of consideration, can even vary with time for the same decision maker. As one would expect, the consequences of the decision we make can be different, depending on the number of dimensions or perspectives we take into or can afford to have for consideration; in other words, the level of optimality can vary. By viewing from another perspective, it becomes evident that a human being's best neural system performance is not achieved by processing the exact symbol sequences that conventional computers handle so well. Rather, our brains are exceptionally good at dealing with complex, ill-defined, and novel challenges, the kinds that people have to deal with in the real world. That is, humans are extremely flexible in adapting to new conditions.

CONTRIBUTION OF PROPERTIES OF THE SITUATION AND INDIVIDUALS IN DECISION MAKING

The choices or decisions we make are not merely inherent in the situations at hand. They are a complex interplay between the properties of the situations and our individual properties such as aspirations, doubts, and histories or simply neural networks of knowledge we hold (Baars and Gage 2010). The prefrontal cortex (PFC) is central to such decision making or evaluation, as it is connected to many other brain regions, accommodating and gathering related information. On the other hand, finding solutions for deterministic situations often is accomplished algorithmically or by following steps routinely. These tasks are increasingly delegated to various devices such as calculators, computers, and the like. However, in the absence of inherently correct solutions, making judgements remains, at least for now, in a uniquely human territory. Thus, through learning, an individual must develop the capacity to have the flexibility to adopt different perspectives on the same situation at different times. The organism must be able to disambiguate the same situation in multiple different ways, depending on the information available or knowledge possessed and to have the capacity to switch between them at will. We, as learners, need to be mindful of the fact that we hold certain positions on certain things at certain times depending on the neural networks of knowledge possessed at the point in time, but not because the positions we held were fixed and ultimate facts. As a result, when we evolve through human development, changing the neural networks of knowledge we hold, we are likely and willing to change our positions or adopt a different stance as required.

Frontal lobes of the brain hemispheres play a significant role in dealing with these ambiguous situations.

DECISION MAKING OR PROBLEM SOLVING IN SCIENCE STREAMS AS A CREATIVE PROCESS

Science usually works from a third-person perspective (Baars and Gage 2010). We assume that there are hard facts of science, and scientists will have to unravel these facts through the extensive, monotonous task of searching. In other words, it is as if scientists randomly select a hypothesis and perform an infinite number of experiments until the hypothesis or a variation is proved satisfactorily. In effect, we have disregarded the significance of the role of identifying a feasible or appropriate hypothesis (as opposed to using a random one) by scientists as creative human beings. It means that researchers adopt an objective point of view and see all evidence as a physical object. Even human beings are seen as objects, not as living beings who have creative minds and can think. In fact, researchers have found that the above approach to science education has created disengagement of learners from the discipline (Tytler 2016).

It appears that goals of and approaches to science education, in general, have shifted recently. Scientists interested in consciousness have begun arguing for an additional way of conducting and approaching science that appreciates and accepts data gathered from a first-person perspective (i.e., representing phenomenological data from introspection or self-report). In a second-person perspective, the other person is viewed as a subject rather than an object, as someone who has mental states (Baron-Cohen 1995; Frith and Frith 1999). In other words, we start to realise that science is a human creation, rather than an object found through searching. Scientists, as human beings, relate their experimental findings to their existing neural networks of knowledge to produce scientific discoveries. Consequently, the mental states of these scientists or neural networks of knowledge they possess are of immense value when they produce ground-breaking discoveries. We tend to see the differences in approaches used in teaching-learning environments of hard and soft sciences disappear. That is, there is no reason why educators cannot use a higher-order learning approach targeting the high end of Bloom's spectrum for science education as well.

Differentiating Machines and Human Brains in Regards to Learning

Selectionist and Instructionist Operations

Human brains are identified to be selectionist (Baars and Gage 2010; Edelman 1989), in which new neural connections can always be created or grown by making new synaptic connections amongst a vast number of neuronal dendrites present. On the other hand, conventional computers are said to be instructionist, where a limited set of instructions or symbols are used to perform a limited set of tasks. Consequently, we say human brains are creative because they can create an infinite number of neural networks or pieces of knowledge theoretically. Further, conventional computers are better in operating sequentially or algorithmically within a limited scope in finding answers to problems where there are exact or predefined answers (Baars and Gage 2010; Beale and Jackson 1990). Some examples would be to multiply two large numbers or balance an account book. Generating an exact answer where there exists only one possible answer similar to the above exercises is referred to as veridical decision making. Based on the left- and right-hemispheric characteristics mentioned before, you may observe that the left-hemispheric brain is more involved in veridical decision making. On the other hand, human brains are better suited for making a judgement or choice where there is no one correct answer. These answers can vary from person to person, context to context, and time to time. Consequently, the same individual can make different decisions on the same problem at the various stages of his or her life.

MACHINES AS MINDLESS DEVICES LACKING METACOGNITIVE ABILITIES

Machines or conventional computers are mindless devices lacking emotions or metacognitive abilities. Consequently, they cannot develop self-awareness as to what they are doing, how they are doing it, how others think, or how their minds work. Unlike human beings, who can self-regulate their actions in a sophisticated manner, machines are typically not capable of performing self-control in their operations, outside any pre-programmed instructions.

THE ROLE OF PREFRONTAL CORTEX (PFC) IN HUMAN/CREATIVE DECISION MAKING

Depending on how many dimensions are taken into consideration, the outcome varies. That is, human beings can learn and unlearn, taking different perspectives of an issue into consideration. This type of optimal decision making human beings are more capable of is known as *adaptive (creative) decision making*. Based on the previous characteristic listing, you may see that the right-hemispheric brain is more involved in adaptive (creative) decision making. The PFC—which is considered as an essential component of human civilisation—plays a vital role in such decision making or making choices in ambiguous situations (Baars and Gage 2010; Fuster 1997; Goldberg 2001; Ingvar 1985; Luria 1966). It has been observed that when the PFC is used for an integrative decision-making activity, the process is relatively slower or takes more time. Even identifying which dimensions or perspectives are appropriate or lie within the problem scope to start with can be time-consuming.

Another related concept is automaticity, in which involvement of cortical resources from various brain regions is reduced significantly when a highly practiced activity is carried out (Chein and Schneider 2005; Coulthard, et al. 2008; Langer and Imber 1979; Raaijmakers and Shiffrin 1992; Schneider 2009; Shiffrin and Schneider 1977). These observations explain the reason why conventional computers or machines are better at carrying out routine tasks much quicker than a decision-making process involving a novel task by a human being. One of the goals of education is to convert explicit problem solving to the implicit type, in which we may use fewer cortical resources. However, due to the plasticity nature of human brain (Scholz, Klein, et al. 2009; den Ouden, Friston, et al. 2009), once a solution or activity is mastered to a level of automaticity, ideally the individual needs to shift the focus, so as to concentrate or utilise cortical resources in solving a different, novel problem mastering a different activity. This lifelong process of learning by moving the focal points to newer areas or domains should continue throughout one's lifespan, to yield the full benefits of specieswide human inheritances. In fact, the capacity of the continual growth of neural networks or creativity could be the most important feature that differentiates human beings from machines such as typical computers. In fact, machines or conventional computers do not evolve or learn new activities with time; instead, they perform the same set of actions repetitively throughout their useful existence.

To Sum Up

Sometimes, it is enlightening to understand a validating scientific basis for our learning processes or concepts. In this chapter, we have attempted to achieve that goal. We came to know that our working memory, which has a limited capacity and a time for contents in it, performs better when we group or chunk information and minimise specific details. Consequently, we do our best in a teaching-learning process to first highlight abstract concepts that are rich in information, before presenting additional details—only if required for better understanding. To create lasting memories through enhanced learning, we encourage learners to make sense and meaning by engaging in elaborate rehearsal. That is, learners attempt to link the information presented or detected to their existing knowledge bases by processing them for an adequate time in the working memory, so that a firm grounding in the knowledge they created is formed. When such a firm grounding of the knowledge is built, learners are likely to achieve the transfer of learning in which they can use the learned knowledge in a creative manner when circumstances arise. Enhanced learning through transfer can be supported by educators when they use relatively longer wait times in presenting contents in a teaching-learning session by asking questions. This practice is widely observed in the constructivist approach to teaching or facilitation. Learner motivation is an essential requirement for enhanced learning, and the higher the level of motivation, the better the level of attention learners pay for the teaching-learning process. More specifically, an intrinsic motivation based on a lasting value is required for learners to stay focused on learning in a lifelong manner en route to enhancing consciousness or wisdom, as opposed to being extrinsically motivated to achieve short-term goals. One of the purposes of education or learning is to make learners better problem solvers and decision makers; particularly, they have to become better adaptive or creative decision makers, as opposed to veridical decision makers, through learning. Veridical decision making engages in algorithmic or routine procedures and is the domain of machines or typical computers. Even though machines or conventional computers are good at performing repetitive tasks very fast using a limited-capacity instructionist approach, they find it difficult to produce creative or adaptive solutions as done by human beings following an infinite-capacity selectionist approach.

Some Learning-Related Measures: Intelligence, Emotions, and Creativity from the Viewpoint of Educational Neuroscience

•   •   •

THIS CHAPTER DISCUSSES SOME COMMONLY used learning-related measures or indicators—intelligence, emotions, and creativity—from the standpoint of educational neuroscience. The measure of intelligence is usually used to refer to some general cognitive ability of an individual, while high emotions are seen as a negative indication as a whole or as something that distorts human thinking, albeit quite inappropriately. The third measure of creativity is usually received positively by our societies, even though we find many academic environments that do not foster it in our learners appropriately. By relying on some neuroscience-based evidence, we will endeavour to understand these learning indicators in more depth in the following sections.

INTELLIGENCE

WHAT IS INTELLIGENCE?
The term *intelligence* is commonly used as a measure of general human ability. For example, if one refers to a particular person as an "intelligent individual," it implies that he or she is a capable individual in an overall

sense and is likely to succeed in life. However, it is interesting in recognising how neuroscientists more formally use the term. Evolution of intelligence is viewed as an increase in the ability to apply specific functions from different regions of the brain to life situations (Rozin 1976). For example, Broca's and Wernicke's areas, in the left-cerebral hemisphere, may be used in increasingly different ways for language production and reception respectively (Baars and Gage 2010) over the years, resulting in an increase in verbal-linguistic intelligence. The motor cortex may be used in various bodily-kinaesthetic exercises over the years, increasing the respective intelligence.

In other words, during a human lifetime, more specialised functions can become available for new adaptive purposes or become intelligent for new uses. That is, more specific neural networks are differentiated during the lifetime, and these differentiated systems can be utilised on their own or possibly in an integrated manner to adapt to new situations. Consequently, we see some overlapping concepts in the inferential abstractions of consciousness and intelligence as we saw being described. Notably, the integration process of neural networks of knowledge from diverse brain regions is one essential feature of consciousness, while it is less explicitly stated or emphasised in the definition of intelligence. Within our current social context, what we commonly observe is that we may learn a particular skill or develop a special intelligence or knowledge base within a domain area relatively early in life and continue to use it repeatedly as a career, possibly with some improvements, throughout a working life. That is, we may utilise our whole dispensable time on a particular skill, domain knowledge area, or intelligence. As a result, we may not develop other relatively new skills or domain knowledge, mainly because we are not motivated to do so, not because we as human beings do not have the capacity to develop as creative individuals and extending our knowledge and skill bases. These patterns were clearly observed by the famous psychologists Abraham Maslow (1968, 1993) and Kazimierz

Dabrowski (1970, 1972, and 1977) and stated in their respective human-development theories that many human beings do not reach the possible higher levels of enhanced consciousness or wisdom due to lack of conducive environments.

MULTIPLE FACETS OF INTELLIGENCE

The 1980s work of Howard Gardner and Robert Sternberg appeared to have changed the concept of intelligence from a singular entity to a multifaceted aptitude that varies even within the same person (Sousa 2011). The different facets of intelligence Gardner (2006) initially identified were verbal-linguistic, logical-mathematical, visual-spatial, interpersonal, intrapersonal, bodily-kinaesthetic, and musical intelligence. He defined intelligence as an individual's ability to use a learned skill, create products, or solve problems in a way that is valued by the society of the individual. This approach expands our understanding of intelligence to include divergent thinking and interpersonal expertise. According to this broad definition, as long as an individual has a well-developed skill or domain of knowledge that can be used successfully and in an acceptable manner within the society, then he or she can be identified as an "intelligent" person. As you may observe, the definition of intelligence in this way is a subjective measure in regards to the perception of the society the individual lives in; in effect, as long as a particular skill is useful, appreciated by the society, and can be developed, the individual can be referred to as an intelligent person. The definition does not address the features of consciousness in which individuals can reach to higher levels of human development as an ongoing process of learning. A person's combined intellectual capability, according to Gardner, is the result of innate tendencies (the genetic contribution) and the society in which that individual develops (the environmental contribution). Gardner also suggests that each intelligence facet is semiautonomous.

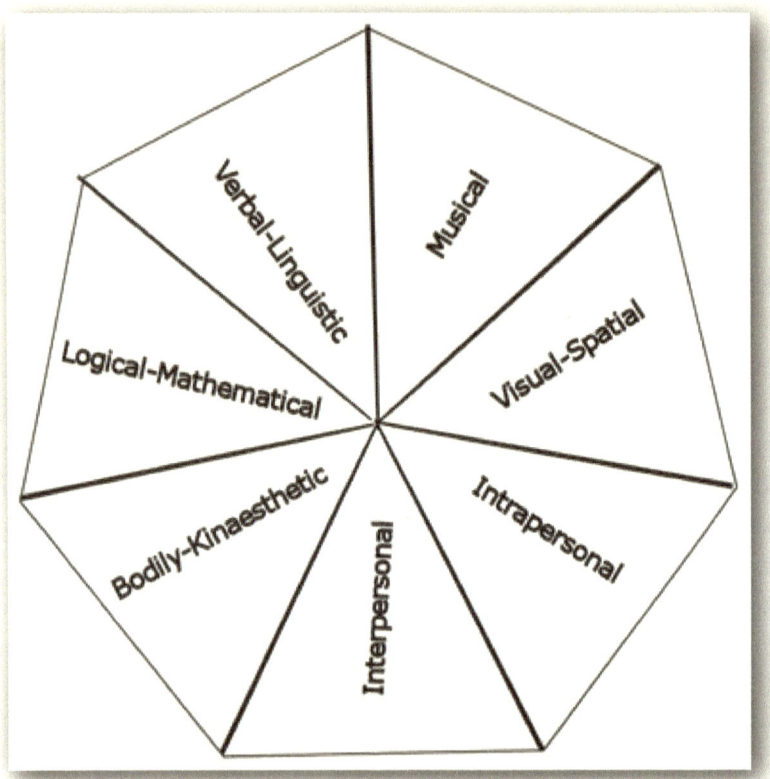

Multiple Intelligences (as Defined by Howard Gardner)

MULTIPLE TYPES OF INTELLIGENCE AND BRAIN LATERALISATION/ SPECIALISATION

As mentioned before, the theory of multiple intelligences (Gardner 2006) indicates that there are a number of basic human ability areas or types of intelligence, so to speak, as opposed to a single measure of ability or intelligence. Interestingly, from the viewpoint of neuroscience, these types of intelligence are most likely to be associated with different functional areas of the brain, either individually or in a collection (Luria 1976; Geschwind 1979; Edelman and Mountcastle 1978). For example, broadly, the verbal-linguistic ability is associated with the left hemisphere, while the visual-spatial ability is associated with the right hemisphere (Silverman 1998, 2002). Wernicke's area, in the left upper part of the temporal lobe, is associated with receptive language or speech perception (Baars and Gage 2010; Friederici 2002; Hickok and Poeppel 2007). An important point to note here is that it is possible an individual possesses some of the types of intelligence or capabilities, and the associated functional areas are developed better than the other regions. To recall, as Donald Hebb highlighted, "neurones that fire together, wire together" or the phenomenon of "use it or lose it."

In other words, we may have asynchronous developments across multiple types of intelligence or functional areas within an individual (Silverman 2002; Webb, et al. 2005). For example, one may possess very well-developed verbal-linguistic abilities (which are left- hemispheric oriented) skills, while lagging behind in visual-spatial abilities (which are right- hemispheric oriented). Taking another example, one may demonstrate well-developed intrapersonal skills more successfully than one might in interpersonal relationships. Using the definitions in neuroscience, and more specifically the one related to the integrated theory of consciousness, it suggests that only a limited number of functional areas may have been differentiated well. From an education viewpoint, the key point to understand is that all types of intelligence or capabilities mentioned above are highly important for the overall development of an individual by enabling achieving a higher level of consciousness. These specieswide abilities or types of intelligence that appeared—possibly as a result of the evolutionary process—are there for a purpose, for human beings to make use of as needed. Therefore, we should encourage and guide individuals to take part in activities that enable the above-mentioned holistic human development. To implement these measures, it will require educators to identify strong and weak areas of development or types of intelligence within each individual systematically and put forth appropriate learning plans to improve on the lagging areas while relying on the stronger ones as pathways and motivational factors to achieve it. To reiterate, we should avoid pinpointing only the most potent ability or intelligence of an individual early in life and relying excessively on that to make a career out of it, neglecting all the other areas of intelligence and ability. If such a path is followed, we will produce human beings of one-sided development instead of individuals of holistic development.

DEVELOPING MULTIPLE TYPES OF INTELLIGENCE AND HUMAN DEVELOPMENT

As we have already seen, many researchers suggest it is better to think of the brain as having a number of cerebral systems that are primarily responsible for processing a particular content associated with each intelligence facet. We have broadly more convincing proofs for such a rationalisation, such as the left hemisphere has an auditory-sequential (or verbal linguistic) bias, while the right hemisphere has a visual-spatial bias (Sperry 1966; Silverman 2002). Further, we have a large number of neural networks of knowledge or synaptic connections formed as a part of creating long-term memories. We can expect that these neural networks are associated with some particular area of intelligence. For example, one may form a neural network related to having strong interpersonal relationships or a neural network associated with a mathematical-logical derivation, and so on and so forth. It is worth noticing that with respect to an area of intelligence or intelligence in general, there is an environment-based contributory factor in addition to a genetic factor, as stated before. As a result, educators should do their best to provide a right environment for learners to develop their respective types of intelligence. In regards to human development, we want to and should support individuals to form as many such useful and meaningful neural networks as possible and then integrate or connect them in every feasible and meaningful way. This kind of support would lead to enhanced wisdom or consciousness within individuals.

INTELLIGENCE AND NEURAL EFFICIENCY

Research studies show that people who score high on tests of reasoning and intelligence show less cerebral activity than people who score lower (Baars and Gage 2010). These results imply that intelligence may be primarily a matter of neural efficiency, whereby the brain eventually learns to use fewer neurones or networks to accomplish a repetitive task (Neubauer, Grabner, et al. 2004; Restak 2003). One important implication of defining intelligence as a matter of neural efficiency is that it entails the significance of timing factor in intelligence tests; during the test, one has to provide highly practised answers in a premeditated manner rather than using as many neural resources as possible in finding answers or solutions on the fly. To provide an explanation, we may recall the related phenomenon of automaticity, in which cortical resources are released for other purposes once a task is practised to an expert level, where subcortical organs take control. We can see a clear distinction here when intelligence tests are conducted in a manner that examines neural efficiency, which is essentially time-based; it does not measure one's ability to provide the optimal solution based on recalled information from various brain regions, which is a measure of consciousness, in effect.

INTELLIGENCE AND DYNAMIC PROPERTIES OF THE CORTEX

More studies on intelligence have revealed some notable findings. That is, a high intelligence quotient (IQ), a means of measuring intelligence, was associated with a thinner cortex, especially in frontal temporal lobe areas, in early childhood. But by late childhood, the opposite pattern was found, with high IQ associated with a thicker cortex (Shaw, et al. 2006; Baars and Gage 2010). The researchers concluded that differences in grey-matter density did not lead to children with superior intellectual abilities; rather, they suggested that the dynamic properties of the development of the cortex corresponded to the level of intelligence, a feature that perhaps enables the child to extract more information from his or her environment. As we could see here, there are possibly both genetic as well as environmental factors playing a role in enhancing intellectual abilities.

EMOTIONS

WHAT ARE EMOTIONS?

Emotions, as we know, are an inseparable part of human life. After some basic functions such as breathing and heartbeat that provide life, emotions make human existence and survival possible through directing and urging some important human activities. One fundamental difference between human beings and machines such as typical computers is that the former possess emotions, while the latter do not. Positive emotions such as pleasure make human beings function more efficiently, while negative ones such as sorrow and anger lower the level of efficiency of human functioning. On the other hand, machines or computers operate at a consistent degree of efficiency in general, devoid of fluctuations. As a result, we may ask ourselves whether we need emotions in human lives. Can human beings function consistently without ups and downs—as machines do? We should highlight one important difference between machines and human beings at this stage: human beings are naturally creative living beings, possessing a theoretically infinite capacity to develop into highly creative individuals, extending their neural networks of knowledge throughout the lifespan, whereas machines can perform only a limited number of operations in a routine manner.

As a result, human beings, with the right mixture of appropriate emotions, could overcome challenges to take our planet to new heights that we have not seen before. Further, as we discussed in the section on metacognition, human beings have the capacity to regulate emotions appropriately through well-developed cognitive systems by achieving higher levels of consciousness or wisdom. In other words, we can be more emotionally intelligent by becoming more knowledgeable through enhanced consciousness or developing denser neural networks of knowledge.

ROLE OF EMOTIONS

For centuries, an interesting and important philosophical question people tried to answer was the role of emotion and how it relates to cognition and learning. A long-held belief was that intellect was of high significance and emotions have a secondary or minor role (Sylwester 1998), if at all, from the perspective of learning; in fact, it was believed that emotions were associated with the heart instead of the brain. Now we know that the limbic system, also known as the emotional brain, is associated heavily with emotions and related functions (Zull 2002, 2011). From the research findings of neuroscience and other related areas, it has become clearer that the previously held belief that emotions have a secondary value was not quite accurate. It is now understood that we cannot disentangle intellect or cognition from emotions; rather, they are more intertwined and inseparable from each other.

For example, what are the drivers of our learning? What urges us to overcome challenges faced in reaching towards our goals? Undoubtedly our positive or rightly balanced emotions. Without these emotional drives, we would be quite ordinary creatures with lacklustre functioning, even if we survived. Historical studies, including the one involving Phineas Gage (Damasio 2005; Zull 2011), prove that damage to brain areas related to emotions cause difficulty in certain decision making; similar brain-damaged patients seem to demonstrate myopia for the future or concern only about the short term. Another important function of emotions is that they can produce quicker responses than the rational ones and can direct us away from dangers, sometimes life-threatening ones; that is, dangers sensed from sensory organs can go directly to the amygdala, bypassing the sensory brain for the purpose of a quicker response.

As Robert Sylwester (1998) pointed out, there is no act of downshifting to emotions from intellect or that intellect is superior to emotions, as had previously been perceived. On the contrary, all physical parts of the brain, including the cerebral cortex and limbic system, are important in its operation as a whole. Emotions, in fact, guide or drive this holistic process. In other words, many parts of the brain are coordinated together when emotions are in operation. Neuroscientists have identified that there are neural connections between emotion-related areas of the brain (namely, the amygdala) and the other parts of the limbic system and the neocortex (the cognition-related part of the brain), indicating that signals travel in both directions of the two brain components. The outgoing connections from the amygdala travel primarily to the front and back integrative cortices, suggesting that the amygdala, as an emotion-related part of the brain, influences memory, ideas, plans, and judgement. Further, the existence of more connections from the amygdala to the neocortex than in the opposite direction implies that emotions tend to overpower cognition rather than the reverse (Zull 2002).

POSITIVE EMOTIONS AND FRONTAL LOBE ACTIVATION

Further, as mentioned before, when human beings are dealing with positive emotions, biochemical endorphins are released in the brain (Sousa 2011). Endorphins produce a feeling of euphoria and stimulate the frontal lobes that connect to almost all the other functional units of the brain. As a result, individuals can function at a higher level, more efficiently or more creatively, by integrating neural networks of knowledge from diverse brain regions. We get to see here the significance of learner emotions or simply the comfort in a particular teaching-learning environment or in learning in general, as positive emotions or relaxed environment help learners to engage in higher-order learning by activating the frontal lobes, towards a path of enhanced consciousness. Conversely, if they are in a situation of mental stress and possess negative emotions, a hormone called cortisol is released in the body. Cortisol travels throughout the brain and body and activates defence behaviours, such as fight or flight. As a result, the frontal lobe activity is reduced, possibly disconnecting with many other regions of the brain, to direct focus on the most urgent matter of identifying the cause of stress and how to deal with it. We see here how emotions control human functioning appropriate to the environmental conditions to which individuals are exposed.

EMOTIONS, HIGHER-ORDER PROCESSING, AND LONG-TERM MEMORY FORMATION

Through findings from neuroscience, one of the defining features of emotion-related systems is that emotion-related circuits can influence higher-order processing. The amygdala appears to play a role in determining how unattended but significant stimuli gain access to consciousness by providing temporary feedback to cortical areas involved in receiving sensory inputs. This action of the amygdala can make the cortical areas momentarily more receptive to certain adaptively important stimuli (Phelps and LeDoux 2005; Panksepp 1998). Further, the amygdala and hippocampus are two structures in the brain that are mainly responsible for long-term remembering, and they are located in the emotional area of the brain. The interactions between the amygdala and hippocampus ensure that we remember for a long time those events that are important and emotional. What we see here is the positive role played by emotions in learning or creating long-term memories. It gives us an explanation as to why gifted individuals, who necessarily demonstrate high sensitivities including emotional sensitivity, show profound abilities in learning, as we elaborate further later.

EMPATHY AS AN IMPORTANT EMOTION

In regards to the study of emotions, empathy is considered a significantly related phenomenon. Empathy carries the sense of feeling the feelings of others. The theory of mind (TOM) (Baron-Cohen 1995) is used to highlight the idea that we normally have complex metacognitive understandings of our own minds as well as the minds of others. Similarly, Frith and Frith (1999) introduced the term *metallising* to capture the idea that, when we have a well-developed mind, we understand ourselves and others, not just as sensory objects but also as subjective beings with mental states. In other words, as mentioned before, if we possess higher levels of consciousness or wisdom achieved through a process of extensive learning or human development, we are likely to become more empathic individuals. Again, it provides us with some explanations as to why gifted individuals, who demonstrate high emotional sensitivities, are highly empathic individuals who can better understand the feelings of others. That is, gifted individuals seem to show well-developed interpersonal intelligence per se, as referred to in the theory of multiple intelligences.

EMPATHISING AND THE FUNCTION OF MIRROR NEURONES

On a related matter, researchers have discovered that some clusters of neurones in the premotor cortex fire just before a person carries out a planned movement (Sousa 2011). Interestingly, the same neurones fired when a person saw someone else perform the same action. That is, similar brain areas process both the production and the perception of movement. The neurones involved are called mirror neurones, and they allow us to recreate the experience of others within ourselves and to understand others' emotions and empathise. In other words, when emotional expressions on other people's faces are observed, it causes mirror neurones to trigger similar emotions in us. The concept of mirror neurones highlights the fact that emotions such as empathy are an integral part of human beings as a species with structural support, even though some individuals such as the gifted, demonstrate related features at heightened levels.

CREATIVITY

WHAT IS CREATIVITY?

Generally, creativity is a positively received notion in our contemporary societies, even though in some situations individuals get into troubled waters by trying to be creative, possibly beyond certain limits. For example, when we promote higher-order learning, targeting the high end of Bloom's Taxonomy, we encourage our learners to be creative. In general, there is a tendency to use the term "creativity" in regards to arts and craft-type work or pieces of literature, such as a novel or poem; for example, we may refer to a creative artist or creative writer more commonly. That is, they can create something novel such as a painting, craft item, story, or poem. It is also not uncommon that we associate the term "creativity" with some product, especially in the commercial arena, where we always have new products being designed or developed and manufactured. Based on customer or user feedback, the manufacturer designs new products as an evolutionary process. When one is producing a creative-writing piece or painting, he or she is likely to approach it with a completely open mind, with minimal self-regulation, letting the imagination go anywhere. However, when one develops a product in a commercial arena based on customer feedback, he or she is likely to be less open-minded and more confined within a set of constraints. Consequently, we tend to get a more monetary or commercial value in the second scenario than the first one.

Differentiating "Big C" Creativity and "little c" Creativity

In literature, there is also a differentiation made between "Big C" creativity and "little c" creativity. "Big C" creativity leads to changes or transformations in the domain, and as a result, "Big C" creators become eminent personnel. On the other hand, "little c" creativity refers to how human beings lead their everyday lives, meeting their requirements and solving problems; as a result, "little c" creators do not necessarily have to be well known. Humanistic psychologists are more prominently "little c" creativity advocates (Piirto 2004). Further, "Big C" creativity is more long term, results oriented, and reflection based, whereas "little c" creativity is more short term, process oriented, and intuition based (Knoop 2008). Consequently, we can see that "Big C" tasks or projects should provide a high level of freedom for the creators involved to make decisions as well as a comfortable means of funding. In contrast, "little c" creators will have to function within more constraints found in the environment, and a source of funding may not be required in many cases, other than having some means of making ends meet. Also, we can rationalise that if we provide freedom, a comfortable means of funding, and encouragement required for those who demonstrate "little c" creativity to function in a more open-minded manner, we have a better chance of transforming them into "Big C" creators.

DIFFERENTIATING CREATIVITY AND WISDOM

Researchers also distinguish between the phenomena referred to as creativity and wisdom, the latter as an advanced form of the former (Claxton 2008). Accordingly, creativity requires domain-specific expertise and constitutes focus strength, whereas wisdom requires broader knowledge about everyday life and represents balance strength (Simonton 2008). Creativity and wisdom are essentially human qualities that are not clearly present in other species or machines. From an educational point of view, we earnestly want our learners to develop creativity and wisdom. We focus on higher-order practices aimed at the higher end of Bloom's Taxonomy in teaching-learning, to encourage learners to make sense and meaning through elaborative and distributive rehearsal practices. From the viewpoint of neuroscience, the information or knowledge learners create is represented and stored in the form of neural networks (Kuhn 1962).

Consequently, creativity can be understood as integrating neural networks within a somewhat limited number of functional brain areas, possibly in a localised manner, while an act of wisdom would result when a highly integrated neural network is formed across a larger number of brain regions, even ones that are spread more widely. Wisdom is clearly a concept that goes hand in hand with consciousness, as defined in neuroscience. The degree of consciousness indicates how efficiently information stored in the brain is differentiated in each individual area and, at the same time, integrated across those multiple areas (Balduzzi and Tononi 2008; Koch and Tononi 2008; Tononi 2008). As a result, we can say that an individual who demonstrates a very high level of wisdom is someone with a high level of consciousness. In other words, since the evolution of consciousness is regarded as the highest expression of the developed brain, as discussed before, an individual can be humanistically and biologically at his or her best when a very high level of consciousness or wisdom is developed. Such highly evolved persons, at the highest level, were referred to as self-actualised individuals (Maslow 1968, 1993) and at level five, the highest level, of the human development process presented by Dabrowski (1970, 1977). The challenge in our social and educational systems is to identify ways in which we can improve creativity and wisdom in individuals and how we can recognise and utilise these high human abilities so that society will benefit from them. In a contemporary society in which economic development is valued predominantly ahead of human development, the million-dollar question would be what revolutionary changes do we need to make to encourage the self-actualisation of human beings? Following Maslow's theory of self-actualisation—hierarchy of needs—it is imperative that the basic and safety needs of learners are satisfied first before they can embark on a path to self-actualisation. In other words, we have to make learners emotionally stable before we get them to learn with a higher-order focus leading to self-actualisation. To recall, when learners are emotionally stable and in a positive mood, the frontal lobes are stimulated, enabling them to integrate neural networks of knowledge from diverse brain regions.

CREATIVE ACTIVITIES AND FRONTAL LOBE ACTIVATION

Some other neuroscientists also recognise that wisdom entails extensive learning, broad experiences, and profound thought (Diamond 2000). They also suggest that creative thinking involves communication amongst many brain regions that do not normally interact with each other during non-creative thinking. Most creative activities involve the brain's frontal lobe, although researchers agree that there is no single brain area responsible for creativity (Heilman et al. 2003; Chavez-Eakle et al. 2007; Fink et al. 2007). Further, it has been observed that when more complex problems are processed, different parts of the brain are activated (Cole et al. 2010; Kelly et al. 2006). Problems we solve become more complex when there are no identified routine procedures to follow until a solution is reached. In effect, problem solvers will have to devise novel approaches and pay more attention and thought to determine connections or relationships amongst pieces of knowledge or neural networks. Consequently, it indicates that when more complex problems are solved, a higher level of creativity or wisdom is used.

CREATIVE ACTIVITIES, INDIVIDUALITY AND SELF-EXPRESSION, AND MINIMISATION OF INHIBITION OR SELF-REGULATION

Research studies show that the areas of the brain responsible for inhibition and self-regulation are much less activated during a creative activity than during a purely memorised or routine operation; instead, the activity in the brain areas associated with individuality and self-expression is increased during a creative task (Limb and Braun 2008; Sousa 2011). As mentioned before, when we perform creative activities, we become open minded in our approach, allowing all possible neural networks in our possession to fire, whereas we become more constrained in our expressions during a memorised routine activity. It gives us the understanding that when we turn off the brain areas involving inhibition and self-regulation, it leads us to produce less focused attention but more enhanced spontaneous and creative behaviour. We usually refer to the process of turning off of inhibition and self-regulations to express openly as *brainstorming*.

It may be rationalised here that in our social contexts, we would find ourselves in both situations where we have to express ourselves either open-mindedly or in a more constrained manner. We put forth this need to have a balance between an open mind and self-regulation when we introduced the term *metacognition*. Metacognition is essentially about developing self-awareness for the purpose of controlling emotions that impact on cognition and vice versa. To be a fully functioning human being, we should develop the capacity to judge or reflectively think when it is appropriate to be open-minded and when it is required us to express ourselves in a constrained manner. More importantly, we should develop the skill to switch between these two important modes at will to make our operations more efficient. For example, if we always operate in a constrained manner, we would never perform as creative human beings; if we attempted to be open-minded all the time, we may get ourselves into trouble or conflict when the environment does not support or understand such an approach.

Teaching Creativity

As we have seen, most definitions of creativity seem to include the notion of thinking outside the box. That is, we need to suggest solutions from outside the standard or conventional frameworks of thinking. It includes the ability to use divergent or open-minded thinking to probe deeply and to find alternative solutions to a problem that were not previously considered. Although creativity comes naturally to some individuals, there is growing realisation that it can be taught (Sousa 2011). Throughout this text, we have highlighted the need to focus on higher-order processing, targeting the higher end of Bloom's Taxonomy as a means of fostering creativity and wisdom in our learners, following a scientific basis or evidence-based approach. It means putting limits on the common instructional approach in contemporary classrooms that revolves predominantly around convergent thinking—finding one correct solution to a problem following a predefined sequence of steps—and where rote memorisation prevails and is assessed over thorough understanding.

To Sum Up

Despite the fact that intelligence is used to measure some general ability, scientists have identified multiple facets of it, resulting in situations where individuals may develop only one or a few of these aspects to a high level of competence. Because there are multiple types of intelligence and associated respective regions of brain specialisation, we tend to value each type of intelligence on its own, individually, unlike in the case of the phenomenon of consciousness, where an integrated, holistic operation of the brain is highlighted. Some of the facets of intelligence also clearly demonstrate cerebral lateralisation that enables us to identify individuals as left-hemispheric oriented, auditory-sequential learners and right-hemispheric oriented, visual-spatial learners commonly. In some definitions, intelligence is also viewed as means of achieving neural efficiency in which through highly specialised regions, the brain can operate in high cognitive speeds while maintaining high neural resource utilisation levels. Although strong emotions are generally negatively received in our societies, positive emotions are capable of stimulating the frontal lobes that enable enhanced learning in addition to their role in creating lasting memories.

Researchers have identified empathy as a higher form of emotion that utilises neural resource across the whole brain as a quality that is possessed by individuals at higher levels of self-actualisation or human development. Further, empathy in human beings is structurally supported by the availability of neural resources referred to as mirror neurones. Creativity is a feature supported by the human brain through its selectionist operation that enables forming an infinite number of neural networks theoretically. It allows learners in self-expression and individuality by minimising inhibition and self-regulation. Researchers identify wisdom as an advanced form of creativity in which information from multiple domains is linked to form useful inferences. Despite the fact that creativity is usually understood to be a natural instinct, educators have observed that it can be taught or enhanced systematically if appropriate instructions and content designs are used.

CHAPTER 5

Popular Learning Theories from the Viewpoint of Educational Neuroscience

• • •

In this chapter, we will introduce readers to some widely used learning theories by viewing them from the perspective of educational neuroscience. In almost all of these theories, we find many overlapping concepts, and they all seem to have a convergence towards achieving higher-order learning as the outcome. In this section, we put forth the additional dimension of educational neuroscience to review some selected learning theories. In doing so, we make a more compelling case in pursuit of higher-order learning. The learning theories we discuss in particular are Kolb's experiential learning cycle, the constructivist theory of learning, theories of deep/surface/strategic learning, gifted-learning theories, auditory-sequential and visual-spatial learning preferences, and Bloom's Taxonomy.

KOLB'S EXPERIENTIAL LEARNING CYCLE

Kolb's experiential learning cycle is widely used by researchers and practitioners of pedagogy to describe a complete learning process (Kolb 1983). It defines four stages of learning: concrete experience stage, reflective observation stage, abstract conceptualisation stage, and active experimentation stage. From the viewpoint of neuroscience, the important point to understand is that we encourage learners to use different functional areas of the brain, namely the sensory cortex, back integrative cortex, frontal lobes (most importantly), and motor cortex to achieve a complete learning in Kolb's cycle (Zull 2002). For example, signals from concrete experiences such as observing and hearing are received in the sensory cortices (visual and auditory), while active experiments can be performed by signalling the areas of motor cortex. Integration of different sensory inputs such as auditory and visual signals for enhanced comprehension takes place in the back integrative cortex (parietal lobe).

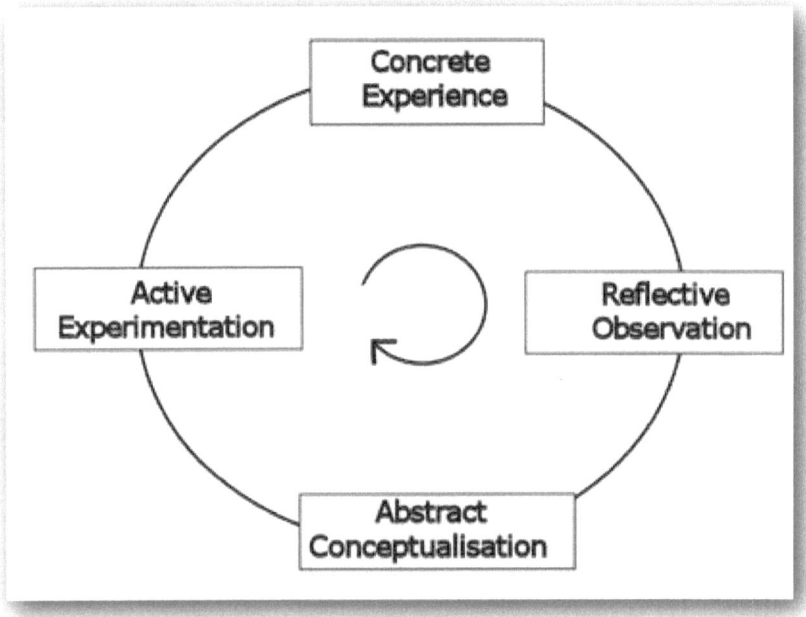

Kolb's Experiential Learning Cycle

Of particular note are the two stages of reflective observation and abstract conceptualisation in which higher-order learning functions such as creation and evaluation (as described by the high-end functions of Bloom's Taxonomy) take place (Watagodakumbura 2013). These stages essentially perform the integrative roles of the learning activity. The prefrontal cortex in the frontal lobes plays an important part in these integrative processes (Baars and Gage 2010; Fuster 1997; Goldberg 2001; Ingvar 1985; Luria 1966) by allowing learners to make sense and meaning through elaborative and distributive rehearsal. In the reflective observation stage, the learner will attempt to reflect by relating the new contents to his or her previous learning; in the abstract conceptualisation stage, he or she will endeavour to use the learnt concepts or patterns to more novel situations, enabling transfer of knowledge, as we have discussed before.

It is important to note that the frontal lobes have played a significant role in the evolution of human civilisation, and getting them essentially involved in the learning process directs us towards achieving higher-order learning. That is, they help learners to build widely integrated neural networks as part of their learning. To recall, enhancing consciousness—the highest expression of the developed brain as put forth by scientists—necessarily requires the integration, as mentioned earlier, from wider areas or domains of the brain. Viewing from another direction, we get to realise that the abstract conceptualisation stage of Kolb's cycle—which uses the frontal lobes—plays the most important role in human learning; it is the stage at which human creativity and wisdom play a significant role. If learners engage in rote rehearsal or lower-order learning practices such as sensing input signals and reproducing them as is, using the motor cortex without elaborate processing amalgamating learners' retrieved personalised knowledge, the treatment in the abstract conceptualisation stage will be at a very minimal level, if at all. It suggests a minimal involvement of frontal lobes, the most important brain region in regards to higher-order learning.

DEEP, SURFACE, AND STRATEGIC LEARNING

Education researchers have identified and revealed that learning can take place in the form of deep learning, surface learning, or strategic learning (Biggs 2003; Entwistle 1998). In general, we expect all students to follow a deep-learning path, in which students maximise the effectiveness of learning outcomes. In deep learning, when new information or concepts are presented, learners link them to their existing knowledge bases to make sense and meaning. In effect, they essentially engage in elaborate rehearsal, constructing individualised meaning that enables them to create lasting memories. Going by Kolb's experiential learning cycle, deep learning essentially involves reflective observation and abstract conceptualisation stages.

In surface learning, learners do not necessarily attempt to link new information or concepts presented to their existing knowledge bases; they do not attempt to make sense and meaning per se. Instead, they engage in rote rehearsal to commit the contents to short-term memory for them to be reproduced in the exact form in examinations or assessments. One reason learners may engage in surface learning is that they may have developed a fear that if they try to link the new information or concepts to the existing knowledge bases, the latter may get exposed or disturbed, making the learners confused. Another possible reason is that they may be getting ready hurriedly for a forthcoming examination and do not have adequate time to link the contents to the existing knowledge bases.

Strategic learning occurs when assessments or examinations are constructed to enable learners to score well on them without necessarily engaging in deep learning. Surface- and strategic-learning approaches are likely to emphasise a concrete experience stage of Kolb's experiential learning cycle, in which the learner senses a large quantity of information, and possibly the active experimentation stage, bypassing or emphasising less on the reflective observation and abstract conceptualisation stages. We can infer that reflective observation and abstract conceptualisation functions utilise relatively longer times, and if learners are not motivated to invest that much time on learning, they would bypass or put less emphasis on these tasks. By doing that, they engage in strategic or surface approaches to learning in anticipation of a "quick" return, targeting the short-term, if that is possible.

CONSTRUCTIVIST THEORY OF LEARNING

In the domain of pedagogy, one of the learning theories discussed widely is the constructivist theory of learning (Brooks and Brooks 1999; Biggs 2003). According to the constructivist approach, learners construct or make meaning individually from what they take in. They link new information or concepts they sense to their existing knowledge bases and create new personalised knowledge altogether. That is, learners create new neural networks of knowledge by connecting newly sensed information with the existing neural networks, as in the case of making sense and meaning discussed before. Every learner brings a unique set of experience to the teaching-learning arena; based on that, he or she creates unique, authentic meaning or knowledge from new learning. Consequently, the knowledge learners create is subjective, despite the fact that everyone in a learner cohort takes in the same information. It is a process of constructing knowledge by active and fearless learner engagement in the learning process.

In effect, the learner engages in looking for various ways to relate or connect newly sensed information to any of his or her retained neural networks, creatively and with an open mind. We see here that the learner is in control of his or her learning process and should enjoy the freedom he or she has to link new information presented to prior personal knowledge in a unique manner (Zull 2011). The positive frame of mind developed here in generating creative ideas or relationships is crucial for activating the frontal lobes, resulting in enhanced learning. This process is what exactly happens in deep, effective learning, as discussed before.

It contrasts with rote rehearsal or surface learning, in which learners do not necessarily link the newly sensed information or concepts to their existing knowledge bases adequately to create new insights; instead, they commit the sensed information to short-term memory to reproduce them in the exact form, possibly a few hours later at most. Further, to put the constructivist theory into practice in a teaching-learning session, educators need to use an appropriate delivery mode such as dialectic approach along with an appropriate pace accommodating learners to construct knowledge accessing and linking knowledge already retained in long-term memory. To access and connect diverse neural networks of knowledge from different brain regions, we essentially have to stimulate the frontal lobes, as discussed before. When the frontal lobe participates in the learning process, we achieve better learning outcomes, even though the operations take place relatively slowly.

GIFTED LEARNER CHARACTERISTICS/OVEREXCITABILITIES

WHAT DOES IT MEAN TO BE GIFTED?

Imagine that an individual possesses the measures we discussed earlier—intelligence, emotions, and creativity—in more excessive levels than the average in any combination. For example, he or she will have high intellectual capacities in general, be highly imaginative in ideas, while being at the same time susceptible to negative emotional setbacks. Fortunately, Polish psychologist and psychiatrist Kazimierz Dabrowski has done extensive studies and research on such individuals in the past. He coined the term *overexcitabilities* to highlight the neural characteristics demonstrated by highly sensitive individuals (Dabrowski 1970, 1972, 1977). These individuals show particular overstimulation to senses, compared to others in the areas Dabrowski identified as intellectual, emotional, imaginational, psychomotor, and sensual.

The individuals commonly characterised as gifted mostly demonstrate intellectual, emotional, and imaginational overexcitabilities. As highlighted before, an intellectual ability relates to a well-differentiated functional area in the brain (Rozin 1976), and high intelligence indicates the dynamic properties of the brain that help the development of respective regions in the neocortex into denser neural networks (Shaw, et al. 2006). When

a higher number of types of intelligence or capabilities and related functional brain areas are differentiated and integrated at the same time, individuals develop denser neural networks, and this results in a higher level
of consciousness or wisdom and creativity. Further, the limbic system of
the brain—the region that plays a significant role in human emotions—is
highly connected with the neocortex, enabling emotions to control cognitive operations, as we discussed in the section on metacognition.

Conversely, we should encourage and guide highly sensitive gifted
learners to engage in metacognitive practices of raising self-awareness
through self-reflection, to enable them to regulate their emotions through
thinking or cognition. Also, emotions that mostly produce implicit memories through incidental learning make individuals learn in a deeper sense
(Baars and Gage 2010; Panksepp 1998). Therefore, we can rationalise
that gifted individuals possess inherent capacities to develop denser neural networks across the whole neocortex by extracting large quantities of
information from the environment, as they demonstrate intellectual and
emotional overexcitabilities (Dabrowski 1970, 1972, 1977; Silverman 2002;
Webb, et al. 2005). That is, these individuals have the abilities to develop
higher levels of consciousness that lead to enhanced ability in decision
making or problem solving and seeing reality as is. As a result, gifted individuals are also highly creative, as they can identify unusual connections
or relationships amongst their existing denser neural networks of knowledge, as explained by the notion of imaginational overexcitability.

VULNERABILITIES OF GIFTED INDIVIDUALS
However, despite all of the above positive aspects about giftedness, expos-
ing these individuals to vulnerabilities that erupt from their high emotional and other sensitivities (Daniels and Piechowski 2008; Ellsworth 2012;
Jackson 1997; Jackson and Peterson 2004; Piechowski 2006; Tolan 2012;
Webb 2008) has become an operation of a knife edge in the existing social
contexts. Their inherent perfectionist or idealistic attitudes portraying

highly fair, just, and empathic behaviours are usually not properly understood or received positively by imperfect, highly competition-oriented social contexts. Especially considering that most of our learning is implicit, educators have to pay particular emphasis to the way they recognise and assess gifted learners accurately, as well as how to help and support them to reach their full potential.

Of particular note are the challenges educators face in identifying the asynchronous and implicit development of gifted individuals (Eide and Eide 2004; Webb, et al. 2005); it is more common that gifted individuals demonstrate high levels of visual-spatial abilities, which are also right-hemispheric biased (Silverman 1998, 2002). That is, they have a natural tendency towards better engaging in higher-order learning. In a contemporary education system that is mostly based on valuing left-hemispheric features such as verbal-linguistic abilities, the challenge is to identify and recognise visual-spatial abilities, as well as implicit learning or knowledge of gifted individuals. As a result, we see a significant number of healthcare professionals and organisations promoting for special-education programs for gifted learners. By taking into account the neurological differences amongst individuals in a teaching-learning environment through broader understanding, we should be able to address some of the issues related to what is referred to as neurodiversity (Armstrong 2011).

AUDITORY-SEQUENTIAL AND VISUAL-SPATIAL LEARNING PREFERENCES

LEFT- AND RIGHT-HEMISPHERIC ORIENTATION OF AUDITORY-SEQUENTIAL AND VISUAL-SPATIAL LEARNERS RESPECTIVELY

It is widely observed that different learners have different preferences or styles they mainly use for learning. Auditory-sequential and visual-spatial learning types (Silverman 1998, 2002) are referred to in one such very useful categorisation done by some psychologists. The two preferences are differentiated mainly on the likelihood of using the left- or right-hemispheric brain functions more predominantly, respectively. Auditory-sequential learners demonstrate strengths, as expected, in auditory skills; relate well to time; prefer analytical and sequential operations; are good in short-term memory and rote memorisation; are comfortable with one right answer; and are able to overcome emotional setbacks quickly.

On the other hand, visual-spatial learners have strengths in visual skills, relate well to spatial tasks, learn concepts all at once, perform well in synthesis tasks, have good long-term memory, dislike drill and repetition, and demonstrate higher emotional and other sensitivities. As you may have noticed, the left-hemispheric brain appears to function similarly to a typical computer or machine in a routine manner, while the right-hemispheric brain can function more creatively, synthesising more optimal solutions and taking into consideration many perspectives. Further, visual-spatial learners are more likely to be identified as gifted individuals and are usually introverts who are better in internal processing, while auditory-sequential learners are generally extroverts who are better at arousing attention to deal with outside stimuli.

Consequently, we can rationalise that visual-spatial learners are better in metacognitive practices of developing self-awareness through self-reflection, as they are better in internal processing ahead of paying attention to external stimuli. From the viewpoint of neuroscience, auditory systems differ from the visual systems in that all sound processing occurs over time. This fact explains why auditory-sequential learners have a better sense of time and do well in sequential activities. Further, it is observed that the auditory cortex is activated during speech perception as well as speech production. That implies that auditory-sequential learners perform well in both listening and speech. This inference explains why auditory-sequential learners are usually extroverts who are more active and fluent verbally, while visual-spatial learners are introverts. It is worth noticing that musical interests are of a particular type of auditory skill that integrates more parts of brain mapping sound onto meaning and emotions (Peretz and Zatorre 2005). Consequently, visual-spatial learners are also found to get involved in musical activities actively.

INCLINATION OF VISUAL-SPATIAL LEARNERS TO ENGAGE IN HIGHER-ORDER LEARNING

When going through the above characteristics, you may observe that visual-spatial learners are comfortable in engaging in higher-order learning targeting the high end of Bloom's Taxonomy. In fact, as mentioned before, they struggle in traditional teaching-learning environments that emphasise auditory-sequential instructions and rote rehearsal. We have to clearly understand here that both auditory-sequential and visual-spatial learning types have useful sets of abilities in their own rights. However, in regards to learning, educators need to focus on higher-order learning enabling learners to develop wisdom and consciousness so that they become better decision makers and problem solvers. Auditory-sequential skills should be a means by which higher-order learning can be pursued, rather than an end itself. Consequently, educators need to encourage learners to develop holistically, enhancing both left- and right-hemispheric skills as appropriate, whilst always pursuing the strategic goal of human development to higher levels or towards self-actualisation.

BLOOM'S TAXONOMY AND ITS APPLICATIONS FROM THE VIEWPOINT OF EDUCATIONAL NEUROSCIENCE

COMPLEXITY LEVELS OF BLOOM'S TAXONOMY

Bloom's Taxonomy is one of the most popular models used for evaluating the level or quality of learning for some years (Sousa 2011; Biggs 2003). The original model of Bloom's Taxonomy (Bloom, et al. 1956) had six levels of learning, referred to as complexity levels: knowledge, comprehension, application, analysis, synthesis, and evaluation, in ascending order. By looking at Bloom's levels of complexity from the viewpoint of neuroscience, we can infer that the first few levels—knowledge, comprehension, and application—have a focus on rote rehearsal activities in which contents introduced will be taken into short-term memory in the exact, unprocessed form. Even though we can refer to different levels of comprehension and application, in Bloom's Taxonomy, it appears that these functions were used in their basic forms. That is, when we achieve a higher level of comprehension by relating the contents being learnt to previously acquired content retrieved from the long-term memory or effect a relatively unusual application instead of a more straightforward one, they become parts of higher levels of complexity, such as synthesis or evaluation.

The other important phenomena we have discussed so far in this text—such as making sense and meaning, transfer, and elaborate rehearsal—are essentially associated with moving more towards the complexity levels at the higher end of Bloom's Taxonomy, namely analysis, synthesis, and evaluation. In the original Bloom's Taxonomy, it held that the six levels were cumulative; a lower level needs to be satisfied before one may move to a higher level. We identify a major limitation in this hypothesis, as we do not classify rote rehearsal as a means of effective learning within a broader sense and the context of our presentation throughout this text. Consequently, we cannot say that a learner has first to engage in lower-order learning using rote rehearsal before he or she engages in higher-order learning.

What we want to see in any teaching-learning environment is the essential emphasis on higher-order learning or the high-end functions of Bloom's Taxonomy; this focus on higher-order learning should start right from the time when new contents are initially presented to learners. More recently, a more appropriate revised model of Bloom's Taxonomy was introduced in 2001 (Anderson, et al. 2001) retaining all of the six levels. In the revised taxonomy, names of all levels were changed to a verb form, three levels were renamed, and two were interchanged to a classification of remember, understand, apply, analyse, evaluate, and create. In contrast to the original model, the strict hierarchy in the 2001 revision has been loosened to allow levels to overlap one another.

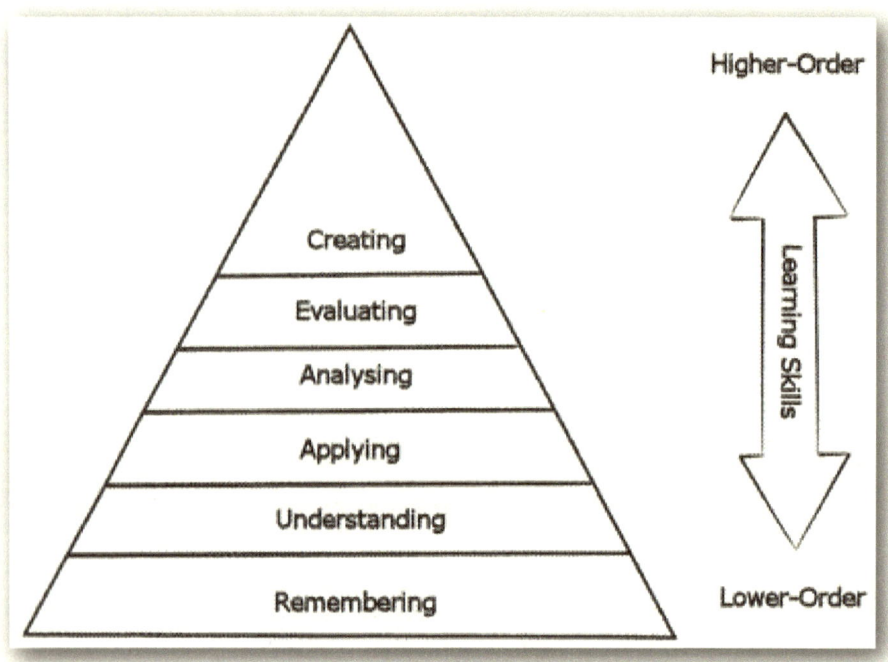

Levels in Revised Bloom's Taxonomy

DEDUCTIVE AND INDUCTIVE REASONING AND BRAIN LATERALISATION
Recent neuroscience studies have found different cerebral regions were involved in solving problems of logic and sequence (deductive reasoning) than in addressing open-ended problems with multiple answers (inductive reasoning) (Jausovec and Jausovec 2000; Mihov et al. 2010; Parsons and Osherson 2001). For example, as mentioned before under brain laterali-sation, the left-cerebral hemisphere is associated with sequencing/timing and analytical processing, while the right-cerebral hemisphere is involved

in processes of creativity/synthesis/generalisation. We have also highlighted existing individual differences depending on an individual's preference to use the left- or right-cerebral hemisphere more predominantly.

These categories of learners were referred to as auditory-sequential and visual-spatial learners respectively. We emphasised in our previous discussions on the topic that the involvement of the right-cerebral hemisphere is essential in any teaching-learning environment when higher-order learning is focused, while the left-cerebral hemisphere can be made use of appropriately in achieving the above goal. The above evidence weakens Bloom's original notion that one type of thinking is dependent on the prior activation of lower-order thinking. More specifically, cognitive psychologists have observed that the thinking skills at the upper levels were a lot more fluid than Bloom's rigid hierarchy suggested (Sousa 2011). For example, when a learner creates a useful new idea by making new connections amongst neural networks of knowledge, he or she will have to evaluate it with other similar existing ideas or neural networks of knowledge so that the new idea is verified to be the most optimal outcome out of many. Here we see creation and evaluation as two inseparable functions of a higher-order learning process.

Convergent/Lower-Order and Divergent/Higher-Order Thinking
In a further categorisation, cognitive psychologists have generally divided thought into two categories: convergent (lower-order thinking) and divergent (higher-order) thinking (Sousa 2011). The lower three levels of Bloom's Taxonomy describe a convergent thinking process whereby learners recall and focus what is known and comprehended in its exact form to solve relatively simple problems through some limited use of the application function. For instance, learning to drive a car is an appropriate example here—you have to follow what the instructor says in its exact form. The learner will have to follow instructions one after the other (sequentially) until the outcome, usually a fixed one irrespective of learner differences,

is achieved. The upper three levels of the taxonomy describe a divergent-thinking process in which the learner comes up with new insights and discoveries or relationships that were not part of the original information introduced. Learners connect new learning to his or her previously learnt contents that were retrieved from long-term memory in an idiosyncratic manner. That is, learners construct new meaning or knowledge based on their previous learning and unique experiences and backgrounds.

BLOOM'S TAXONOMY IN GENERAL FROM THE VIEWPOINT OF EDUCATIONAL NEUROSCIENCE

From the standpoint of neuroscience, synthesis/creation is a process through which we form new knowledge as new neural networks are created, possibly connecting knowledge from multiple domain areas. By enabling integration of different parts of the neocortex or stored neural networks of knowledge, as that happens in enhancing con-sciousness, we can allow learners to engage in the process of synthesis/creation at the highest level of learning. Synthesis/creation, in other words, is the process of making new inferences (Baars and Gage 2010) by linking neural networks together. Similarly, the process of evalua-tion can be achieved at the highest level by allowing learners to make a comparative judgement from the knowledge or information spread in different parts of the neocortex; remember here that we are comparing different neural networks of knowledge (Kuhn 1962), ideally from different domain areas.

The functions at the lower half of Bloom's Taxonomy (revised version)—remember, understand, and apply—may visibly lack the connecting and integrating aspects with different brain functional areas. Thus, we get to an understanding that in high-order learning functions such as synthesis/creation and evaluation, the most important process is the integration of knowledge from different brain functional or domain areas. Recall here the definition of wisdom as a higher level of creativity that integrates knowledge from various domains. Further, at a higher level of consciousness, neural networks of knowledge across wider brain areas communicate together.

From another point of view, in deep learning (Biggs 2003; Entwistle 1998) and critical thinking (Paul and Elder 2000), we make learners engage in higher-order learning activities such as synthesis and evaluation by creating new neural networks of knowledge and comparing them with other existing knowledge bases for validity. It enables forming lasting memories in contrast to committing to short-term memory through rote rehearsal is the outcome in surface or strategic learning. Further, in critical thinking, new learning or knowledge created is viewed more objectively, as opposed to subjectively, by seeing or evaluating them from a number of perspectives or dimensions so that a high degree of objectivity is achieved. As a result, the possible subjectivity that results is due to omitting or minimising many perspectives or dimensions. Put differently, the knowledge, comprehension, application, and analysis functions of Bloom's Taxonomy should not be the ends of learning; instead, they can be the means in some instances by which synthesis and evaluation functions are achieved or higher-order learning is directed. Consequently, it is imperative that educators set assessment tasks, primarily summative ones, to focus on the higher end of the Bloom's spectrum.

HIGHER-ORDER LEARNING AND FRONTAL LOBE ACTIVATION

As expected, recent research studies show that elaborative rehearsal involving higher-order thinking skills engages the brain's frontal lobe. Further, they indicate that different parts of the brain are involved as more complex problem-solving tasks are handled (Cole et al. 2010; Kelly et al. 2006). That is, we can rationalise that as the frontal lobe connects to almost all the other parts of the brain, it can activate and gather related memories stored in those parts to form more meaningful, deeper inferences. Once again, it is evident that the integration of related information stored in many parts of the brain is the key to higher-order learning. One thing we become assured of is that for a learner to readily recall appropriate piec-es of information from across the brain to support an item being learnt, those pieces of information need to be retained firmly in a well-connected manner, as opposed to as isolated pieces. Consequently, when we intro-duce new learning contents to learners as educators, we should do our best to help them to connect them to as many other contents or existing neural networks as possible. It will enable learners to easily recall the retained information in many related situations that demand them.

USE OF THE CONSTRUCTIVIST THEORY OF LEARNING AND TARGETING UPPER LEVELS OF BLOOM'S TAXONOMY

It is interesting to note that constructivist teachers, more specifically, ask open-ended questions and continually encourage students to analyse, evaluate, and create (Brooks and Brooks 1999). To answer open-ended questions, learners will have to scan their whole brains in search of related information towards a possible solution, in the absence of a definite step-by-step procedure leading to an exact answer. That is, it appears that teach-ers who consistently target the upper levels of Bloom's revised taxonomy are essentially demonstrating constructivist behaviours. According to the constructivist theory of learning, learners construct or create meaning by relating what they learn to their individual knowledge bases or neural networks.

This task of forming or creating meaning or knowledge is essential-ly a higher-order learning process that is supported by the open-ended questions posed by the facilitator. However, we observe schooling still de-mands mostly the lower-order processing levels of convergent thinking. Common pedagogical practices and assessment focus on content acquisi-tion through rote rehearsal, rather than on processes of analysis, synthe-sis, and evaluation. Repeating the exact answers becomes more important than the higher-order processes used to get the answer. Even though it is possible for learners who adjust well to these negative conditions to obtain high grades, these extrinsic goals do not always lead them to higher levels of human development with enhanced wisdom or consciousness.

DIFFERENTIATING BETWEEN COMPLEXITY AND DIFFICULTY LEVELS OF BLOOM'S TAXONOMY

In regards to Bloom's taxonomy, the terms *complexity* and *difficulty* are used to describe different levels or types of mental operations (Sousa 2011). However, we often find them being used synonymously, somewhat incorrectly. In Bloom's Taxonomy (revised), we say there are six levels of complexity: remember, understand, apply, analyse, evaluate, and create. Complexity describes the thought process or a level of thought that the brain uses to deal with information. In fact, by looking at them from the viewpoint of neuroscience, we see that lower-order functions of Bloom's Taxonomy are more associated with left-brain operations, while the higher-order functions are associated with the right-brain activities. By promoting our pedagogical practices towards the higher end of the spectrum, we are encouraging learners to engage predominantly in right-brain-oriented activities. It is implied here that brain functions involving the right-cerebral hemisphere (such as evaluation and creation) are more complex than the ones mainly performed by the left-cerebral hemisphere (such as following a routine procedure in a predefined manner to find a solution).

The phenomenon of difficulty, on the other hand, refers to the amount of effort and possibly time that the learner must expend, usually within a single level of complexity, while engaging in learning. It is worth realising that a particular learning activity can become increasingly difficult without becoming more complex. For example, if in the first scenario, we get learners to multiply two numbers with each number below ten, and in a second scenario, multiply two numbers with each number over one hundred, the difficulty in the latter case is higher, even though both scenarios are at the same level of complexity as defined in Bloom's Taxonomy. It is interesting to note that even though the repetitive task of multiplying two large numbers is difficult for a human brain, it is a relatively simple task for a machine such as a typical computer. What we see here is that machines or computers are better at performing lower-order repetitive or sequential tasks to produce a definitive result, while human brains are better at parallel processing tasks that integrate relatively a larger number of inputs and produce many possible outcomes.

If you consider a higher-order function such as create of Bloom's Taxonomy (revised), it also can have different levels of difficulty. For example, one can create an idea or inference by connecting knowledge or neural networks associated with one domain or disciplinary area, while another can do a similar but more difficult task by combining knowledge or neural networks from diverse domains or disciplinary areas. To carry out the more difficult latter task, we need a highly developed human brain with enhanced wisdom or consciousness. Unlike in the previous example of multiplication of two large numbers, a computer will not be able to perform a more difficult task of the higher-order function. As educators, the lesson we can learn when setting up assessments is that we should not use lower-order tasks with a higher level of difficulty to accurately evaluate learners. Since such tasks usually take a longer time, they not only eat up the valuable time available for assessment but also misguide learners to resemble machines by engaging in rote rehearsal. Further, the validity of such assessment is very limited.

HIGHER-ORDER RIGHT-BRAIN ACTIVITIES AND LOWER-ORDER LEFT-BRAIN ACTIVITIES

It has been observed that if teachers understand and follow the revised Bloom's Taxonomy correctly, all members of a learner cohort, irrespective of individual differences, can be sent through a process of higher-order learning. When higher-order learning is focused in a consistent and ongoing manner, it gives learners a clear message of the significance of right-brain activities. That is, learners will not get confused as that happens when there is no clear distinction made between higher-order, right-brain-oriented parallel processing and lower-order, left-brain-oriented sequential processing. Referring to the previous example of multiplying two numbers, educators should not give a higher standing for multiplying two larger numbers, such as each over one hundred, ahead of multiplying two numbers below ten. Regarding learning the concept or principle of multiplication, the two examples stand on par, as verified by having them both at the same level of complexity in Bloom's spectrum.

One way to make higher-order learning practically possible is to review the curriculum and remove the topics of the least importance to gain the time needed for practising at higher-order levels of Bloom's Taxonomy. It is worth noticing that pursuing higher-order activities is more time-consuming initially compared to lower-order activities requiring rote rehearsal. However, we have to understand that spending more time initially on forming more integrated neural networks of knowledge (as opposed to isolated, standalone ones that are likely to be forgotten very quickly) is an investment for the future towards lifelong, continuous human development as individuals with enhanced wisdom and consciousness.

On the other hand, if we focus on the quantity of contents covered in a substandard and rapid manner, we will be engaged in a futile effort; learners will be left with very quickly forgotten memories as opposed to lasting ones. Another approach to focus on higher-order learning is to integrate the new concepts introduced with previously taught material and connect them to appropriate concepts in the other curriculum areas to the best possible extent. We emphasise here that concepts we highlight in any domain are not isolated pieces of knowledge that stand alone; rather, they are and can be connected to other areas of knowledge or existing neural networks. By doing this, we create more integrated neural networks of knowledge within our learners. Further, we are necessarily supporting a process of transfer in which learners become capable of readily using the concepts learnt in different situations, as discussed before.

To Sum Up

In this chapter, we investigated some of our commonly used learning theories from the additional perspective of educational neuroscience. In Kolb's experiential learning cycle, we identified that reflective observation and abstract conceptualisation stages were crucial in linking sensed information to other existing knowledge bases or making sense and meaning that enable transfer of learning. In these stages, the frontal lobes are used to integrate information or knowledge, performing elaborate rehearsal, thus putting learners on a path to higher levels of human development. When we engage in these two stages, we further say that we get involved in deep learning while resorting to surface learning if only to pursue the stages of concrete experience and active experimentation stages, bypassing the other two.

In surface or strategic-learning exercises, sensed or experienced information will be reproduced as is, as a concrete experimentation following rote rehearsal. Consequently, in this case, no transfer of learning takes place; only achieving a short-term goal of passing an assessment or examination (if that is accommodated by the type or nature of the assessment or examination) is possible, devoid of a lasting value of learning. In the constructivist theory of learning, for learners to engage in higher-order learning, they have to link the sensed information to their other retained knowledge bases, by making sense and meaning to construct or create personalised or subjective knowledge. Again, this is a deep learning exercise as we saw in abstract conceptualisation and reflective observation stages of Kolb's experiential learning cycle. Gifted learners demonstrate overexcitable or highly stimulant characteristics mainly in the areas of intelligence, emotion, and imagination. As a result, they possess higher learning abilities that enable them to engage in an accelerated path to higher levels of human development or self-actualisation. However, they are highly vulnerable to emotional shocks they receive due to their higher intensities including intellectual and imaginational ones.

The commonly used Bloom's Taxonomy (revised) directs us as educators to target the high end of the spectrum containing the complexity levels of evaluation and creation. These are the levels that we get our learners to perform elaborate rehearsal by linking sensed information to their existing knowledge bases, enabling the transfer of learning. When learners are guided towards this high end of Bloom's Taxonomy, they engage in divergent and inductive thinking processes, yielding higher-order learning.

On the other hand, if the focus in a teaching-learning process is on the low end of Bloom's Taxonomy, then the learners will engage in convergent and deductive thinking exercises resulting in lower-order learning. When the high-end functions of Bloom's Taxonomy are focused, educators make learners use their right-cerebral hemispheric characteristics along with the frontal lobes more, enabling them to achieve higher levels of human development or self-actualisation in a lifelong learning process. Further, we differentiate between complexity and difficulty levels in regards to Bloom's Taxonomy. When we move towards the high end of the spectrum, we essentially move higher in complexity levels while difficulty levels can be increased while at the same level of complexity. In effect, we may get our learners to perform more difficult routine or repetitive, machine-like activities utilising more time in some instances, but not necessarily getting them to engage in higher-order learning.

Reflecting on the Goals of Education, Taking the Concepts of Educational Neuroscience into Consideration

• • •

When we conjecture on the purpose of education, we may find that different notions are present from various stakeholders. Some of these purposes can have a short-term focus, while some others will have a lasting value, as it should be. In this chapter, we look at this topic from the viewpoint of educational neuroscience or from the basis of what human beings can achieve biologically as a species through education. Consequently, you may see that our discussion essentially entails providing a lasting value of education. The goals we highlight are: making learners better problem solvers and decision makers; providing learners with an opportunity with human development resulting in enhanced consciousness; transforming explicit learning to implicit memories; making implicit learning explicit; and fulfilling fairness to neurodiverse learning cohorts.

PRODUCING BETTER PROBLEM SOLVERS AND DECISION MAKERS AS A GOAL OF EDUCATION

WHAT DOES BETTER DECISION MAKING OR PROBLEM SOLVING MEAN?
Not many will disagree if I say broadly that one of the primary goals of education should be to develop learners into better problem solvers and

decision makers while gaining a deeper perception of reality through enhanced creativity and wisdom. Wisdom is understood here as an advanced form of creativity (Claxton 2008) that penetrates into the interconnected knowledge of multiple domain areas. In this regard, the decisions we make are broader, taking into consideration inputs from multiple domain areas or various dimensions. As a result, they are more sustainable in our personal and social evolution. These better decisions we make are neither egocentric nor based on short-term gains; they are selfless by nature and will have long-term or lasting benefits to us individually as well as societally.

Even if we have made decisions focusing on egocentrism and short-term gains in the past, we should be able to develop metacognitive abilities to reflect and improve on them in future. We solve problems and make decisions of different levels of complexity in a pervasive manner in everyday life situations; some are in our personal lives while the others are associated with our professional lives. How can we evaluate and make sure that we make the right decisions? How can we judge that one decision is better than another, and what is the benchmark? Can the education we receive or all the learning we do make us better decision makers naturally?

ENHANCED CONSCIOUSNESS AND BETTER DECISION MAKING OR PROBLEM SOLVING

From the standpoint of neuroscience, enhancing wisdom implies enhancing consciousness, as mentioned before. Further, while wisdom is a more general term, consciousness will have to be viewed from the basis of neuroscience, as it has been a phenomenon highly researched in the area of neuroscience in the recent past (Baars and Gage 2010). As presented in the integrated theory of consciousness, we can understand consciousness as the integration of a vast number of differentiated sets of neural networks of knowledge from many brain regions, possibly spanning multiple domain areas of knowledge. The brain regions referred to need to essentially include both the left and right-cerebral hemispheres, as they both perform different but vital functions in human operations. That is, as highlighted before, both auditory-sequential and visual-spatial characteristics (Silverman 2002) need to be developed holistically.

Usually, high-level, broader, and conceptual knowledge is easier to integrate across multiple domains, while more specific information is difficult to integrate across domains due to its narrowness or limited scope. Also, broader, high-level concepts are retained in memory longer as semantic memories, as discussed before. Benefits of an integrated view need no elaboration; when information from multiple domains is integrated, we see a broader, better, and more balanced picture of a situation. Further, when we integrate information, we do it in a manner that maintains consistency, removing any possible inconsistencies in pieces of information and their relationships on our own, in a reflective manner. That is, through the process of integration of knowledge, we tend to become essentially more metacognitive in our practices. We aim to develop more meaningfully interconnected, denser neuronal networks physically in individuals as they evolve through learning.

Transfer of Learning and Better Decision Making or Problem Solving

From another perspective, we achieve the transfer of learning, as discussed before, through education (Sousa 2011). The transfer of learning is another well-understood objective of education. In that, once concepts are learned or mental representations are formed, in regards to one or a few situations, learners should be able to use the knowledge gained in relatively novel and different situations successfully while solving related problems or making decisions. Learners have to recognise connections between the learned context and new and different situations. Learners should be able to recall appropriate information, retained possibly in various regions of the brain, readily and whenever necessary to achieve this goal of transfer.

This retrieval of memory traces is made easy when we have highly differentiated and integrated neural networks of knowledge across many of our brain regions, as is the case with enhanced consciousness. In general, broader, high-level concepts stored as lasting semantic memories are easier to be related to any arbitrary and novel situation, as opposed to specific details retained in short-term memory. By attempting to meet the requirements of the transfer function in learning, we give a broader and lasting meaning to learning or education, beyond the short-term goals of scoring high in assessments, not appropriately set in many situations. Through the transfer of learning, we create lasting and firm memories en route to a higher level of human development, as we will discuss in the next section.

ROLE OF METACOGNITION IN DECISION MAKING OR PROBLEM SOLVING

It is not difficult to understand that for effective decision making and problem solving to occur, we have to have our emotions well regulated. We often hear the advice not to make decisions when you are emotional, as resulting decisions may not be optimal. Consequently, having a sound control between cognitive and emotional activities through metacognitive practices, such as developing self-awareness and self-regulation, is important when it comes to making decisions or solving problems. Further, having an enhanced consciousness through the development of cognition not only supports viewing problems in a multidimensional perspective but also help learners to regulate their emotions through extensive knowledge. Conversely, when one possesses well-regulated emotions, he or she can better decide where to direct cognitive resources or prioritise and select the problems that need to be solved.

Pursuing Human Development as a Goal of Education

Human Development to Higher Levels as a Lifelong Learning Process

By enhancing consciousness, we also say that we achieve human development (Dabrowski 1970, 1972, 1977; Colman 2006) into self-actualising (Maslow 1968, 1993) human beings. Following the conceptualisations of Kazimierz Dabrowski, Abraham Maslow, and Carl Jung (Beebe 2006; Casement 2006; Colman 2006; Hauke 2006; and Stevens 2006) we use the term *human development* to indicate the evolvement of human beings as more creative and empathic creatures in this book. These highly evolved individuals possess a higher level of wisdom and enhanced capacities to see and accept reality as is. These higher levels are what we, as human beings, can biologically achieve as a means of our evolution. We see here a direct relationship to the term *developmental psychology*, especially how it is used more lately to include human potential development throughout the lifespan of human beings.

In this process of human development, individuals essentially broaden their knowledge base or become more learned or educated in a deeper sense, including raising self-awareness through metacognitive and reflective practices. They tend to see more relationships amongst the knowledge bases they have formed over the years or develop multidimensional perspectives of the world. When individuals engage in the process of learning in a lifelong manner, they continue to add additional dimensions of views to their repertoire. As a consequence, they become better problem solvers and decision makers, as we highlighted in the previous section. One important aspect of seeing human development as a goal of education is that we become strategically or long-term oriented, in contrast to having short-term goals of passing examinations or finding employment. As many business organisations essentially have their strategic goals well defined, we can have individuals focusing on strategic goals so that they can stay directed even in the face of unavoidable challenges they encounter.

HUMAN DEVELOPMENT AND PHYSIOLOGICAL CHANGES IN CEREBRAL CORTEX

It is interesting to see how psychologist and psychiatrist Kazimierz Dabrowski, who conducted many studies on gifted individuals, recognised the relationship between human development and growth in the cerebral cortex decades ago, before the emergence of many facts of neuroscience available now. He mentioned that when higher levels of human development are achieved, the underlying functions stimulate the cerebral cortex, indicating physiological changes to the neural system. That is, we can infer that individual knowledge bases or neural networks get connected to each other more, forming more meaningful integrated knowledge. These changes are responsible for enhancing consciousness in humanistically evolving individuals. In human development, changes occur in both cognitive and emotional domains. For the purpose of controlling each other for the best, the essential interconnection between cognition and emotion is the outcome of enhanced metacognitive practices. Empathy is identified as one of the prime emotions developed in the individuals at higher levels of developments (Battaglia 2002), through the metacognitive approach to reflection. Possibly, when human beings achieve a broader and connected view of the world and its phenomena along with its constraints and limitations, they become inclined to accept the reality as is, more empathically and with more tolerance.

HUMAN DEVELOPMENT AS DEFINED IN DABROWSKI'S THEORY OF POSITIVE DISINTEGRATION (TPD)

Dabrowski, et al. (1970) have highlighted the phenomenon of psychoneuroses that leads to the Theory of Positive Disintegration (TPD), in which he identified individuals with a high developmental potential need to disintegrate from lower levels of development or psychological status before re-integrating at higher levels of development. The phrase positive disintegration is used to indicate the fact that moving to higher levels of human development is, in fact, something positive, even though the process involves some disintegration from lower but stable development or psychological status. We can infer here that if individuals become economically stable by having a means of income, they can become integrated at the primary level, which has relatively low stability. If they are to move beyond this primary integration level, they will have to challenge their own existing frameworks of thinking by identifying their constraints, resulting in a disintegrated state.

As we can see, the individual will have to possess a key motive to disintegrate from a relatively stable state and think and work courageously towards more rewarding higher levels of integration. In Dabrowski's theory, he identifies five levels of human development, the fifth being the highest level at which humanistically highly evolved individuals exist. At this highest level, individuals have highly empathic, creative, and autonomous personalities, so to speak, and have achieved a secondary integration, following the disintegration from the primary level. Gifted individuals with higher overexcitability or sensitivity characteristics usually have great potential to develop to higher levels, even though this is not an automatic process (Lovecky 1997; Moyle 2005; Silverman 2012). That is, despite possessing a high developmental potential, due to lack of environmental and social support, gifted individuals may fall short of achieving it. For example, if they face life-threatening situations in which they struggle to find their basic needs for living, they would be forced to sacrifice the human development pathway for the purpose of making ends meet.

PRIMARY INTEGRATION AS DEFINED BY DABROWSKI AS A BARRIER TO HUMAN DEVELOPMENT TO HIGHER LEVELS

Dabrowski's research findings (1970, 1972, and 1977) show that a significant portion of our population continues to stay at the development level of one, the lowest level of development in Dabrowski's theory, without moving to higher developmental stages. It was a result that was also observed by Maslow in his study of self-actualising individuals. Once one is firmly integrated at the lowest level of development (*primary integration*), he or she needs a profound shake-up or disintegration process of psycho-neuroses before moving up to a higher level. This shake-up process can sometimes be critical, according to Dabrowski, as he found through au-tobiographical studies of individuals, as some end up in suicidal attempts. But Dabrowski highlighted that even personal or other tragedies could result in accelerated development humanistically, causing them to disinte-grate from the primary integration level (Battaglia 2002).

Moving to a higher layer from a lower layer necessarily involves a dis-integration or psychoneurosis process. Further, the process of *developing as a human being* is not the same as *developing individuals in economic perspec-tives*; it is about developing into a more creative, empathic, and content human being, even though financial stability, at least to fulfil basic needs, helps in reaching this status. However, whether or how such human quali-ties are understood, valued, and encouraged in our contemporary society is a different matter for discussion. If the goal of education or learning is narrowly and extrinsically defined merely to obtain employment or finan-cial stability, learners will not pursue lifelong learning in diverse domains to enhance consciousness, which results in human development. Possibly aiming at a goal of a lower level than what is humanely accommodating can be a primary contributory factor for the majority of social members not to develop beyond level one as defined in Dabrowski's theory. On the other hand, if we can motivate learners intrinsically towards a broader goal of achieving a higher level of human development through enhanced con-sciousness, they are likely to face and overcome associated barriers more wilfully and courageously.

HUMAN DEVELOPMENT AS DEFINED IN MASLOW'S THEORY OF SELF-ACTUALISATION

The famous humanistic psychologist Abraham Maslow referred to per-sons with high growth potential as "self-actualising individuals." At the highest possible level of human development, these individuals become highly creative and self-actualised human beings who become aware of and accept reality as it is, facing it courageously with much less whining (Maslow 1968, 1993). As the name implies, self-actualisation is a process of developing a self-insight of one's strengths and weaknesses in regards to our environment and coming to an acceptance of it. As you may observe, this is a metacognitive process of high reflection that raises self-awareness. As mentioned before, to achieve this higher level of self-awareness, one needs to have inter-supported cognitive and emotion functions. The road to the ultimate goal of self-actualisation is a hierarchical process of fulfilling individual developmental needs.

Maslow outlined some significant external or environmental factors that contribute towards the self-actualisation process of individuals. At the lowest level of the above hierarchy, we have the fulfilment of basic needs (food and shelter); above that, we have the feeling of security (created through employment and other means); further up, we have the needs of love, respect, and belonging from family and society, before reaching the highest level of self-actualisation with a higher level of autonomy. It is important to understand that the above needs at each level are necessary requirements, but not essentially sufficient ones; that is, fulfilling the needs of a lower level does not necessarily mean that an individual would automatically progress to a higher level of human development. Moving to a higher level always becomes a challenge; the ability to leave a lower level of stability and move into a relatively new territory depends on the personal decisions of the individual. For example, if an individual is gainfully employed with resulting financial stability, why would he or she take the trouble of learning to develop more integrated, denser neural networks of knowledge, especially if there are formidable barriers to overcome? Unless the individual is intrinsically motivated to learn to see the reality or world as it is and to self-explain it more accurately, he or she would have no desire to change the status quo or perceived level of comfort.

Abraham Maslow's Hierarchy of Needs towards Self-Actualisation

SELF-ACTUALISATION AND HEALTHY AND SICK SOCIETIES AS PRESENTED BY MASLOW

Self-actualisation is an idiosyncratic process, as every individual is different from the others. That is, each individual will have to embark on the process to self-actualisation in an individualised manner. Importantly, Maslow also observed high sensitivity, especially emotional sensitivity, in self-actualising individuals. Self-actualisers also have high moral sensitivity and develop content states of mind overall. As discussed earlier, gifted and creative individuals are the more sensitive member group of our society and have the potential to be in an accelerated process to self-actualisation. Maslow further pointed out that most of our social members do not reach higher levels of development or self-actualisation inherent to human nature due to lack of conducive social and educational environments (Maslow 1993). He stressed the point that for human beings to self-actualise, it is essential that we have good social conditions, that is, a society that promotes and values human development, as we described here. He referred to societies that negatively contribute the self-actualisation process of individuals as "sick societies" as opposed to "healthy societies." We may have to ask the question ourselves here whether we hold back our high-potential individuals from self-actualising through our improper social practices, such as setting a humanistically lower ceiling of increasing economic gains as the ultimatum; this may conspire against promoting the development of healthy and sustainable societies.

HUMAN DEVELOPMENT AS DEFINED IN JUNG'S THEORY OF ANALYTICAL PSYCHOLOGY (JUNGIAN PSYCHOLOGY)

In the theory of analytical psychology presented by Carl Jung, the human psyche is divided into conscious and unconscious parts (Hauke 2006). You may see that this notion is similar to the explicit and implicit memories we discussed before in regards to neuroscience findings. According to Jung's theory, the process of human development (or *individuation*, as he referred to it) is achieved by making the human psyche fully conscious by integrating the unconscious and conscious psyches. This process of individuation strives towards psychic wholeness or totality represented by what is referred to as the self (Colman 2006). We can see here that the self is a state of mind similar to the highest level of self-actualisation presented by Maslow and the highest level of the five defined in Dabrowski's theory of human development. Jung's theory also supports the notion that reaching the highest level in human development is a process of enhancing consciousness, as we discussed before while introducing the phenomenon of consciousness.

We can see the integration process of the unconscious and conscious highlighted above in forming a psychic wholeness; it is very similar to the process of integration we highlighted when defining the phenomenon of consciousness. Further, there are four functions of consciousness: thinking, feeling, sensing, and intuition, described in analytical psychology (Beebe 2006). According to Jung's theory, an individual may demonstrate an inclination towards one or more of these functional characteristics. *Sensing* is the conscious function that registers reality as real. *Thinking* is the function that defines what we perceive; to define what we perceive, we may relate what is perceived to some basic knowledge networks or frameworks we hold. *Feeling* is the function that assigns a value to what we have perceived; we may infer here that for us to assign a value or provide quantification, we should relate and link what we have perceived to broader knowledge networks we hold than in the previous step of thinking function. *Intuition* is the function that defines the implications or possibilities of the thing that has been perceived empirically.

Further, the functions of feeling and intuition appear to be very closely related notions, as we usually understand them. From the viewpoint of more recent knowledge of neuroscience, we can see that sensing and thinking functions relate to cognition, while feeling and intuition functions focus on emotions. The thinking function is associated more with the frontal lobes, and the sensing function makes use of posterior part of the neocortex. In addition to having an inclination towards one or more of the above functions, an individual will also have a more inclined attitude type, so to speak; the two possible attitude types Jung presented were *introversion* and *extroversion*. We may notice here, based on our previous discussions, that the functions of sensing and thinking correlate well with the characteristics defined for left-hemispheric oriented, auditory-sequential learners, while the functions of feeling and intuition correlate well with the features of right-hemispheric oriented, visual-spatial learners (Watagodakumbura 2014a, 2014b). Interestingly, recent research (Silverman 2002; Sperry 1966) also reveals that the former category of individuals is more extroverted, while the latter group is more introverted, unlike purely independent attitude types defined by Jung.

THE PROCESS OF INDIVIDUATION BY BECOMING CONSCIOUS OF THE
SHADOW AS DESCRIBED IN JUNG'S THEORY OF ANALYTICAL PSYCHOLOGY

As long as a function we defined in the previous section is undifferenti-
ated, it cannot be deployed in the conscious manner of a directed mental
process. The process of individuation is the progressive differentiation of
the various psychological functions of consciousness (Colman 2006). As
we can see, the formal definition we used before for consciousness—the
integration of large sets of information that are differentiated—aligns well
with Jung's theory. Further, Jung's theory highlights the need to have both
cognitive (sensing and thinking) as well as emotion (feeling and intuition)
functions differentiated well for the individuation process to progress.

We can see here that gifted individuals, who more specifically demonstrate intellectual and emotional overexcitabilities, as Dabrowski put
forth, are well equipped to advance in an individuation process, as they
possess well-differentiated cognitive and emotion functions. Another definition found in analytical psychology is the shadow (Casement 2006); it
is complementary to consciously held attitudes and can be both personal
and collective. The personal shadow may be conceived of as the repository
of all the aspects of a person that are unacceptable or distasteful (envy,
aggression, greed, laziness, jealousy, and shame) to him or her. The individuation process starts off by the individuals becoming conscious of their
shadow, which can be painful, although there is a positive gain: to acquire
self-knowledge, one has to tackle the shadow.

It is important to embody the shadow in consciousness; otherwise, if
it is repressed and isolated from consciousness, it remains uncorrected and
liable to erupt in a moment of unawareness. In other words, we see that in
the process of human development to higher levels, we need to be courageous and challenge ourselves to identify our limitations and constraints
so that we can take appropriate measures to overcome them or at least
to accept them uprightly, consciously following some metacognitive self-
refection. In other words, Jung highlights the need have a self-awareness

or metacognitive knowledge on one's weaknesses (shadow) to take appropriate measures of rectifying them.

HUMAN DEVELOPMENT AS A HOLISTIC PROCESS AS OPPOSED TO A ONE-SIDED ONE

This process of self-actualisation or human development to higher levels can be lifelong; it indicates the additional goal of education in which individuals need to learn self-reliance in accommodating lifelong learning. That is, individuals need to be on the road to enhancing consciousness by forming integrated neural networks of knowledge. As we can see, we have a broader goal of education that goes beyond merely training individuals to develop a limited set of skills in a particular career path. In the theory of multiple intelligences (Gardner 2006) presented before, we have identified many of types intelligence a human being can possess. In our main goal of education, we want individuals to develop many areas of intelligence across multiple brain regions. For example, individuals need to develop characteristics of both (left- and right-hemispheric brains; auditory-sequential and visual-spatial skills) as referred to before. That is, individuals need to evolve continuously, getting introduced to new domains of knowledge and identifying the connections amongst them; getting into a career path, with a narrow scope in many cases, should not confine an individual to an expert in a single domain. In short, we want individuals to develop holistically, internalising knowledge in multiple domain areas, as opposed to in a restricted, one-sided manner.

TRANSFERRING EXPLICIT LEARNING TO IMPLICIT MEMORIES AS A GOAL OF EDUCATION

In a teaching-learning environment, learners engage in explicit learning; teachers give instructions on what to learn, and learners attempt to grasp what is instructed by some possible means. When novel material is presented long enough, possibly from diverse perspectives, the contents become clearer to learners, and we say that the brain has "achieved magical learning." Now, if clarity is achieved to a high degree, possibly with the help of some practical or real-life applications, what is learned explicitly becomes implicit. It means that our brains can implicitly or unconsciously apply the concepts learned in a similar but different situation spontaneously; this is what we refer to formally as *achieving the transfer of learning* or somewhat informally as *the internalising of knowledge*. The important point to note here is that educators as well as learners need to make sure that we take that extra step to improve the clarity of what is learned to an adequate level with regards to the framework of knowledge we already possess.

When clarity is achieved by forming more connected neural networks of knowledge, we are more likely to make those neural networks more efficient as well, possibly through getting rid of redundant or least-used connections. That is, we achieve a higher level of neural efficiency, as described in literature (Zull 2011) in addition to making more connections. When this sufficient level of clarity is not achieved, the knowledge we gathered will not become implicit through a process of transfer, resulting in an incomplete process of learning. To achieve the transfer of learning, we need to associate sense deeply to new concepts learned through elaborate rehearsal. That is, we need to relate the new contents learned to as many existing knowledge bases of the learners as possible, so that these integrated pieces of knowledge can be retrieved to working memory from long-term memory for processing and constructing new knowledge or meaning in future.

It is possible that some of these knowledge bases retrieved from long-term memories are implicit by nature, possibly accessed through some priming activity; by elaborate rehearsal in the working memory, these implicit memories can become more explicit, as we will discuss in detail in the next section. To get motivated to spend time in performing elaborate rehearsal, learners need to have a meaning in what they learn; that is, learners need to see some value, especially a lasting one, in what they learn to be motivated to learn. In regards to a teaching-learning environment, the goal of education is to transform explicit learning to implicit learning. This process of transformation from explicit to implicit learning should continue endlessly; once some concepts are transformed from explicit to implicit memories, we do not stop there, assuming the target is achieved. Rather, we look continuously for more concepts for similar transformation to be performed. The neuroplasticity feature of our brains plays an important role here; neuronal networks in human brains can grow endlessly, explaining the concept of creativity associated with human beings, compared to noncreative machines or computers (Beale and Jackson 1990). To recall, we have seen that human brains are selectionist, compared to conventional computers, which are instructionist.

Transferring Implicit Learning to Explicit Memories as a Goal of Education

Even though we mostly refer to learning when we engage in explicit learning in formal environments, most of our learning is identified to be implicit (Bowers, et al. 1990; James 1890; Metcalfe 1986; and Yzerbyt, et al. 1998). That is, we learn from day-to-day life situations we encounter by just paying attention. In these situations, we do not learn explicitly in a selected domain per se but retain traces of implicit memories in diverse domains, depending on the experiences we undergo. More specifically, we have evidence that gifted individuals learn implicitly or incidentally more naturally (Eide and Eide 2004), clarifying more the purpose of using the term "gifted" on them. It may be because gifted learners can pay attention deeply to the experiences they encounter and form new neural networks of knowledge.

As a consequence, learners bring a wealth of implicit memories or experiences to a classroom or formal learning environment where explicit learning takes place, albeit to different degrees depending on personal characteristics. The question we need to answer now is how useful are these traces of implicit learning, or can we make them useable? Even though we may not be able to elaborate precisely on these implicit or somewhat semiconscious traces of learning, we may be able to recognise them when some priming functions are available. Consequently, another important goal of learning or education is to transform these implicit memories to more explicit or declarative memories. In this way, we can make these implicit traces of learning more useable in our day-to-day operations. We can achieve this goal by helping learners to associate sense to new concepts learned. Further, it can be accomplished more elaborately by relating the new concepts introduced to diverse situations in multiple domains. Then, learners will be able to use and express this tacit knowledge more elaborately when appropriate circumstances arise. To reiterate, as educators, what we need to do in a teaching-learning session is to relate the new concepts introduced to as many neural networks of knowledge as learners possess, including the implicit ones, instead of keeping these knowledge networks apart from each other as separate pieces.

By helping to transform learners' implicit memories to explicit ones, we make somewhat unusable knowledge of learners readily usable in appropriate situations. From another perspective, we make learners' experiential learning over time count towards more formal learning by providing them with a vocabulary and established theories for describing their learning. Interestingly, decades ago, the education philosopher John Dewey (1957, 1963) highlighted a similar notion of the significance of experiential learning. Further, a similar idea of making implicit memories explicit was presented in Jung's theory of analytical psychology we discussed above; when individuals progress in human development towards the self through a process of individuation, what they essentially do is integrate the unconscious with conscious and become aware and accepting of one's unconscious shadow.

BECOMING FAIR TO ALL LEARNERS OF A NEURODIVERSE SOCIETY AS A GOAL OF EDUCATION

We live in a neurodiverse society (Armstrong 2011); every individual is neurologically and psychologically different from the others. In a broad and useful categorisation, some learners are identified to demonstrate visual-spatial abilities, while others show auditory-sequential abilities more predominantly. Amongst many available categorisations, we would like to highlight this particular one, as it is based on how learners are inclined to perform the right or left-cerebral hemispheric activities predominantly, respectively. The former category of learners is more likely to be identified as gifted individuals (Silverman 1998, 2002; Webb 2005, 2008) who usually demonstrate overexcitable characteristics (Dabrowski 1970, 1972, 1977) such as emotional, intellectual, and imaginational. The two categories exhibit significantly different psychological and neurological features and learning preferences.

It is widely discussed in the literature that visual-spatial learners are disadvantaged in a contemporary educational setting where higher-order learning is not specifically pursued. We cannot just resort to the presumption that learners who are more comfortable with higher-order learning practices are equally comfortable with lower-order practices. In fact, research findings show that visual-spatial learners struggle with lower-order practices such as rote memorisation and time-dependent sequential operation. By taking into consideration the broad concept of neurodiversity, a goal of education is to provide a unique, systematic, and fair form of education to every individual, despite his or her inherent psychological and neurological differences. As mentioned before, we want all our learners to undertake a higher-order learning path that essentially uses the right-hemispheric characteristics, while valuing the holistic operation of both hemispheres in achieving the goals.

We need to send neurodiverse learners through a process of transfer of learning in an individualised manner and subsequently assess them reliably and meaningfully. We need to essentially avoid a situation commonly described in Aesop's fable of the fox and the stork (At the fox's home, the stork was given soup in a bowl that the stork found difficult to drink with its long beak. At the stork's home, the fox was given a meal in a narrow-necked vessel that made it difficult for the fox to reach the food. Similarly, every human being is different from others and needs individualised attention to succeed in learning). This elusive goal of education can be a real challenge to achieve in a contemporary social environment.

To Sum Up

In this chapter, we have discussed a number of goals of education from the viewpoint of neuroscience. However, they are not mutually exclusive ones; rather, they are mostly overlapping to a good extent. For example, transforming explicit learning to implicit memories (or vice versa) is directly connected with the goal of producing better problem solvers and decision makers. More explicit or conscious memories allow us to make better decisions, and transforming explicit learning to implicit memories will enable us improve our neural efficiency and direct our resources to solve new problems. In turn, becoming better decision makers or problem solvers means moving towards a higher level of human development with enhanced consciousness. The bottom line is that they all trend towards enhancing learner consciousness, the brain resources and neural networks of knowledge integrating phenomenon identified as the pinnacle of human evolution and parallels with the development of the frontal lobes.

In fact, enhancing consciousness through education or learning is clearly highlighted in all three human-development theories we discussed: Dabrowski's theory of positive disintegration leading to human development, Maslow's theory of self-actualisation, and Jung's theory of analytical psychology. In all these theories, it is highlighted that individuals need to develop a self-awareness, identify and accept one's constraints or limitations courageously and be motivated, and sacrifice a lower level of stability to achieve a higher level of human development or psychological status. To enable progress in human development, we aim to make learners utilise their retained knowledge bases across multiple domains, areas, and regions readily and spontaneously for diverse and complex problem-solving and decision-making tasks.

As mentioned at the start of the chapter, one challenge faced by learners is to find the means of evaluating and judging their decisions and solutions to problems for the level of quality they achieved, especially in the presence of large sets of related information. Usually, the higher the number of sets of information integrated, the better and more balanced, multidimensional, or critical the decisions and solutions become. Further, the higher the number of dimensions we take into consideration for our decision making or problem solving, the more objective our decision or solution becomes, deviating from a narrower level of subjectivity. There are different degrees of objectivity we can reach, depending on the number of dimensions we consider, and at the highest level, we have the objective of making personally as well as socially more sustainable decisions or solutions. Finally, we highlight the need for providing a fair system of education for our neurodiverse cohort to thrive as a goal of education. As we discussed, a fair system would be one that promotes higher-order learning indiscriminately across the board and one that does learner evaluation accordingly.

Useful Pedagogical Practices and Study Skills from the Viewpoint of Neuroscience

• • •

CHAPTER 7

Delivering Learning Content Following the Concepts of Educational Neuroscience

• • •

IN THIS CHAPTER, WE FOCUS on some useful pedagogical practices that can be used while delivering new content to learners during a teaching-learning session. To provide them with a scientific basis or make them evidence based, these practices are viewed and validated from the perspective of neuroscience. The areas we discuss below are emphasising high-level concepts as opposed to specific details, the significance of the pace of delivery, asking questions as part of content delivery, using longer wait times for learners to respond, the task of motivating learners, and getting learner attention in the teaching-learning process.

HIGHLIGHTING HIGH-LEVEL CONCEPTS AHEAD OF MORE SPECIFIC DETAILS DURING A TEACHING-LEARNING SESSION

As facilitators during a teaching-learning session, one of the critical parameters we have to be conscious of is the level of detail we need to introduce to our learners. In one extreme, we can present a large volume of specific details related to the content; at the other extreme, we can present a limited number of high-level concepts and how these concepts relate to each other. Let us examine what the findings of neuroscience tell us in making an educated decision.

HIGHLIGHTING HIGH-LEVEL CONCEPTS TO MAKE USE OF LIMITED-CAPACITY WORKING MEMORY EFFICIENTLY

When delivering new content to learners in a teaching-learning environment, we need to emphasise the high-level concepts we present, instead of focusing on more specific details. By doing this, we will be able to utilise the learners' limited-capacity working memory more effectively following the phenomenon of chunking, as discussed before. That is, when grouped or generalised information is presented as a small number of concepts, instead of a larger number of specific detailed items, learners will be handling only a smaller number of knowledge-rich items in their limited-capacity working memory. As a result, the initial rehearsing process of knowledge, making sense, or connecting information presented to existing neural networks of knowledge will be more efficient. Further, high-level concepts are retained in memory longer as semantic memory, which is independent of time and space contexts, as discussed before.

On the other hand, specific details are stored as episodic memory, which is more susceptible to forgetting; these specific details usually have references to time and space, and their validity can be subjective or have a relatively limited scope. We highlight this fact not to deny that there are situations where more specific details are useful (especially when a high-level concept is put into practice or to a real-world implementation); we rely heavily on more specific details. Additionally, if a particular high-level abstract concept is difficult for learners to grasp, we may provide more specific details related to it, to enhance clarity. However, when we introduce a topic area to our learners, we need to make sure that we do not clutter our learners' minds with large quantities of specific details. We need to help our learners to grasp the limited number of fundamental concepts related to the content area first and into lasting memories. We should not forget that this is the age of information and related technologies; large volumes of information reach our desks very quickly and relatively economically. As a result, if learners need any specific details at any time, they can look for them on the World Wide Web. It is important to grasp the fundamental concepts initially and how they relate to each other as well as to learners' existing knowledge bases. From another perspective, if more specific details are likely to be forgotten easily, why should we emphasise them unnecessarily to engage in a futile task? If high-level concepts are retained longer, why shouldn't we stress on them in a teaching-learning session? In a nutshell, let the learners "see the forest for the trees," and introduce detail on a need-to-know basis to clarify, using a session regulated by learner feedback.

HIGH-LEVEL CONCEPTS AS KNOWLEDGE CROSSING MULTIPLE DOMAINS

Since high-level concepts are usually more generalised knowledge, they tend to penetrate through various domain areas of knowledge as well. To accomplish the knowledge-transfer process, we can link these concepts into as many domain areas or diverse situations or examples as possible. Consequently, by emphasising high-level concepts, we not only create more lasting memories through a process of transfer; we also enable the interconnection of knowledge in multiple domain areas. Further, when we relate the content presented to multiple domain areas, we necessarily move learners from a restrictive, lower-order, and convergent thinking exercise to a more creative, higher-order, and divergent-thinking exercise, as discussed before.

To reiterate, to enhance wisdom in learners, we have to let them create knowledge across multiple domains. Here, we are penetrating across knowledge silos into more fluid learning modes, and the integrated and lasting knowledge that can be retained and recalled readily is the result. Looking from a different perspective, we encourage and provide necessary foundations for learners to be creative, divergent, or inductive in their thinking; we are targeting higher-order thinking or learning to focus on the high end of Bloom's Taxonomy. From the viewpoint of neuroscience, we are en route to enhancing learner consciousness, the phenomenon of brain resources and neural networks integration for enhanced usability.

It is also worth noticing here that different parts of the brain work in inductive and deductive or abstract and detailed reasoning; the right hemisphere is likely to be heavily involved in inductive and abstract reasoning, while the left hemisphere focuses on deductive and detailed reasoning. Consequently, following the revised Bloom's Taxonomy, we can get learners to pay attention to generalised concepts without necessarily introducing extensive specific details, as discussed before. Further, we have highlighted that visual-spatial learners prefer to use the right-cerebral hemisphere, while auditory-sequential learners prefer to rely on left-cerebral-hemispheric thinking. As a result, we are avoiding a typically disadvantaged situation faced by visual-spatial learners in a traditional educational environment where auditory-sequential instructions are the norm. By encouraging both learner categories to use right-hemispheric creative and divergent thinking more predominantly, we put all learners on a path to a higher level of human development through enhanced consciousness.

RELATING HIGH-LEVEL CONCEPTS TO INDIVIDUALISED KNOWLEDGE IN UNIQUE WAYS

To reiterate, when we introduce new high-level concepts, we have to help learners make sense or link them to their existing knowledge bases. Existing knowledge bases that can be recalled easily would most likely to be the concepts based on the day-to-day life phenomena, spreading across multiple domains. Recall that most of our learning is implicit and learned through our daily experiences from multiple domain areas. Consequently, through teaching-learning procedures, we have to make these implicit or semiconscious memories more explicit or conscious. In this way, we support learners to build more lasting and more integrated knowledge bases, instead of isolated pieces that are domain specific and susceptible for forgetting. Researchers have observed significant student disengagement resulting from facilitators not paying attention to connecting classroom studies to real-world applications (Larkin 2016). Also, when new concepts are presented, we can guide and get learners to link the new concepts on their own to their existing personalised body of knowledge. That is, learners attempt to identify relationships between their existing and new knowledge as we encourage them to do it on their own.

The important point we highlight here is that learners bring individualised knowledge bases to the teaching-learning environment, depending on an individual's unique background. As a result, the linking process of new knowledge to their existing knowledge bases may ideally be done by the individual learner on his or her own, rather than by an outsider. In fact, we can get them to do this as a secondary, elaborate rehearsal task after the teaching-learning session, during a learner's leisure time, to enhance retention and the ability to recall. What we as facilitators can do is to encourage learners to be bold and courageous in the presence of new information and avoid any inhibitions and self-regulation, and to be creative, divergent, or inductive in reasoning or learning; this will activate a learner's brain areas of individuality and self-expression, as discussed before. The result is that learners engage in the process of creating personalised knowledge, as highlighted at higher levels of Bloom's Taxonomy and in the theory of constructivism—and they do so in a relatively autonomous manner that would enlighten them on how to proceed with a process of lifelong learning continuously.

MANAGING SESSION TIME EFFECTIVELY ONLY HIGHLIGHTING HIGH-LEVEL CONCEPTS WHILE GIVING DETAILS ON NEED BASIS

Before a teaching-learning session, educators can prepare by identifying which high-level concepts out of many probable will be introduced during the time-constrained session. Further, we can decide what specific details related to the selected concepts will be presented, ideally on a need basis, to help learners to grasp the abstract concepts. We may also have some real-life examples or anecdotes handy in case some learners request an additional explanation. Provision of a clarification on the difference between high-level concepts and specific details and why high-level concepts are more useful and retained in memory longer would also be helpful for learners who need guidance on our presentation, as well as to direct their learning appropriately during the teaching-learning session. With the help of this clarification, learners will be able to differentiate between high-level concepts and specific details and the pieces of information that are more important to pay attention to and understand deeply.

ASKING QUESTIONS AS A MEANS OF PRESENTING FOLLOWING THE CONSTRUCTIVIST THEORY OF LEARNING

For learners to identify the mentioned relationships amongst pieces of knowledge or information, we can direct them by asking a series of open-ended questions to guide them towards the target; learners will get to the goal of identifying connections by answering or just attempting to respond to these questions. It is essentially the technique followed by constructivist theory practitioners. The questions we ask need to be thought-provoking or open-ended ones that can stimulate learners' brains. From time to time, we should get them to develop self-awareness through self-reflection by asking some metacognitive questions. These questions would be about their learning and how they engage in the learning process. In constructivist theory, we say each learner constructs meaning individually, depending on his or her existing knowledge base. That is, knowledge each learner constructs within is subjective, not objective. Also, instead of being passive listeners, learners will make attempts to actively construct answers to the questions posed by retrieving and linking information from their neural networks of knowledge. As mentioned before, learners get the pleasure of having control of the learning process to generate new ideas or relationships, by linking the newly introduced information to their existing knowledge bases. Such positive emotions are likely to activate the learners' frontal lobes to enable enhanced learning. Further, we can make use of some related analogies or anecdotes to enhance clarity of the concepts presented.

These figurative language examples usually represent high-level concepts concisely; as a result, it would help learners to grasp abstract concepts better. The key point here is that we make them identify relationships between existing and new knowledge on their own, rather than relating them to learners for them to commit to memory, as in a rote rehearsal exercise, which is unlikely to give a lasting impact. The significance of this approach is that learners are in control of their learning and enjoy the freedom of creating knowledge, resulting in better learning outcomes (Zull 2011). Even when we present our learners with a well-established theory or law, we should mimic the thinking process that would have gone through in the mind of the creator of this theory or law; the creator may have inquired him- or herself in numerous ways, asking various questions against his or her existing knowledge bases before confirming the hypothesis. We should lead our learners in a similar path of self-inquiry, mimicking a process of construction of knowledge, making sense and transfer during a teaching-learning session.

CONTROLLING THE PACE OF PRESENTATION APPROPRIATELY FOR ENABLING LEARNERS TO CONSTRUCT KNOWLEDGE

As a facilitator of a teaching-learning session, have you ever reflected on the need for an appropriate pace of presentation? The faster the pace of presentation, the more content we can probably introduce to our learners. But how effective are we regarding learner retention during a rapid content-delivery process? Have you heard learners say, "The contents flew over my head"? Let us now find out what educational neuroscience reveals to us.

DECIDING THE PACE OF PRESENTATION CONSIDERING THE RELATIVE SLOWNESS IN ENGAGING THE FRONTAL LOBES

We need to present new content to learners in a manner that they can link to their existing knowledge bases. It is the process of making sense during an initial rehearsal process, as we have described before. The existing knowledge bases or neural networks may be associated with multiple domain areas of knowledge and may have been spread across multiple physical regions of the brain, depending on individual neurological and psychological differences (Watagodakumbura 2013). Some of these knowledge bases can be implicit or semiconscious, formed through more prevalent implicit learning. In effect, they may not be very explicit or conscious and not be readily retrievable.

To reach out to neural networks of knowledge in multiple regions, we need to necessarily send messages to the frontal lobes, which are highly connected to all the other areas. However, findings from neuroscience reveal that when knowledge is processed in the frontal lobes and connects with the knowledge bases in the other regions, this whole task takes relatively longer, making the process slower. This slowness, we can infer, could be due to the parallel processing and communication that takes place across multiple brain regions. This is a divergent or inductive thinking process in which learners will have to scan across all of their brain regions to identify any related neural networks of knowledge, as highlighted in the high end of Bloom's Taxonomy, as we elaborated before.

The process is different from finding a directly and clearly associated piece of knowledge as in a convergent or deductive thinking process. The slower time comparison done here for the divergent or inductive thinking process is usually made in regard to modern machines or conventional computers composed of electronic circuits that run sequentially in repetitive cycles at very high speeds. Also, we have to remember that frontal lobes are considered to be the organ of civilisation; that is, any processing involving frontal lobes or resulting in higher-order processing has the impact of a deeper and better learning experience, as highlighted before. Consequently, when presenting new content to learners, we have to present it at an appropriate pace, taking into account the relative slowness in processing that involves the frontal lobes. Especially when learners make somewhat unfamiliar connections between new concepts and rather vague or implicit exiting knowledge bases, it is possible that longer rehearsal times are required.

HIGHER WAIT TIMES AS A MEANS OF ENSURING HIGHER-ORDER LEARNING

Interestingly, some researchers who have worked independently on wait times have formulated interesting and related results to the topic. They observed that higher wait times after asking a question from learners resulted in better and higher-order answers. Further, as a corollary, they identified that educators who tend to allow higher wait times are likely to ask thought-provoking, higher-order questions as well, encouraging learners to pursue divergent or inductive thinking. What these research results may reveal is that with appropriately longer wait times, learners, as well as facilitators, have an adequate time to utilise their frontal lobes for better communication amongst various other regions of the brain that result in a more integrated neural-resources operation. In other words, educators can induce higher-order thinking in our learners by ourselves engaging in higher-order questioning.

APPROPRIATE PACE OF DELIVERY FOR CREATING LASTING MEMORIES

Looking from another point of view, we see that frontal lobes are usually involved with the process of abstract conceptualisation, as highlighted in Kolb's experiential learning cycle (Kolb 1983; Watagodakumbura 2013; Zull 2002). As a result, when new contents are presented with the aid of introducing new concepts, we need to allow learners adequate time to understand or conceptualise them. It contrasts from presenting contents to learners rapidly so that they have to commit them to short-term memory, involving in a convergent thinking exercise, for them to reproduce the content in the exact form (i.e., rote rehearsal) later on, not necessarily getting the frontal lobes involved appropriately. That is, when new materials are presented, the initial elaborate rehearsal process in working memory helps learners to construct new knowledge; it sends and retains them in long-term memory for recalling readily later. In other words, making sense and transfer of knowledge, as elaborated before, is done more efficiently within learners when an appropriate pace of presentation is maintained. Further, by keeping an appropriate pace of presentation, we allow learners to create new knowledge or identify new relationships, sometimes very creative or intriguing ones, by essentially making use of the right-cerebral hemisphere; this will facilitate visual-spatial learners to engage better in the learning process.

MOTIVATING LEARNERS TO ENGAGE IN DEEPER LEARNING BY GIVING FACTS FROM EDUCATIONAL NEUROSCIENCE

Despite having sound facilitation and learning resources, some learners do not participate in the teaching-learning process satisfactorily or to the best of their ability. In this section, let us try to understand the significant role of learner motivation and how this essential requirement can possibly be fulfilled by viewing it from the point of educational neuroscience.

INTRINSIC MOTIVATION AS A MEANS OF ACHIEVING A HIGHER LEVEL OF ENGAGEMENT

For effective learning to take place in a teaching-learning environment, learners will have to engage well in the learning process. More specifically, they have to be intrinsically motivated in learning; that is, they have to see some long-lasting and highly objective value in learning. It is not pursued merely for the purpose of getting through approaching examinations or even for purely making way for their future careers, but for something more meaningful in general in everyday life throughout life. That is, learners have to see some useful and lasting meaning, as elaborated before, in what they learn, for them to develop a motivation intrinsically. For example, if learners realise that deep learning, as highlighted throughout this text, leads to enhanced consciousness and wisdom that enables them to become better decision makers or problem solvers, they are more likely to be intrinsically motivated to engage in it. In fact, researchers have found that attention or focus is at the highest possible level when learners are intrinsically motivated, as discussed before. Also, if learners can identify a significant meaning in what they learn, they will be more inclined to perform more elaborate rehearsal, both initially and secondarily, resulting in a better transfer of learning.

LASTING VALUE OF LEARNING TO DEVELOP A HIGHER LEVEL OF CONSCIOUSNESS AS THE MOTIVATOR

In order to motivate our learners to engage deeply in the learning process or gain lasting meaning in what they learn, educators can provide them with some useful and unravelling facts about learning, in general, related to educational neuroscience. Let us discuss some examples. As discussed before, our brains use more neural resources in learning new material, and learning new material is relatively more engaging as well as challenging. Learners should be more prepared and focused when new contents are presented. However, even difficult contents can be mastered by simply paying attention for a longer period (i.e., elaborate rehearsal); then the brain will do the wonder of learning—making lasting connections with the existing knowledge base as well as creating new relationships.

The elaborate rehearsal exercise can also be attempted at a secondary stage, leisurely, if learners see some meaning in expending this time or are motivated adequately. Elaborate rehearsal in working memory will help to improve the clarity of even new or challenging content, enabling a more efficient transfer process. In other words, to enable a better transfer process, learners are advised and encouraged to simply spend more time on any content that does not make a clear sense initially or is unclear. Rather than keeping away from such content in fear, possibly in anticipation of distorting the existing framework of knowledge, they can be instructed to avoid forced inhibitions and self-regulation and be bold in engaging in a creative, divergent-thinking process.

Also, our brains have the natural property of neuroplasticity that help us to create new neural connections or networks altogether, provided that we rehearse the contents for an adequate amount of time. In fact, researchers have found that human beings are novelty-seeking creatures who are naturally motivated to create new neural connections, as discussed before. That is, we can be creative and develop wisdom if we try to understand new concepts deeply by linking them to other existing concepts or frameworks, more specifically from multiple domain areas. Further, the task of learning is a lifelong process that does not end at the completion of examinations or formal studies.

Ideally, learners should not be narrowly focused on short-term goals; instead, they should have broader and highly objective goals in learning and life in general. The concept of distributed rehearsal, as discussed before, is applicable here; learners go through or revise some contents they have learned before, after an extended time gap of months or even years. They can see the knowledge they have gained before with a new set of eyes, through all the other learning they have done since, improving clarity following a process resulting in neural efficiency (Zull 2011), and enabling them to make new useful connections. As we move on with our lives, we develop more integrated, useful neural networks that cross the boundaries of domain areas, thus enhancing consciousness and wisdom into higher levels of human development. In this way, we can become better general problem solvers and decision makers, seeing the reality better by recalling well-retained memories readily whenever needed, as an evolutionary process over the years of our lifespan. This idea of an ever-extending and integrating neural network (provided we engage in learning deeply performing elaborate rehearsal routines) can be a significant contributing factor for creating intrinsic motivation within learners. Every unit of effective time one spends on learning will give that person an improved opportunity to see reality or the world more broadly or as it is.

CREATING POSITIVE EMOTIONS AS MEANS OF MOTIVATING

By providing positive facts about learning and content presented, we can create positive emotions (such as pleasure) in the minds of learners. At the same time, we can get rid of any negative emotions (such as fear) from the minds of learners with appropriate instructions and behaviour. For example, if learners get a feeling that the contents are not difficult to master and a systematic approach is utilised, they may not be fearful of them. If the teacher presents a nonauthoritative figure, like that of a facilitator, in front of the class, learners will be more comfortable and prepared to learn, with no negative emotions. These positive emotions lacking negative ones help learners to be more specifically motivated in the learning process, transforming a convergent thinking process focusing on safety to a divergent one that supports bold enquiry. In other words, considering the hierarchical responding nature of the human brain, in the absence of life-threatening and highly emotional situations, learners are well aligned to engage in and pay full attention to the teaching-learning environment. It is worth noting that positive emotions release the biochemical endorphins in the brain that stimulate the frontal lobes, broadening the scope of attention and enhancing critical-thinking skills. In contrast, negative emotions release the hormone cortisol, activating defence behaviours such as fight or flight, thus narrowing the frontal lobe focus towards identifying the cause of stress, as discussed before.

GETTING LEARNER ATTENTION ENTIRELY ON THE TEACHING-LEARNING PROCESS OR DISCUSSION

In addition to motivating learners appropriately to get their attention to the teaching-learning process, what other measures can we as facilitators take, especially in the presence of findings from educational neuroscience?

BINOCULAR RIVALRY AND THE NEED TO FOCUS ON ONE THING AT A TIME
We have heard some people brag about their ability to multitask—attending to two or more things at the same time. It is not hard to understand a situation where a person walks while listening to music with a portable music player. However, what would be our capability to attend to two tasks that each has a high demand for brain resources? Neuroscientists have identified a concept referred to as binocular rivalry, as discussed before, that explains that human brain can concentrate or pay attention completely to only one thing at a time. We can make use of this principle appropriately in our teaching-learning environment by asking learners only to listen and to see by paying full attention and engaging in the discussion. By doing this, we allow learners to participate in initial rehearsal, as discussed before, entirely, during the teaching-learning process by attaching sense to the content learned. During this initial rehearsal, we have the contents processed in learners' working memory. Working memory has two components: the phonological loop (for processing auditory signals) and the visuospatial sketchpad (for processing visual-spatial signals), as discussed before. If we make learners concentrate on auditory and visual-spatial signals in an integrated manner by talking about what we show them, they are in a better position to pay full concentrated attention to a single task. In fact, we have structural support in our brains for integrating multisensory signals; to be more specific, the parietal lobe in the neocortex does multisensory integration and has also evolved much larger in humans.

MINIMISING HARMFUL ANXIETY AND DIVIDED ATTENTION
Further, learners can be provided with summaries of the discussion, and if possible, a voice or video recording of the same for their reference later on; this will reduce harmful anxiety, as discussed before, created due to the possibility of missing important points highlighted during the teaching-learning points. Still, if they want to write down some notes in their own words, we can provide note-taking times separately for this purpose. It

will avoid a multitasking situation where learners will have to listen and to view visuals subconsciously while note taking. Also, it is different from jotting down the presenter's exact words to be reproduced later on at the examinations or assessment (i.e., rote rehearsal, as discussed before). We are trying to avoid learners having to undergo a situation of divided attention that would have an adverse impact on deeper learning or elaborate rehearsal, resulting in better-connected neural networks of knowledge. In this way, we encourage learners to be fully vigilant by paying attention to the discussion, constructing meaning, and creating abstract conceptualisations (Kolb 1983) by linking new knowledge to existing knowledge bases. That is, we encourage learners to extend a possible convergent, lower-order thinking exercise to a divergent, higher-order one by utilising more productive time.

RAISING HELPFUL ANXIETY TO GET LEARNER ATTENTION
Further, we can get learners' attention towards what we present by asking related questions to build curiosity, instead of performing a narration; these questions can relate the concepts we highlight to day-to-day phenomena for inter-domain integration. By generating curiosity, we raise the level of concern to a helpful anxiety level, creating a positive atmosphere. In fact, constructivist theory practitioners engage in the teaching-learning process by asking open-ended questions to learners regularly, as highlighted before.

To Sum Up

If we spend some time reflecting on how our brains learn, we will be able to identify those subtle means we can use during a teaching-learning session for enhanced learning. One of the most important tasks we should undertake as educators is to organise the contents presented in a hierarchical manner: high-level concepts at the top, with more specific details at the bottom. Further, we need to put the emphasis on the high-level abstract concepts because human beings are better at grouping and chunking information and identifying patterns. We also need to make learners differentiate between high-level concepts and details themselves and pay more attention to the former. Highlighting mainly high-level concepts would help us to manage our presentation time well, while learners are given a better opportunity to create lasting memories through better understanding.

When new concepts are presented to learners, we should direct them to identify the important points or features related to the concepts on their own by asking them a series of questions in guiding them towards the understanding—the practice commonly followed by the constructivist theorists who allow learners to create knowledge internally. Further, the pace of content delivery, including the time allowed for responding after raising a question, needs to be carefully and thoughtfully decided. From time to time, during the presentation, we should attempt to motivate learners in learning by highlighting the lasting value of learning. By doing this, we make learners intrinsically motivated, as opposed to extrinsically, focusing on short-term goals. When learners are properly motivated, they are likely to pay attention to the teaching-learning session better. We can help them to give full attention by aligning or synchronising the visual contents with the auditory ones and allowing them to separate note-taking time (if required) so that harmful anxiety is minimised.

Assessing Learners Following the Concepts of Educational Neuroscience

• • •

IN THIS CHAPTER, WE WILL identify some useful pedagogical practices to use when setting up valid assessments. The validity of these practices is discussed from the viewpoint of educational neuroscience. Since learners are primarily guided by assessments in the way they involve in the learning process, it is imperative that valid and well-justified principles are used for constructing them. Our discussion will include: the need to focus on assessing higher-order learning and conceptual understanding; discouraging rote rehearsal exercises; the significance of recognition tests ahead of associative recall; assessment encouraging adaptive decision making ahead of veridical decision making; setting an appropriate time period for assessments; taking into consideration of having to the use of the frontal lobes for providing answers and assessment that lead learners towards developing consciousness or wisdom into a higher level of human development.

Forming Open-Ended Conceptual Questions Minimising the Need for Rote Rehearsal and Associative Recall

To Direct and Encourage Learners to Provide Unique, Individualised Answers

When setting up assessments, we need to consider ways in which we might involve learners' frontal lobes, which essentially connect multiple brain regions, in providing solutions. By doing this, we can test how well learners were able to engage in deep learning (Biggs 2003; Entwistle 1998) or elaborate rehearsal by constructing individualised meaning (Yero 2002). We as educators should discourage every single learner from providing identical answers, exactly in the form we presented to them, following a rote rehearsal exercise. To achieve this important objective, we can ask relatively novel and open-ended conceptual questions (Watagodakumbura 2013). We deviate from asking questions that require regurgitation of factual and exact, recalled information; that is, we keep away from asking questions that need associative recall in providing answers.

Some possible examples of associative recall type questions are "What is the capital city of Australia?" or "Who is the president of China?" Such questions only require a rote rehearsal effort from learners. Further, answers to these questions can be instantaneously provided if learners have rote rehearsed them well; they require little processing involving multiple brain regions including the frontal lobes in preparing the answer. Also, if learners have access to modern technology in the form of the World Wide Web or the Internet, finding answers to associative-recall questions can be a trivial task. Consequently, by making learners memorise answers to such questions, educators may be wasting valuable learner time for no purposeful gain regarding learning, per se.

Open-ended conceptual questions allow us to test learners' higher-order learning abilities developed as a result of involving in high-end functions such as creation and evaluation of revised Bloom's Taxonomy. High-level conceptual questions help us encourage learners to provide generalised answers that cross multiple domains; these are the traces of semantic memory that are retained longer. In other words, we encourage learners to engage in adaptive decision making instead of veridical decision making, even when answering examination questions. Learners adapt to open-ended questions in an individualised manner to provide idiosyncratic solutions. We ask appropriate open-ended questions from learners to discourage them from providing premeditated or habitual answers. If they have responded to a similar question before, they may provide a habitual answer; the brain plays an automaticity function here, bypassing the engagement of cortical resources including the frontal lobe appropriately. Consequently, even during the examination time, learners engage in a process of elaborate rehearsal, integrating information from multiple brain regions, using the frontal lobes. Based on the clues given to the open-ended questions, learners will have to retrieve retained information from appropriate areas of the brain; to do this, they must perform a widespread scan to make valid and creative inferences.

Encouraging Learners to Provide Creative or Higher-Order Answers, Even in Science Education

We would like to emphasise that the discussion in the above paragraph can be applied equally well even to science education, not only for areas of social-science education. Science usually works from the third-person perspective, adopting an objective point of view. In fact, researchers have found that the above approach to science education has led to disengagement of learners from the discipline (Tytler 2016). However, recently there is a shift in seeing science from a first-person perspective, in particular by the scientists interested in studying consciousness. In this approach, phenomenological data is viewed from introspection or self-report. Consequently, what we have discussed in the preceding paragraph can be applied to science education environments equally well, encouraging learners to develop creativity and wisdom. In other words, assessments in science education do not have to focus on veridical decision making or asking questions with exact or precise answers; questions can be so constructed that learners can provide subjective answers, engaging in a divergent-thinking process, without violating the rules or laws of a broad framework of knowledge.

DECIDING AN APPROPRIATE TIME DURATION WITH DILIGENCE FOR ASSESSMENTS

From the perspective of Bloom's Taxonomy (revised), we encourage learners to engage in the functions of creation and evaluation or divergent-thinking exercises. In the end, we evaluate the transfer of learning in regards to the learner. As a result, the time allocated per question becomes a key design factor of an examination. As we are not expecting premeditated, habitual answers requiring fewer brain resources, we need to assign adequate time not only to write down but also to create the response, utilising as many brain resources as possible through a scan across the board, engaging in a divergent-thinking exercise. In timed tests or assessments, since we have a limited time to evaluate our learners, it is important that we create questions at higher *complexity* levels, clearly not at higher *difficulty* levels. Questions at higher difficulty levels may utilise more time and a lower-order effort from learners' point of view, whilst not necessarily testing higher-order thinking abilities or transfer of learning. Further, since we have only a limited time to conduct timed tests or assessments, these tests become a form of statistical analysis that allows only a sample set of questions to be included rather than all possible questions. At the risk of not allowing learners adequate time to formulate and write down answers, we should take a special care to not to overload the examination paper with too many questions.

Assessing Higher-Order Learning and How It Helps Form Lasting Semantic Memories

Assessment Focusing the High End of Bloom's Taxonomy

As educators, we have a general understanding that assessments should test what we commonly refer to as higher-order learning. The term *higher-order learning* relates well to the high end of the hierarchy of levels described in Bloom's Taxonomy, a favourite tool amongst educators used for classifying the type or quality of learning, as discussed before. In the revised Bloom's Taxonomy, we have evaluation and creation at higher levels, while comprehension and knowledge are at lower levels; analysis and application functions are found in the middle. When we refer to assessing higher-order learning, we necessarily want to assess our learners for their ability to create and evaluate. In creation, a learner formulates relatively novel answers on the fly by integrating pieces of knowledge he or she possesses in regards to the question asked. This process contrasts from making learners merely recall what someone else said or as the textbook presented it; rather, it is a personalised and accurate view or judgement of the learner.

In the process of evaluation described in Bloom's Taxonomy, a learner compares and contrasts contents with and from other related memories, usually high-level concepts he or she has retained. Again, this is a task done on the fly, instead of providing a highly practised or premeditated answer. To engage in creation and evaluation tasks, learners will have to take part in a divergent and inductive thinking process by scanning across the brain to locate probable or more closely related answers. This thought process contrasts from directly associating a definitive answer stored at a particular location of the brain, as that happens in a convergent or lower-order thinking exercise. Looking at this from another perspective, we want our learners to demonstrate their understanding of underlying abstract concepts. When abstract concepts are well grasped, they can be readily associated with many relevant areas or contexts.

ASSESSMENT GUIDING LEARNERS IN FORMING LASTING SEMANTIC MEMORIES

To reiterate the need to emphasise high-level concepts, in Kolb's experiential learning cycle (Kolb 1983), abstract conceptualisation is considered as the most important stage in learning (Watagodakumbura 2013; Zull 2002). This stage of the learning process is the one in which learners spend time absorbing abstract concepts deeply, relating them to as many contexts as possible. This premise of highlighting abstract concepts in both learning as well as assessment can now be validated by the evidence available in neuroscience. Our high-level knowledge or abstract concepts are stored in our brains as semantic memory, the type of memory that lasts longer. On the other hand, more specific or narrower details about particular situations are stored as episodic memory and are more susceptible to being forgotten quickly (Baars and Gage 2010).

Further, episodic memory is associated with sources of time and space, whereas semantic memories are independent of sources of time and space. Now we see that high-level concepts are generalised summaries of knowledge or facts that are valid beyond the time and space of occurring. As a result, they are applicable in many broader contexts. Consequently, in assessments, it is justified that we test learner understanding of these abstract concepts associated with semantic memory ahead of more specific details linked to traces of episodic memory that are valid only within limited contexts of a particular time and space. Also, generalised concepts have the capacity to penetrate into other domains of knowledge and application; a deeper and more critical understanding (Paul and Elder 2000) of them have a greater lasting value into the future, justifying the investment of an adequate time.

Designing Assessment Taking Constructivism and Implicit Learning into Consideration

Taking into Consideration the Subjective Nature of Knowledge in Assessment

The constructivist theory of learning, as discussed before, indicates that during a teaching-learning process, every learner creates knowledge internally and independently. That is, every learner creates subjective knowledge based on his existing knowledge base. The term *existing knowledge base* refers to what the learner has retained in a lasting manner and could also be readily recalled when required. From the standpoint of neuroscience, when new knowledge is created internally, learners create new neural networks and associate them with the existing neural networks. Associating newly created neural networks to existing neural networks is crucial to the creation of lasting memories, making sense of what is learned, and accomplishing a function of transfer, as discussed before. We clearly understand two important points here: knowledge is subjective (Yero 2002), not objective, and learning has a physical meaning, which indicates the growth of neurones to make more connected neural networks, as discussed before. Knowledge is subjective because every individual carries different knowledge bases or neural networks that he or she can associate readily or spontaneously to newly learned knowledge. Consequently, the resulting connected neural networks formed are different from one individual to the other.

Taking into Consideration Implicit Learning in Assessment

Evidence from neuroscience shows that the most of the learning we do as human beings is implicit, as discussed before. In academic environments, we mostly have explicit learning in which the teacher tells learners what to learn, to try to get brain resources focused on the particular task being introduced or learned. On the other hand, implicit learning takes place unconscious to the learner and does not have to take place in an academic or teaching-learning environment. Even in an academic environment, an individual learner can engage in implicit learning, by creating subjective individualised knowledge, not usually intended by the facilitator or curriculum.

Another related term we use is *incidental learning* (Eide and Eide 2004), in which human beings learn implicitly by observing an incident or undergoing a certain situation. Now, we see an interesting relationship between constructivism described in the previous paragraphs and implicit learning. Since learners make subjective knowledge internally and individually and most of our learning is implicit, in assessments, educators have to accommodate learners to provide their subjective responses, followed by an evaluation of their validity. That is, we have to be mindful that even in a formal teaching-learning environment, learners can learn certain pieces of knowledge implicitly, depending on their background and engagement level. In other words, learners may create new insights that the teacher may not have implied or given out directly.

Considering this situation, asking objective-type questions where there is generally one correct answer will not encourage our learners to be creative and unique in providing their responses; it does not allow us to evaluate learners on the level of higher-order learning or divergent thinking achieved. Rather, it promotes a rote-learning environment in which learners tend to commit facts to short-term memory, exactly as given by the teacher or textbook, in preparation for assessment tasks.

ACCOMMODATING INCLUSIVENESS IN ASSESSMENT

In short, we have to set assessments in a manner that encourages learners to respond subjectively as well as to demonstrate their implicit learning, which should then be evaluated for the level of higher-order learning demonstrated. These assessment questions are generally open-ended and in contrast from the ones that prompt learners to merely reproduce particular memorised facts. It is also worth noticing that gifted learners (Silverman 1998, 2002) are highly capable in incidental or implicit learning (Eide and Eide 2004). They will not be disadvantaged, as that happens in traditional classrooms if assessments are set in the manner mentioned above, encouraging and giving the opportunity for them to provide their subjective responses. By providing a better learning environment for gifted individuals who demonstrate a higher level of overexcitable characteristics (Dabrowski 1970, 1972, 1977), we can be more inclusive (Goleman 2005; Webb 2005, 2008) in our pedagogical approaches within a neurodiverse (Armstrong 2011; Watagodakumbura 2013) society.

Designing Assessment Encouraging Adaptive Decision Making/Recognition Tests ahead of Veridical Decision Making/Associative Recall

We have seen that learners construct subjective meaning from what they learn, and most of the learning is implicit or unconscious to the learner; sometimes what the learner has grasped may not have been implied by the teacher. Further, we have recognised that higher-order learning or high-level concepts learned last longer in learners' memories, are more useful in general, and are not valid restrictively for particular sources of limited time and space. In the presence of this evidence, the challenge now is to identify ways to construct assessments that appropriately yield validity. Evaluations need to focus on testing higher-order learning or the ability to create and evaluate, which is essentially retained in long-term memory.

We have to note that human brains are selectionist, unlike conventional, instructionist computers (Baars and Gage 2010). That is, computers are relying on a limited set of symbols to identify a predefined solution; human brains can produce new solutions altogether by forming new neural networks that did not exist before, on an ongoing basis and without a limit in a timeframe. That is why human beings are identified as creative, while conventional computers are not (Beale and Jackson 1990). The term *higher-order learning* is used to highlight that we create new connections amongst neural networks to create new knowledge when we learn. In other words, human brains are better or more naturally inclined in adaptive decision making, while computers are better in veridical decision making; that is, human brains can adapt to new situations in an entirely novel manner, while computers can only find an existing or predefined solution.

In adaptive decision making, you usually take a large number of inputs into consideration and come to an optimised solution rather than a 100 percent correct solution with a limited scope. In contrast, in veridical decision making, when we generally take a relatively lower number of inputs into consideration, we may come to a 100 percent correct answer, albeit one with a limited scope. We can see here that when we take lower-number inputs into consideration, coming to a definite or clear conclusion is not difficult. The answers human brains are better in producing will not have a single "right" answer; rather, the answer will be dependent on the way learners have argued or evaluated to make a valid judgment on a somewhat ambiguous situation.

In most of our life situations, we make adaptive decisions in the presence of ambiguous conditions. More importantly, as individuals, we will adapt to a given situation in different ways, due to our individual differences; some will take a lower number of inputs or dimensions into consideration, while others will take a higher number into account. Further, the same individual may take a different number of inputs or dimensions into consideration at various stages of his or her life, resulting in different adaptive decisions at different times. This approach is different from applying a routine algorithm on a relatively limited number of inputs to come to the same answer again and again, as conventional computers do. We now have some clues on how we have to direct our assessments so that learners are better guided to engage in their learning, as well as to improve the validity of assessments in a lasting manner. We have to give learners the opportunity to provide creative and individualised responses and then evaluate them for the level of quality and degree of validity. In other words, we have to design and ask open-ended questions that require subjective or more optimised answers, instead of objective-type questions that yield one correct answer from all of our learners. Further, these open-ended questions will be inherently based on testing the understanding of abstract concepts rather than specific details; this is because specific details generally yield from a veridical decision-making process.

We essentially avoid associative recall questions and incline towards recognition tests. In the former type, reproduction of exact, memorised facts is done; in the latter, awareness or understanding of a high-level concept is demonstrated in the presence of some clues or priming content. Recognition tests are more common in our lives, as we have to have the ability to recall previously learned concepts readily when the circumstances require—if we have done learning effectively. On the other hand, an associative recall task may only be useful for a limited time immediately following a rote rehearsal activity; consequently, associative recall tasks should not be part of a valid assessment component. In summary, in an authentic assessment, educators should be able to differentiate and give a higher standing for an appropriate recognition activity that consumed more time than an associative recall that was produced relatively quickly.

Negative Implications of Multiple-Choice Questions Mostly Focusing on Testing Associative Recall

One of the favourite tools of assessment used by many educators is multiple-choice questions. Answers to multiple-choice questions are usually less time-consuming to mark, and the evaluation is fair across the board, as there is only one uniquely correct answer per question. However, mostly as a test of associative recall, multiple-choice questions push learners to engage in rote rehearsal. In providing answers, learners will do very little processing in formulating answers or judgements; instead, they rely on instant memory recall of factual information. Another limitation of multiple-choice questions is that they do not give learners the opportunity to provide their individualised or subjective answers based on how each learner uniquely processes the related information. Consequently, we promote conformity in learners instead of encouraging them to be self-expressive or creative.

Multiple-choice questions with a slightly modified focus can be used to get learners more involved in processing and providing their answers. In these modified questions, we can ask learners to select the least accurate or the most accurate statement out of four or five complete statements that are very closely matching in regards to the degree of accuracy. Further, we emphasise complete statements here, as they provide some contextual information, compared to isolated pieces of information as given in partial statements.

RETHINKING ON THE TIME FACTOR IN ASSESSMENTS WHEN INDIVIDUALISED, UNIQUE ANSWERS ARE EXPECTED UTILISING THE FRONTAL CORTEX ESSENTIALLY INSTEAD OF SUCCUMBING TO AUTOMATICITY

We now understand that most of the decisions we make in day-to-day life situations are adaptive in nature. To improve the quality of our adaptive decisions or to make the most optimal decision, we have to take into consideration as many possible dimensions of the problem at hand as we can. There are no strict procedures or predefined routine actions to carry out until one specific answer is obtained, as in the case of veridical decision making. In adaptive decision making, in the presence of ambiguous conditions, the frontal cortex of the brain gets involved extensively, resulting in more executive control (Baars and Gage 2010). Considering that the frontal lobes played a significant role in the evolution of human civilisation, the use of our frontal lobes in our regular decision making is indeed a positive sign; that is, we take advantage of highly evolved physiological resources and human qualities for optimal decision making.

It is interesting to note that when the frontal cortex gets involved in decision making, the process takes longer. The reason for this longer time could be because the role played by frontal lobes as an organ connecting most of the other parts of the brain. As a result, they integrate information received from many other parts of the brain, making it an understandably slower process. When we get involved in routine activities for a longer duration, such as in the case of habituation, the phenomenon known as automaticity results; when this happens, voluntary actions become automatic and fewer cortical resources are used for the underlying process. Consequently, the time required to complete a routine task that has been practised to a level of automaticity becomes relatively short. Now we can apply this timing concept to formulate our assessments better. First, we want to conclude that we need our learners to engage in an adaptive decision making or optimising process on the fly, thus deviating from providing a premeditated or habitual answer. Further, we need to set our assessments in a manner that learners have to provide individualised or unique answers after making evaluations and judgements on a somewhat ambiguous situation during the process. To achieve this task, learners will have to connect to as many related neural networks as possible to get the most optimal decision.

This process essentially utilises the frontal cortex and understandably requires relatively longer time. We should not set our assessments in a manner that learners are only required to regurgitate premeditated or practised answers quickly; instead, learners should be required to provide novel solutions to the reasonably novel questions we set. When answers are provided to novel questions, cortical resources are utilised better; this avoids the phenomenon of automaticity, as discussed before. Considering this situation, educators have the responsibility to provide adequate time for learners to construct their subjective answers to the open-ended questions we set and also to write them back on the paper; sound judgement from educators is essential on this assessment timing matter (Watagodakumbura 2013).

CONSTRUCTING ASSESSMENTS THAT HELP ENHANCING LEARNER CONSCIOUSNESS AND WISDOM INTO A HIGHER LEVEL OF HUMAN DEVELOPMENT

As educators, we have understood the need to set assessments to test understanding of abstract concepts. Since abstract concepts are summaries of generalised knowledge, they have the power of penetrating into many domain areas and applications of knowledge or neural networks. That is, a single abstract concept has the propensity to be utilised in many applications across multiple domains. Since the brain consists of a vast number of differentiated functional areas, it is highly likely that knowledge pertaining to different domains is stored in various regions of the brain. Consequently, when we focus on evaluating the understanding of abstract concepts in assessment, we inadvertently encourage learners to use multiple brain regions or functional areas to provide responses; that is, they are encouraged to use a larger number of neural networks across the brain. When this happens, learners are directed to use their frontal cortex more elaborately, as it is the part of the brain that connects most of the other regions.

Further, when we set our assessments in a manner that learners have to answer open-ended and novel questions with somewhat ambiguous conditions, the frontal cortex gets essentially involved. As presented by neuroscientists, consciousness is the phenomenon in which multiple, differentiated brain areas and functions are integrated, and evolution of consciousness is considered as the highest expression of human development, as discussed before. Consequently, when we focus on open-ended questions targeting abstract concepts, we are directing our learners on a path to enhance consciousness, a prime human quality as understood by scientists; that is, we are guiding our learners to become the best they can be as human beings. Similarly, when we integrate knowledge from multiple domain areas and possibly functional areas to make useful inferences, we develop what educationists refer to as wisdom (Claxton 2008). Wisdom is, in fact, a higher form of creativity that utilises knowledge of multiple domain areas to recall what we discussed before.

The frontal lobe, which is recognised as the organ of civilisation and integrates many brain areas together, plays a significant role in the tasks of enhancing consciousness and wisdom. That is, we have to direct our learners to use the frontal cortex as much as possible through assessment activities. As a result, when educators set assessments focusing on understanding of abstract concepts and ask open-ended questions for learners to thrive, they direct learners to enhance consciousness and develop wisdom, the highest human features achievable in the process of human evolution. We put learners on a path to a higher level of human development or self-actualisation, as discussed before, so that they could see the reality better, similar to having many open eyes, and become better or more optimal problem solvers.

To Sum Up

Educators have to use well-founded principles when constructing assessments in any teaching-learning environment. Otherwise, the validity of the assessment is challenged, and some learners get demoralised, sometimes in a lifelong manner, despite being highly capable academically or other diverse ways. One of the first points we highlighted was to assess learners' conceptual understanding of learning content ahead of rote-rehearsed specific details. Usually, open-ended questions allow us to test a learner's conceptual understanding or the level of higher-order learning, even in science education, as educators have observed recently. Answers to open-ended questions will have to be formed by engaging in the process of adaptive decision making, a more creative process human brains are capable of, ahead of using a machine-oriented, veridical decision-making process.

In particular, educators need to be diligent to avoid using malformed multiple-choice questions that test associative recall, encouraging learners to engage in rote rehearsal. Another compelling reason for this approach is that a conceptual understanding lasts longer as semantic memories; as a result, learners benefit from such lifelong learning or assessment and achieve human development. In effect, learners get to see a lasting value in learning, which motivates them intrinsically, unlike in the case where they are extrinsically motivated to get through an assessment as overcoming a short-term barrier.

The allocated time duration for an assessment, or conversely, the number of questions included to answer in a given time, is a critical design parameter of an assessment component. We need to provide sufficient time for learners to provide well-formulated responses on the fly, essentially stimulating the frontal lobes to provide individualised answers. Further, by guiding and encouraging learners to provide individualised answers, educators get to practice constructivism and are also able to tap into implicit memories formed through common incidental/implicit learning. By setting assessment correctly by adhering to well-founded principles, educators can guide our learners on a path to higher levels of human development by enhancing lifelong consciousness or wisdom.

CHAPTER 9

Curriculum Construction Following the Concepts of Educational Neuroscience

• • •

CURRICULUM CONSTRUCTION IS ONE OF the primary tasks in which educators get involved. It needs to be attended essentially with a high level of reflection and serious thought. In this chapter, we take into consideration some important pedagogical practices we should follow when constructing a complete curriculum. The validity of these practices is again verified by looking at them from the viewpoint of educational neuroscience. The points we discuss include: expectations of a well-set curriculum; coverage within a limited time duration; what teaching-learning materials need to be prepared and distributed to learners (and the nature of material); preparing assessment components giving consideration to the number and type; and creating additional learning activities including practical or real-world exercises in some cases for enhancing learning.

EXPECTATIONS OF A CURRICULUM BASED ON INPUTS FROM EDUCATIONAL NEUROSCIENCE

When a well-designed and -constructed curriculum is carried out within a stipulated duration of time, we expect that the learners will retain lasting new memories or neural networks of knowledge that will be useful in numerous ways. Ideally, these memories or neural networks they would make should not be confined to a single area of study, disciplinary area, or profession; instead, the learners should be able to use the memories retained or neural networks identified more broadly in any appropriate real-life situation. The area of study, in effect, becomes an application or the medium through which some useful real-life phenomena or concepts are learnt. From the findings of neuroscience, we know that high-level or more generalised knowledge or concepts are retained as lasting semantic memories, as opposed to episodic memories. Consequently, it is important that we highlight as many generalised high-level concepts as time sufficiently permits throughout our curriculum. By doing this, we enable transfer of knowledge, as if the protruding neural sensors of learners are waiting to be connected to any related piece of knowledge or application we may learn in the future.

The outcome of the curriculum is not an end in and of itself, but a means by which the learners can make more connections or neural networks of knowledge in the future, as they get exposed to further knowledge and experiences on a lifelong journey. A broadly based curriculum similar to this will attract learner motivation better, as it is useful in a more generic sense. It is not merely because of opening up of a particular career path (which might change significantly over a relatively small duration of time in regards to the prospects) that learners are motivated. Rather, it is because of the opportunity that opens up for becoming better decision makers as a whole or in human development as self-actualising and creative human beings with a higher level of consciousness or wisdom. Engagement in the curriculum at a higher level of motivation, possibly intrinsic by nature, or with some emotional attachment is the key to achieving enhanced learning, the essential means of reaching a higher level of human development.

In the above paragraph, we tried to clearly communicate that a well-designed and constructed curriculum is not one that merely presents a collection of pieces of information of various levels of detail. Instead, it is one that is prepared after giving due consideration to the need of emphasising abstract, information-rich concepts and providing details at the minimum level required for enhanced understanding. In effect, it is constructed by clearly differentiating between high-level abstract concepts and specific details presented and organising them in a hierarchical manner with some conscious or reflective effort.

DECIDING THE CONTENTS OR TOPICS TO BE INCLUDED WITHIN A CURRICULUM

WHAT CONTENTS OR TOPICS NEED TO BE INCLUDED AND WHERE TO FIND THEM?

If we are given the responsibility of constructing a curriculum in a particular area of study, one of the important decisions we have to make is the contents or sections to be included in it. In most cases, we should be able to find a standard textbook in the area of the curriculum we construct. In fact, it is a good idea if we can stick to one selected book, as it provides learners with a clearer direction on the scope of the contents and curriculum. Especially if the curriculum in focus is in a fundamental knowledge area that has been well established, we are in a better position to select a single textbook that serves our purpose of introducing the basic knowledge. By doing this, we will save our learners a considerable amount of time for an elaborative rehearsal of concepts, rather than spend time identifying useful sources of content. If the area of the curriculum we construct is not a well-established one or is still evolving through ongoing research, facilitators should make useful reading references available for the learners. Since the aim of a curriculum is to create lasting memories or neural connections of knowledge for further connectivity in future, we should save learners time for elaborative rehearsals, which is the basis for forming useful internal knowledge networks.

GIVING CONSIDERATION TO THE LIMITED TIME DURATION AVAILABLE FOR CARRYING OUT THE CURRICULUM

An important factor that needs to be considered when deciding the contents to be included in a curriculum is the fact that time available for carrying out the curriculum is limited. As a result, we may not be able to discuss all the subsections in the curriculum area or all the chapters of the selected textbook in detail. We emphasise here that in-depth affirmation of the most critical knowledge areas we choose and introduce is more important than investing time in less-significant sub-areas of content. Essentially, we have to prioritise the high-level concepts we are going to highlight and include them in the curriculum for discussion, starting from the top of the list and covering as many as time permits.

We should never be carried away by the notion that learners only learn what is presented in a classroom environment; as a consequence, as many important concepts or sections as possible need to packed tightly into a curriculum. It is worth paying attention to the fact that most of our learning is implicit, that is, it is not done in a classroom environment. In this era of information and communication technologies in which relevant information is easily searchable and receivable, what is important is to introduce learners to the fundamental knowledge of the curriculum area comprehensively to raise his or her curiosity and motivation levels for furthering this understanding if and when required. We are primarily helping learners to develop a line of thought, a vocabulary with which to relate and see their past, as well as inspire future learning from this particular perspective. In effect, what we should cover in a curriculum is the most important high-level or generalised concepts that can provide within the available limited time with enough emphasis. To highlight high-level generalised knowledge, which is stored as lasting semantic memories, we may have to cut down on and reduce the focus on more specific details or narrower knowledge.

A Curriculum as a Means of Generating Positive Reminiscences towards a Path of Lifelong Learning

As educators, we need to clearly understand that a curriculum is not an end to learning in the area of focus. Rather, it is the means by which an interest is raised in learners, along with an opening of minds to further their knowledge or neural networks en route to a higher level of human development. Consequently, at the end of the implementation of the curriculum following the stipulated time, the learners must be left with positive reminiscences. The implications of negative memories can have severe detrimental impact on learners' future learning as well as human development; they may create permanent barriers on extending learning, especially in the area of focus, albeit quite unrealistic barriers, in a true sense, in most cases. For example, a learner who is capable of learning abstract theories well may not receive a curriculum well if it pays emphasis on a large number of more specific details as opposed to high-level generalised concepts. The result may be an inadvertent but negative attitude towards the area of study by the learner, when the real issue was with the focus or content of the curriculum, despite the learner possessing a highly useful ability to learn abstract theories.

As part of the curriculum itself, we should give learners the opportunity to develop metacognitive knowledge of self-awareness through self-reflection. With this metacognitive knowledge, learners would get to know what things in the curriculum they enjoyed. Otherwise, they could take any appropriate measures to improve the conditions. To achieve this task of developing metacognitive knowledge, we can present learners with questions that raise self-awareness and develop knowledge about their own learning from time to time. These questions can be presented as part of learning material delivery or even as part of assessment, such as reflective journals, diaries, or similar means. Ideally, at the end of the implementation of a curriculum, learners should be left with positive memories of valuable learning that would help them in future in numerous ways.

DECIDING AND DESIGNING THE LEARNING MATERIAL OR DOCUMENTS THAT ARE MADE AVAILABLE TO LEARNERS

WHAT SHOULD WE INCLUDE IN TEACHING-LEARNING MATERIALS OR AIDS WE PROVIDE, AND WHAT IS THE PURPOSE OF IT, PER SE?

In addition to prescribing an appropriate textbook for the curriculum we carry out, we should make summaries of important high-level concepts available to learners for their reference. A learner new to the area of study would find reading the detailed descriptions of a typical textbook useful. However, the learner will benefit from a summary highlighting the important high-level concepts as a second-time reading that can be carried out relatively quickly. A second or third reading could happen by means of a distributive rehearsal, a useful learning technique after a lapse of some time. As a result, learners may not find adequate time to go through the textbook once more. What they need is a useful summary that they can go through relatively quickly. By providing a high-level concept summary as mentioned, we are also helping learners with their time-management endeavours. Further, when reading a comprehensive textbook, it is possible that learners get lost in details, de-emphasising the importance of high-level concepts learned.

Even though more precise, detailed descriptions would help to understand, as the term is used in Bloom's Taxonomy, they may not help learners to make meaning or lasting memories in the form of semantic memories, the residual that would be useful in the longer run. The latter task of making meaning or helping to create semantic memories can be supported by providing a high-level summary of the important concepts. From another point of view, our working memory has a limited capacity; when it is filled with too many specific details (as in the case of reading the book, instead of high-level concepts), we may not be able to relate what we learn to our existing knowledge (and make sense) efficiently. This is because it is easier to make connections with high-level concepts than with specific details, as highlighted before. Consequently, when we go through the high-level concepts only, using the provided summary of concepts that exclude specific details in a second reading, we can fill our limited-capacity working memory with as many high-level concepts as it permits and make connections with existing knowledge networks better or more efficiently.

STRUCTURE AND ORGANISATION OF TEACHING-LEARNING MATERIALS OR AIDS PROVIDED

Another important decision we have to make is how we are going to present the important high-level concepts to learners within the documents or learning aids we provide. We need to compile these documents in such a manner that they can be used as a standalone resource at least for a familiar reader. In other words, because they lack in information that can be connected to the context of discussion readily, we should avoid point-form incomplete sentences; instead, we should highlight concepts using more contextual, complete sentences that help provide meaning in a continuum. Providing complete, contextual sentences instead of isolated pieces of information will help learners to make connections amongst pieces of knowledge or neural networks, even when going through the content after a lapse of an extended period. Isolated pieces of information will only push learners on a strategic learning path with a focus on merely obtaining a higher grade (if assessments permit that by nature), by encouraging them to get these disconnected pieces of information into short-term memory through rote rehearsal. Further, additional specific details we may include for the sake of providing more context or clarity can be provided with indentation on a sub level so that readers identify optional or additional reading content depending on their familiarity with the content area.

Deciding and Designing Diverse Assessment Components of a Curriculum

Deciding on the Type of Assessment

There are many different types of assessment used by educational practitioners for evaluating learners. To determine what types we can use within our curriculum, we first have to understand clearly the intended purpose of our assessment. Ideally, the evaluation should provide an indication of how well a learner has formed lasting memories or neural networks of knowledge that lead to a higher level of human development. In other words, we assess how well the transfer of knowledge or higher-order learning has taken place within learners. For example, using Bloom's Taxonomy, we can evaluate how well learners can perform evaluation and creation tasks that involve divergent thinking or inductive learning. To achieve these objectives, we can use open-ended, novel, and conceptual questions assessing the abilities for adaptive decision making as opposed to assessing capabilities for veridical decision making. These high-level conceptual questions will test the learners' abilities to recall lasting memories stored as long-term semantic memory spontaneously. What we should deviate from is assessing how well a learner has committed facts or specific details in the original form they were presented into short-term memory, mostly crammed just before the assessment. Such evaluations are said to have a focus on what is referred to as rote learning, and encouraging learners to engage in rote rehearsal has little value in making positive attitudinal and behavioural changes within learners.

Deciding on the Number of Assessments in a Curriculum

In addition to determining the types of assessments used, as above, we have to decide on how many assessments we may use during the stipulated time in which the curriculum is implemented. Too many assessments will distract the learners from the primary purpose of the curriculum—learning or creating lasting memories or neural networks of knowledge; the focus will be more on the rituals or overheads of attending and completing the assessments. When carrying out the curriculum, we need to develop a culture within the classroom or teaching-learning environment, so as to intrinsically motivate the learners for learning, rather than introducing assessment items to get them to learn. If assessments are not properly set up to evaluate higher-order learning and learners are extrinsically motivated to obtain a higher grade from such an evaluation, learners will achieve little from their efforts where human development into creative human beings is concerned. They are not likely to create lasting semantic memories or neural networks of knowledge that will be useful in many or generic ways. Consequently, a minimal number of properly constructed assessments as appropriate will put learners on the right track towards achieving higher-order learning.

DECIDING ON THE COVERAGE OF ASSESSMENT

Another important decision we have to make is the coverage of the assessment. Ideally, assessments should cover all the areas highlighted within the curriculum, proportionately to the time spent in each area. This is not to say that we have to ask every possible question within each section covered in the curriculum; rather, it can be considered as a statistical analysis in which a sample set of questions across the whole curriculum is selected to make some valid and useful inferences on student learning. By limiting the size of the set of questions we choose for an assessment, we provide learners a longer time to provide more contemplative and creative answers to the selected questions utilising the frontal lobes of the brain—instead of encouraging learners to provide premeditated or previously practised answers rapidly. This time factor consideration is more specifically applicable to timed assessments. Also, when we cover all the sections of a curriculum in assessments, we discourage learners from following a strategic path to higher grades by selecting only some parts of the curriculum to engage in elaborate rehearsal or deep learning.

Deciding on Having a Balance Between the Theory and Practical Components (if Applicable) of a Curriculum

Some units or courses we teach or set curricula for have essential practical components as part of learning. For these units or courses with practical components, we have to decide on the specific practical elements to be incorporated carefully, as well as the amount of time we expect to expend on them. The intention of introducing a particular component is to get the learners exposed to relevant, real-world experiences or applications. Exposure to these applications or experiences will enable learners to understand or generalise underlying abstract theories or concepts better. While some learners—especially the right-cerebral-hemispheric-oriented ones—learn abstract concepts more easily, those with a left-hemispheric orientation will benefit from practical exposure as it enhances understanding of abstract theories. We make a clear distinction here that our intention is not to make learners highly skilled in the respective practical component; such skills will have to develop over time through continuous practice. As we highlighted before, when we engage in a particular activity for a reasonably longer period, our brains get used to performing them automatically, and as a response, utilise relatively fewer neocortical resources, a phenomenon known as automaticity.

Such a high skill level can be achieved if a learner is interested and motivated in the activity in the longer run, or he or she has a specific purpose for doing it, but our intention is not to make learners master a particular skill within the limited time available for implementing a curriculum. Consequently, it is better to limit the time spent on practical components appropriately, especially if it does not help learners to develop lasting memories or neural networks of knowledge. When human development into creative human beings is the ultimate goal of learning, as we have highlighted throughout, the emphasis in any teaching-learning environment has to be on high-level generalised concepts, while essential practical exposure can be used to enhance the digestion of these concepts.

To reiterate, if a course or unit is mostly aimed at developing a particular motor skill in learners, it will not have the real learning value per se that will retain lasting semantic memories.

PROVISION OF ADDITIONAL LEARNING ACTIVITIES TO SUPPORT ENHANCED LEARNING

As part of the implementation of a curriculum, sometimes we may find extra time allocations available to conduct other activities to help learners in their progress toward better learning. Some of these activities can be part of the practical exercises we highlighted in the previous section. For these situations, including the practical sessions, we will have to prepare the additional set of activities to be carried out by the learners. When preparing them, we have to make sure that we reinforce what the learners have been introduced to by the other components of the curriculum. We especially need to identify which prioritised items need reinforcement through some additional or detailed activities. Once these items are selected, we should develop appropriate activities by making sure that they will enhance learner understanding.

TO SUM UP

At the end of carrying out a curriculum in any teaching-learning environment, we expect learners to retain positive thoughts about the teaching-learning process, motivating them to continue learning in the particular area or otherwise in a lifelong manner to higher levels of human development. Special attention is given to enable learners developing metacognitive knowledge, as it would help them take appropriate measures in future to overcome any shortcomings. The contents introduced need to be the most important, high-level concepts in the area that can be comfortably included in the limited time duration available. When high-level, more generalised concepts are focused, it carries a lasting value for learners, as these lessons are retained in semantic memory, in addition to allowing the generic concepts to be connected with many other diverse domains of knowledge.

While encouraging learners to read any recommended texts, educators can prepare and provide them with well-organised summaries of the essential contents for any subsequent referral, utilising relatively less time. As learners usually get guided by assessments, it is of paramount importance that these assessments are well-formulated, so that they may direct learners to engage in higher-order learning essentially. The number of assessments conducted as part of the curriculum, the type or nature of them, and the time allocated for timed assessments are critical parameters that need to be given due consideration. Additional learning activities, including practical sessions (if appropriate and required) can be prepared and made use of for the purpose of enhancing learning or if an additional emphasis is needed.

Advising Learners on Study Skills Following the Concepts of Educational Neuroscience

● ● ●

As EDUCATORS, WE ARE SOMETIMES required to provide learners with useful information on study skills or practices that would help them to enhance their learning through a systematic engagement in the learning process. In this chapter, we provide some useful study skills based on the findings of educational neuroscience for learners to take into consideration. These include some general educational neuroscience facts that can be used to motivate learners for engaging in deep learning and some other similar points they can follow in regards to a formal learning or education environment.

GENERAL EDUCATIONAL NEUROSCIENCE FACTS THAT MOTIVATE AND ENHANCE LEARNING

VALUE OF LEARNING AND IN PURSUIT OF LIFELONG LEARNING

As educators, we must find ways to get learners to understand that learning has a deeper and lasting meaning that goes beyond passing examination barriers and finding employment. Similar to the strategic goals defined by almost all reputed business organisations, individuals can have a strategic goal achieving higher levels of human development through extensive lifelong learning. If one engages in higher-order learning as described throughout the text, learning can continue producing a positive outcome throughout the lifespan, enabling human development to higher levels of consciousness, wisdom, or self-actualisation. That is, the neural networks of such learners will grow denser, producing more meaningful and connected neural networks within the brain. It enables learners to see reality better as it really is. Consequently, these learners will become better or more optimal decision makers and problem solvers in everything they do. It can be both in day-to-day activities and their professional lives. Further, learning does not always have to take place in a classroom. In fact, most of our learning is implicit, and we can pursue higher-order learning as an ongoing process if we are motivated enough. If we are motivated and believe in a lifelong journey of learning or human development, we tend to pay keener attention to all our experiences in our everyday lives, thereby forming more integrated neural networks of knowledge. In effect, if you spend time every day reflecting on your experiences, you are on a path to human development to a higher level throughout your life. With every day you pass in learning actively, you get to see and understand this world better in more comprehensive and connected ways than before.

GETTING MOTIVATED TO LEARN CONTENTS THAT APPEAR TO BE DIFFICULT

Sometimes we, as learners, find certain new material difficult to understand or relate to what we already know. As a result, we may develop a negative attitude towards that specific content at the very beginning of the learning process or cycle. We may even continue to have these negative attitudes throughout our lives. However, findings from neuroscience tell us that even challenging content can be learnt well by just paying attention and spending more elaborative rehearsal time. Instead of developing a negative attitude towards the content that appears difficult, we should develop a positive frame of mind, be courageous, and try to find more time to spend on the content more diligently. We should see the positives of overcoming an apparent barrier through discipline and commitment, instead of succumbing to it. If we start giving up passively in the face of challenges we encounter in any learning endeavour, we are likely to make a habit of it throughout our lives, thereby nullifying the concept or goal of lifelong learning.

Further, if the source we use to get introduced to the content is difficult to follow, we should use another source so that we can approach the same material from a different angle or perspective. Approaching the same material from different perspectives will enable us to understand the content more deeply and comprehensively. As the clarity of the material we get introduced to improves, or we connect them to as many other knowledge bases we possess, we assimilate a deeper learning into lasting memories. We should not forget that in a modern world that boasts advanced technologies, information is available on your table at a relatively low cost instantaneously. All we need is an urge to learn and an ability to foresee the benefits of human development into creative human beings through enhanced learning.

BE OPEN-MINDED AND UNAFRAID OF THE LARGE VOLUMES OF DATA, INFORMATION, AND KNOWLEDGE WE RECEIVE

Decades ago, data, information, and knowledge were hard to come by; mostly, we had to attend an educational institution where experts in diverse knowledge areas were present or visit a library to have access to data, information, and knowledge. As a result, the process of learning in which we get exposed to new data, information, and knowledge and make new connections with our existing knowledge bases was a relatively difficult task. We, as human beings, spent a relatively small amount of time in learning per se or developing a specific knowledge base. We relied on this particular knowledge base to survive as social beings, through employment, forming a highly restrictive comfort zone to spend a lifetime. Understandably, we avoided the anxiety of finding new data, information, and knowledge or engaging in learning in a lifelong manner en route to higher human development. After all, finding data, information, and knowledge itself was a difficult task.

Things have changed since the availability of data, information, and knowledge in the electronic format has become relatively convenient, instantaneous, and cost effective. We are given a chance to engage in life-long learning—if we are motivated and can foresee the benefits of human development possible through learning. What we need is to be positive about the large volumes of data, information, and knowledge we receive. We must be bold, enjoy accessing this data, and make new connections with the existing knowledge bases with an open mind. We should not close ourselves to new data, information, and knowledge in fear of the possibility that it might contradict our already highly established but limited knowledge bases. Instead, we should be courageous and open to relearning; we sometimes need to leave behind some of our highly accepted and believed rituals. Without getting overwhelmed by the quantity of information to which we have access, try to organise it in a hierarchical manner with high-level concepts at the top, as mentioned before. Learn to clearly differentiate between high-level or abstract concepts and specific details. Try to pay attention to these high-level concepts, whilst making sense in a pervasive manner by just paying attention voluntarily. We should not restrict ourselves to absorbing contents or ideas only in the area of our study or work by closing our senses to all the other areas of knowledge passively. Instead, let your wonderful brains learn through all your experiences, whether positive or negative. They are capable of learning so long as you continue living; in fact, they seek novelty for their growth.

DEVELOP AN UNDERSTANDING OF PERSONALITY TRAITS BASED ON OUR NEUROLOGICAL BIAS, AND BE BOLD IN ACCEPTING WHO YOU ARE

As we have discussed before, there are two main personality types based on the tendency to use the left or right-cerebral hemisphere more predominantly: auditory-sequential learners and visual-spatial learners. Auditory-sequential learners demonstrate more extroverted and emotionally stable behaviours, while visual-spatial learners are mostly introverts who can be more vulnerable emotionally. In a contemporary world, we find the behaviours of auditory-sequential learners are more accepting, while the typical ways of visual-spatial learners are usually received in a negative sense.

However, visual-spatial learners demonstrate a higher capacity as learners and are often categorised as gifted learners. Despite these capabilities, visual-spatial learners encounter challenges from the environment they live in, as these emotionally vulnerable introverts can appear different from the majority auditory-sequential learners. Ideally, we as learners should develop an understanding of what personality characteristics we possess. We should not be discouraged if we tend to demonstrate introverted and more emotionally vulnerable characteristics; strictly speaking, there is nothing negative about those traits, contrary to widespread beliefs. Rather they are just a set of different traits that also entail a highly useful set of positive characteristics.

To reiterate, the famous Polish psychologist and psychiatrist Kazimierz Dabrowski even used the term *psychoneurotics* to refer to the individuals with high development potential or ones commonly known as gifted (Battaglia 2002). Those who are interested may like to go through the poem titled "Be Greeted Psychoneurotics" by Dabrowski that is readily available on the Internet. Generally, no learner should develop any negative thoughts depending on one's personality type based on neurological bias. Both auditory-sequential and visual-spatial personality types possess positive as well as challenging characteristics. We as a society need to embrace neurodiversity broadly. Individuals should not expect to interact with clones of themselves all the time, possessing identical preferences giving you unrealistic comforts.

UNDERSTAND AND APPRECIATE THAT WE ARE BETTER AT ADAPTIVE DECISION MAKING AS HUMAN BEINGS (AS OPPOSED TO VERIDICAL DECISION MAKING); BE PREPARED TO FACE AMBIGUITY AND COMPLEXITY
As discussed in previous chapters, we must encourage learners to appreciate the differences in the way the human brain and typical machines

or computers function. Conventional computers or machines are better in veridical decision making, in which routine or algorithmic procedures are carried out repetitively; human brains are more suited for adaptive decision making, in which they tolerate higher levels of ambiguity and complexity. Human beings should not find solace in finding simple routine answers similar to computers. Learners should be conscious of the type of decision making or tasks with which they are involved. They will see that tasks of adaptive decision making utilising more cortical resources in a more conscious manner, while tasks of veridical decision making can be completed in a more automatic or habitual manner once practised adequately. Consequently, in regards to achieving enhanced learning, adaptive decision making plays a more significant role as it engages more cortical resources in producing more creative solutions. We as learners, decision makers, or problem solvers should be courageous in facing ambiguity, uncertainty, and complexity instead of running away from them passively or in a premeditated manner; the human brain is biologically and physiologically prepared to meet those challenges.

The more we have learned and evolved through the creation of denser neural networks, the better we are prepared to face the challenges of ambiguity, uncertainty, and complexity and to produce more optimal and balanced solutions to the problems we encounter. In these optimal and balanced solutions we deliver, we incorporate the perspectives of as many dimensions as possible; the higher the number of dimensions taken into consideration, the higher the optimality of the solutions we produce, in the absence of one definitive or correct simple answer. Further, learners can make use of this categorisation of veridical decision making and adaptive decision making in evaluating assessment components of a curriculum, for a personal reference or as means of providing feedback. The more you engage in adaptive decision making in assessment, the more higher-order assessment you undergo, thus yielding a higher validity.

Be Willing to Accept the Status Quo That Achieving Human Development Does Not Always Translate into Achieving Economic Development

Throughout this text, we have constantly referred to human development through enhanced consciousness or wisdom. We achieve human development by enhanced learning, through which we develop useful denser and connected neural networks. Consequently, human development is what we are capable of achieving biologically and physiologically as human beings. However, we cannot find a simple equation that converts human development into an individual's economic development under the status quo. When we achieve higher levels of human development, we tend to take more balanced or optimal decisions devoid of bias.

However, we cannot deny the fact that, in most cases, to achieve economic development, we are compelled to take biased decisions with vested interests. Consequently, we see the two roads to human and economic developments mostly diverge from each other (or at least they do not converge). The essential requirement for achieving human development— even to the highest level of self-actualisation—is the fulfilment of basic needs such as food, shelter, clothing, and security. In effect, while achieving economic stability is essential for human development to higher levels, achieving economic development to excessive levels does not necessarily translate into higher levels of human development. We have to understand and accept the current status quo, that human development would not always be equivalent to economic development. Human development to higher levels will make us better decision makers and problem solvers; it will help us to be more content and face real-world challenges more uprightly and realistically. On the whole, we become just and fair citizens who contribute to sustainable societies. Further, because you make more and more useful connections, the expansion of your neural networks of knowledge through learning will accelerate as you move to higher levels of human development. You will tend to see everything is connected to everything else—as declared famously by Leonardo da Vinci.

ENCOURAGE LEARNERS TO DEVELOP A CLEAR UNDERSTANDING OF WHAT LEARNING AND EDUCATION ARE ALL ABOUT AND ENGAGE IN METACOGNITIVE PRACTICES REGULARLY

Especially for adult learners, it is important to have a clear understanding as to what the terms *learning* and *education* truly mean. We should add broader, lasting, or strategic meaning to learning and education, instead of just having narrow, short-term objectives. It can get learners guided along a journey of lifelong learning even in the face of challenging situations. For example, if learners develop an understanding that learning has a physical meaning in which one can develop denser neural networks of knowledge that enable us to engage in creative activities, this would help learners to take appropriate measures to achieve this goal of learning.

When you develop a clear understanding of what learning and education are all about or have a reference model defined (as above), it becomes the starting point of developing the metacognitive knowledge that helps you monitor the progress of your learning. When you engage in metacognitive practices, you develop self-awareness through self-reflection and knowledge of your own learning. Consequently, once you get to understand your strengths and weaknesses clearly, you are in a position to take appropriate actions to direct you to the goals of learning and education you understand clearly by now. Engaging in metacognitive practices is an important step on your journey of lifelong learning; commit to monitor and control its progress. Further, when you develop your metacognitive knowledge, you will be in a better position to control and interrelate your cognitive and emotional activities for your own overall benefit or development.

Useful Facts Related to Enhancing Learning in a Formal Learning or Education Environment

Before a Teaching-Learning Session

Learners will benefit from a teaching-learning session more if they go there prepared. To prepare for the session, they can do a prior reading of any related chapters of a prescribed textbook or other teaching-learning content provided by the facilitator. Such preparation can be a huge task for some of the learners, as it requires a very high level of motivation and initiative. However, learners will benefit immensely if they do so. First, they will be developing skills of self-reliance by taking the initiative to read or study beforehand. Second, the connections made in advance on their own can be verified by engaging in elaborative rehearsal during the teaching-learning session, thus improving the retention capacity. Also, any positive assertion one gets during the teaching-learning session on his or her inferences made during the advance self-study or self-reading session would provide useful metacognitive feedback. In other words, learners would develop some self-awareness and knowledge of their own learning itself. Developing such an awareness or metacognitive ability is the key to pursuing a lifelong path of learning (Zull 2011).

During a Teaching-Learning Session

Pay attention fully to what you see and hear. Remember the phenomenon of binocular rivalry—we can focus on only one thing at a time. You should not try to write down hastily the words the facilitator expresses, to go through them in detail later or even to reproduce them in assessment in their exact form. Instead, try to actively relate what you see and hear to your existing knowledge base or to make sense by engaging in elaborate rehearsal on the fly. Avoid rote rehearsal by trying to memorise what the facilitator says in his or her exact words. Even mere understanding within the context presented may not be adequate for enhanced learning; try to actively relate the contents you are introduced to your personal experiences and knowledge bases, so you comprehend and extend them in a personalised manner. Be courageous in engaging in this process of active learning, and be ready to take the initiative. By doing this, you will be constructing meaning, as suggested in the constructivist theory of learning; you will be an active learner instead of a passive listener. Your preparation in advance by familiarising yourself with the material covered, as highlighted in the previous section, will be very useful in allowing you to participate actively in the learning process.

Further, during the teaching-learning session, try to get the content presented organised in mind in a hierarchical order. That is, differentiate and place high-level concepts at a higher level of precedence and details used to elaborate or explain them at a lower level. Once the concept is understood by utilising details or applications provided, try emphasising the high-level concept. That is, use specific details or applications as a means of understanding more generalised abstract concepts; it is unnecessary to try to memorise specific details. Remember that high-level or more generalised concepts need to be the primary focus, ahead of specific details, as they last in our memories longer as semantic memories. Also, try to understand or generalise the high-level concepts presented as standalone pieces of knowledge, decoupling as much as possible from the details of the application or subject area in which they were introduced. It will help you to reuse the piece of high-level or generalised concepts in a generic sense by attaching meaning in future when the circumstances arise.

The degree of sense and meaning you can make will vary depending on your familiarity with the topic area and the motivation level at which you are engaged. However, you should not panic if new contents are difficult to understand and to attach some sense and meaning at the start. You need to keep concentrating and persevering without giving up. As long as you keep your focus on the content in a disciplined effort, clarity will improve gradually, enabling you to transform what you have grasped into long-term memory.

Go through the summary of concepts, avoiding any specific details at the end of the teaching-learning session. It will allow you to improve your retention of high-level concepts. Your facilitator may assist you in this regard by going through a summary of concepts with you.

If you are given a break in the middle of the teaching-learning session, go out for a brief walk and relax; your blood circulation will improve, giving more food to your brain. It will enable you to start afresh, tuning all your brain resources again for a new, more focused start.

AFTER A TEACHING-LEARNING SESSION

Concepts or contents introduced in a teaching-learning session are most likely to be retained in our short-term memory for some hours or a few days at most. During this time, it is better if we engage in further elaborative rehearsal, to transform our fresh memories to long-term memories. As discussed before, during this elaborative rehearsal process, we should focus on grasping and making further connections with high-level or generalised concepts, as they are likely to be retained in long-term memory as semantic memories. Go through the detailed or specific descriptions only if they help you to understand the introduced high-level or generalised concepts further. The time you need to spend on elaborative rehearsal after a teaching-learning session to achieve enhanced learning can be minimised by spending adequate time on preparation by going through the recommended textbook or other learning material before the teaching-learning session.

Advance preparation can be considered here as an investment that returns time savings following the teaching-learning session, in addition to helping learners develop independent learning skills and an attitude of self-reliance in learning that is likely to yield benefits in the long run as lifelong learners. Converting short-term memories to long-term memories or the process of memory consolidation requires a phenomenon known as protein synthesis that is helped by having an adequate amount of sleep (around seven to nine hours) each night. Consequently, learners are advised to have regular sleep in sufficient amounts to complete the learning cycle with memory consolidation. In other words, manage your time well to allow yourself a good night's sleep.

To further enhance our learning or create more lasting memories, we can perform distributed rehearsal after a gap period of some months from the initial learning. By this time, you will have retained whatever made it into your long-term memory (most likely high-level generalised concepts), and the contents or concepts would not be entirely new to you. Consequently, you will be able to engage in further elaborative rehearsal, making more valuable connections relatively quickly. The time gap from the initial learning will help you to clear your mind of the unnecessary specific detail that would have been forgotten by the time distributive rehearsal occurs, and you will only have retained the more clearly understood high-level or generalised concepts. These more generalised concepts can be connected more easily with other knowledge bases or concepts we hold. Consequently, distributed rehearsal will play a significant role in making more enhanced and effective learning that creates more lasting memories. Further, more distributive rehearsal can be performed even after a prolonged period, say one year, if that is appropriate, for enhanced retention in long-term memory. You may even use different sources for reading than the original resources you used, so that you approach the same contents from a different perspective or direction, thus enabling better retention.

To Sum Up
We as educators should encourage learners regarding the lasting value of learning that allows them to develop to higher levels of human

development. In effect, the goal of learning should be comprehended beyond passing examinations or assessments. Learning, in fact, has a physical meaning, in which we develop more connected and integrated neural networks of knowledge that help us become better problem solvers and decision makers by seeing reality as is. Strategic or surface learning approaches focusing short-term goals need to be avoided, as it will become a futile effort when human development to higher levels of self-actualisation, wisdom or consciousness is taken into account. Human development to such higher levels is a continuous lifelong process of which learners need to be conscious.

Human brains are naturally novelty-seeking organs that are capable of learning even complex or ambiguous contents, provided we persevere, giving enough time for our brains to improve clarity and learn. We should, in fact, be encouraged to see that large volumes of data, information, and knowledge are accessible to us easily and economically, thanks to developments in information and communication technologies. These large amounts of data, information, and knowledge should be received with an open mind, so we can process them to create useful inferences or neural networks of knowledge. This courageous interaction of knowledge will put us on a lifelong path to higher levels of human development.

We as learners need to understand and embrace the concept of neuro-diversity; every learner has unique characteristics and will engage in the learning process differently. However, if we participate in higher-order learning purposefully and continuously, we all can be on a path to higher levels of human development, at a pace defined by our unique characteristics and other environmental factors. Be conscious that human development to higher levels and personal economic development are not necessarily the same in our existing social contexts, even though it is essential to have basic human needs satisfied before an individual develops to higher levels of self-actualisation.

In addition to the above-mentioned generic guides based on educational neuroscience, learners can also plan and get guided by some similar facts to engage in a formal learning environment. Some of these practices include getting prepared for a teaching-learning session, participating actively in the teaching-learning session by constructing new knowledge based on one's existing knowledge bases, and engaging in distributive and elaborate rehearsal after a gap of some time duration, following the teaching-learning session.

• • •

Comprehending Learning and Education in a Deeper Sense

IN THIS BOOK, WE HAVE attempted to grasp learning and education in a more profound sense than we usually do, by viewing them from the additional dimension of educational neuroscience. As highlighted throughout the book, our learning and education should take us on a path to higher levels of human development or self-actualisation. When we progress in human development through lifelong learning, we enhance our consciousness, metacognition, and wisdom. That is, we evolve by forming more integrated and useful neural networks of knowledge and interrelating our cognitive and emotional activities well to become more productive members of society. In effect, we become better decision makers and problem solvers who see and accept the reality as is as we engage in continuous improvement through learning. We become conscious of our mental and physical well-being and pursue a healthy lifestyle by engaging in more reflective or metacognitive approaches to learning. It is likely to achieve by developing brain functions in a holistic manner, involving both left- and right-cerebral hemispheric operations.

The Essential Need to Focus on Higher-Order Learning

As educational practitioners, we have seen the reconfirmation of the need to focus on higher-order learning. It is the basis for creating lasting memories that are useful in generic ways in both professional and personal lives. In other words, we are essentially targeting the high-end functions of the commonly used framework of the revised Bloom's Taxonomy, namely evaluation and creation within our curricula. By systematically following pedagogical practices with a higher-order learning focus, we can foster novelty-seeking creative human brains to grow towards higher levels of consciousness or wisdom. With higher levels of consciousness or wisdom, learners can see a more integrated world of multiple disciplines, and they become more receptive to large volumes of diverse information flowing around them. As educators, we need to clearly keep away from practices of lower-order learning focus that result in a futile effort from the standpoint of both the educator and learner. The biggest challenge faced by educators is the clear differentiation of lower-order and higher-order practices to select and emphasise the latter.

Fostering Creative and Novelty-Seeking Instincts of the Human Brain

We have seen that human beings, in general, get the pleasure of being involved in creative activities and that the human brain is a novelty-seeking organ. Humans find joy in connecting sets of information sensed to each other as well as to other stored information or knowledge. We contrast here with the fact that they get bored if they have to merely memorise or rote rehearse what they have sensed in its exact form. Consequently, educators should make it a point to give learners an appropriate level of freedom and control for them to make creative and valid connections amongst the pieces of information they get to process. It becomes an appropriately controlled process promoting a right level of self-expression as well as self-regulation on the part of learners. We put in place the control and regulatory processes to prevent learners from getting lost in excessively imaginative worlds. As highlighted in this book, in learner evaluation, we get them to answer more open-ended questions, even though it is relatively difficult to implement compared to more objective questions. Objective questions usually have one correct answer, and as a result, we can conduct learner evaluation more equitably—allocating marks or grading depending on the exact right or wrong answers. Consequently, to assess learners following higher-order learning concepts and using more open-ended questions, educators have to be better equipped with appropriate preparation and tools. We should be able to make a judgement on their answers to open-ended questions correctly, as the answers can be idiosyncratic in nature. We should be able to judge the validity of the answers within an appropriate scope and context; this can be a very subtle process, especially if the educator is new to the approach. Further, we have to be in possession of well-interconnected knowledge networks crossing the borders of artificial disciplinary boundaries so we can relate the concepts we emphasise to real-world experiences.

EMPHASISING HUMAN DEVELOPMENT AS A MAIN GOAL OF EDUCATION AND LEARNING

We emphasised that one of the prime goals of learning and education is to give learners meaningful and lasting value by enabling enhanced consciousness or wisdom. What educators can do is to help learners identify as many relationships as possible amongst the pieces of information we introduce that they hold in their memories. Learners enhance consciousness by having this integrated view of information or knowledge bases from diverse disciplinary areas. As we see, we do not confine learners to focus on a single disciplinary area; instead, we encourage them to be courageous in forming relationships across diverse areas of discipline. Educationists have defined the term *wisdom*, which aligns closely to *consciousness*, as a higher form of creativity that links information or knowledge across multiple domain areas. In other words, we should not introduce a significant number of sets of information to learners as isolated pieces and expect them to retain them in long-term memory. As learners engage in lifelong learning, they should continue to grow their neural networks essentially in an integrated manner, identifying a growing number of connections. In this way, they create lasting memories that are more useful in everything they do—a lasting value for learning. When learners are presented with this lasting value that results from a lifelong learning path, they become motivated to engage in the process in a systematic way. We reiterate that learner motivation is a key contributory factor in achieving enhanced learning. Further, as learners progress in lifelong learning, making an increasing number of connections amongst neural networks of knowledge, as one would expect, the process becomes easier. That is, learners possess an increasingly integrated and denser network of knowledge that can be linked to many diverse pieces of information readily, compared to a less connected sparse network.

LIFELONG LEARNING AS AN ESSENTIAL COMPONENT OF INDIVIDUAL WELL-BEING

When we engage in lifelong learning, it contributes to our mental well-being. In fact, it engages our novelty-seeking creative brain in useful mental activities and distances us from diseases such as dementia and Alzheimer's disease (Gates 2016). We should clearly understand that lifelong learning does not mean we always have to be enrolled in an educational institution to engage in learning. In contrast, it is about how we utilise our brains by engaging in learning or mental activities that help us grow our integrated neural networks of knowledge. To recall, most of our learning is implicit. Mostly we learn by just paying attention to day-to-day experiences and situations. What is important is that we have to pay attention and be reflective of our experiences by being conscious of their learning outcomes. In the presence of large volumes of information reaching us, thanks to the developments in information and communication technologies and diverse experiences we encounter daily, we have to be open-minded in the way we receive them, as they give us the opportunity to learn and evolve.

Just because we have become economically stable by being employed in a narrow career path, as many of us are, we should not close our receptive sensors to all the other information reaching us from outside our career path or discipline. We may argue that our careers give us a comfortable living and we should only seek advancement and take the trouble to progress in them; that is the way for us to increase our earnings. It is a narrow, one-dimensional, and lazy view of the world that disregards our overall well-being; it only views from an economic-development perspective but not from a holistic human-development perspective. By being open to learning in whatever ways are possible and the large volumes of information reaching our senses, we can be mentally active so that, most importantly, mental well-being is achieved. For us to be constantly receptive to learning, we should try to develop a state of mind that allows us to relax and be meditative as much as possible, so we are attentive and mindful of our experiences and information sensed. To develop these learning states of mind, we have to be free of various mental stresses and emotional setbacks of different forms. As mentioned before, sometimes we sacrifice our well-being by pursuing one-dimensional economic development, undergoing various mental stresses and emotional setbacks. In effect, for many of us, it becomes a delicate balancing act between human development and economic development.

The Importance of Balancing Economic Development and Human Development

In the modern world, it is not uncommon that we spend most of our disposable time on our employment or career activities. These activities, in many cases, have a very narrow scope or specialisation. As a result, our learning, if any at all, gets confined to a limited domain, as opposed to being broader. As our employment and careers give us economic stability, we tend to close our senses to more extensive learning opportunities available by absorbing various information or knowledge for rehearsing elaborately. We focus narrowly on our career path by only paying attention to the experiences and information related to it. In other words, we do not make ourselves open to learning in a generic way. We become hyper-focused on a relatively short-term goal of career advancement in a narrower sense, rather than focusing on overall long-term well-being through broader learning.

It is a typical situation most of us get trapped in, sometimes consciously sometimes unconsciously. On numerous occasions, we compete with fellow workers in a stressful manner to achieve career advancement, disregarding a healthy lifestyle leading to human development through learning, as we described before. We do not get to see the value of human development or self-actualisation to higher levels, a holistic process of development compared to one-sided development gained in career or economic advancement. It is worth recalling here that, in Maslow's theory of self-actualisation, we learnt that human development to higher levels could be achieved when basic human needs such as food, clothing, shelter, and security are fulfilled. However, even if these lower-level requirements are satisfied, sometimes at excessive levels, there is no guarantee that an individual moves to higher levels of self-actualisation, possibly because of the lack of direction or motivation to expend time on broader learning, resulting in enhanced consciousness or wisdom. That is, the individual may be narrowly focussed or motivated on one-sided economic or career development, utilising most of his or her dispensable time. Sometimes we see religious leaders or hermits who have embarked on that path, as they have almost all of their disposable time to spend on human development in the absence of the goals of economic and career development.

In fact, research shows positive neuroplasticity changes in the brains—especially in the areas associated with metacognition—of religious leaders who have undergone thousands of hours of focused meditation (Gates 2016). The interesting point of discussion is how we as laymen, most importantly, strike an essential balance between economic development and human development. Lacking in the latter form of development by leaning towards the former, as the current trend, is creating disastrous results regarding a sustainable social development. When an individual has a one-sided focus on development, the decisions he or she makes take a narrower or premeditated perspective, as opposed to an open-minded one. Such decisions often get challenged even by broadly knowledgeable individuals outside their discipline, but when they approach them with an open mind. It is a lesson we learn in the fable of "The Emperor's New Clothes" (The emperor was fooled by a weaver who said that the new clothes he made were invisible to those who were stupid and incompetent. The emperor paraded before his subjects in his presumed new clothes before a child in the crowd cried that the emperor was naked, with an open mind, seeing the reality as it was). We reiterate on the matter that we need to emphasise on the overall human development crossing the borders of disciplines, ahead of a one-sided development constrained be disciplinary boundaries.

In Maslow's words (1968, 1993), "when the only tool one has is a hammer, he tends to see everything around him as a nail [to be hammered]." That is, individuals with narrower perspectives, as described above, are highly likely to become arrogant and dominating personalities, devoid of empathy and tolerance, contributing negatively to the development of sustainable societies. Unfortunately, the learning careers of many of us, before starting our first employment, follow a very similar path. Many of our educational programs provided by various academic institutes focus on a relatively short-term goal of preparing learners for a very narrow and specific career path, ahead of a long-term, broader learning path leading to human development. In essence, what the educational institutes do is to prepare learners for a highly industrialised, technological, and streamlined world, lacking creative instincts and human touch.

Meaningful Learning Essentially as an Interdisciplinary Phenomenon

As we have emphasised throughout this text, meaningful learning will have to be interdisciplinary by nature. For example, to enhance consciousness or wisdom, we have to integrate neural networks of knowledge across as many brain areas, as well as domains, as possible. We have seen some progress in some educational systems in regard to this aspect. In them, they focus on systems where there is no division into subject areas or focus on thematic or integrated curricula. In this text, we emphasised relating concepts in a single subject or domain area to as many real-life scenarios or experiences as possible to enhance learning. On a similar point, decades ago, education philosopher John Dewey (1956, 1963) raised the need to overcome the undesirable split between what is learned in the classroom and what is gathered through real-life experiences or between intentional learning and incidental learning. Helping learners to develop integrated neural networks of knowledge in this manner is the key to creating lasting memories towards higher levels of human development through enhanced consciousness or wisdom.

The Essential Need to Develop Reflective and Metacognitive Capacities

When we evolve as human beings through learning-enabled enhanced consciousness or wisdom, we become more receptive to large volumes of information we receive and sensations that reach us. It is because we already possess more integrated neural networks of knowledge that are readily available to be connected to incoming senses and sets of information. In other words, we are in a better position to pay attention to or be mindful of incoming senses and information due to heightened awareness, as long as we maintain a relaxed or meditative state of mind, devoid of other emotional setbacks or mental stress. In effect, we are in a position to be more reflective of our experiences following metacognitive approaches; we do not succumb to the phenomenon of automaticity, in which our actions become reflexive or automatic. If we engage in prolonged repetitive work, our actions become automatic, deviating us from reflection and possibly closing our senses to new experiences. Consequently, we need to develop the capacity to be more receptive to new experiences and information openly and courageously over an extended period of time of effective or deep learning. We may recall that reflective activity of learning new content or facing new experiences requires more brain resources. With enhanced consciousness, we are in a better position to be more reflective or follow metacognitive practices.

As reflective or metacognitive practices essentially make us self-evaluate our thinking and learning, we are put on a path to continuous improvement. As you may have seen, such practices are essential components of the lifelong human-development processes. When one is highly self-reflective and has developed a high level of metacognition, he or she becomes aware of his or her states of mind or develops a high level of self-awareness. As a consequence, he or she is in a better position to direct it to a state that is desired most. Even when this person performs an unavoidable automatic or reflexive activity, he or she still becomes conscious or being aware of it; it is an automatic or reflexive action but not a reflective one. Most importantly, when individuals develop metacognitive abilities, they are in a better position to control their emotions through cognitive activities and vice versa, as discussed before. Consequently, one becomes in control of one's cognitive as well as emotional activities, so that they can be directed for more purposeful tasks.

The Need to Develop Inclusive and Fairer Educational Systems

We cannot turn a deaf ear to some vociferous medical and healthcare professionals who raise the issues of disadvantaging gifted individuals in contemporary educational systems. These gifted individuals demonstrate visual-spatial capacities predominantly and are right hemispheric oriented.

As mentioned before, they have more innate abilities to achieve higher levels of human development through enhanced consciousness, metacognition, and wisdom. In effect, gifted individuals have the potential to develop into individuals with high levels of empathy, tolerance, resilience, and humility over time if accommodating environments are present.

However, despite possessing a higher developmental potential, these individuals suffer at the hands of contemporary educational systems that do not have a strategic focus on human development. Instead, the present systems are more narrowly focused on short-term goals such as passing examinations or finding employment. Consequently, we see a significant number of highly capable or gifted individuals end up as losers of the prevailing education systems. They usually possess intellectual, emotional, and imaginational overexcitabilities, and as a result, are extremely vulnerable to highly competitive educational systems that push everyone on a narrow path of "one size fits all," focusing on one-sided development. As a result of the reactions to these adverse conditions by gifted individuals, they are susceptible to being misdiagnosed and stigmatised, according to some research by medical specialists (Webb, et al. 2005). As highlighted throughout this text, when we have a higher-order learning focus leading to human development in our educational systems, we fulfil the important requirements of being fair and inclusive in our practices. In a world with an increasing number of mental-health problems, pursuing human development to higher levels could be the path to developing sustainable societies.

Consciousness and an Analogy from the Technology Space—Big Data

Let us put forth an analogy from the technology space. The term "big data" has attracted widespread interest, not only in the technology space but also in the business world in the recent past (Schmarzo 2013). Stakeholders have realised the value of large volumes of diverse data available and flowing around us, mostly electronically. As a result, in the field of big data, they are trying to relate or integrate those large sets of data to each other to make useful inferences using the power of high-performance computing. If you conjecture on the phenomenon of consciousness, we see a similar function taking place: the human brain, similar to a high-performance computer, attempts to relate large sets of data reaching it with each other and with other stored information or knowledge.

While we make high-performance computers to relate and integrate large volumes of diverse data in a contemporary world, why can we not educate human brains or learners systematically to do a similar function at the same time over a lifetime? In fact, it can be done in a more efficient and productive way, as the human brain structure and operations are better suited for it than even high-performance computing systems. What we need here, essentially, is a belief and realisation of human or brain capacities we can make use of as a consequence of continuous effective or higher-order learning, resulting in enhanced consciousness or wisdom. I am very excited to foresee the current enthusiasm we have observed in the technology space as a consequence of the emergence of the concept of big data to appear in the education and learning space for the benefit of our societies in a sustainable manner.

Developing Empathy, Tolerance, Resilience, and Humility through Human Development as Essential Qualities of Interpersonal and Intrapersonal Intelligence

I like to get the readers' attention on the quality of empathy as an important human feature. As discussed before, human beings have the capacity, supported by their neural structures, to understand the states of mind of their fellow human beings. We also have evidence that when human development to higher levels is achieved through enhanced consciousness or wisdom, we become more empathic individuals who can better understand the states of mind of others. Religious leaders or hermits, who pursue a path of human development expending their whole dispensable time, usually demonstrate this quality more profoundly. When we become more reflective and self-aware by having an improved degree of metacognition as a result of moving towards higher levels of human development, it is not surprising that we become capable of understanding the states of mind of fellow human beings better or empathise with them more profoundly.

Further, with human development at higher levels, individuals develop highly integrated, diverse neural networks of knowledge, enabling them to see things in more optimal, multidimensional, or balanced ways. With this highly developed cognition, individuals become capable of regulating their emotions better, expressing positive ones more often. With this ability to penetrate through matters, these individuals would become more aware of the constraints or limitations on themselves, as well as the environment, making them more empathic, tolerant, resilient, and humble. We can see that the development of these attributes as a significant enhancement in interpersonal, as well as intrapersonal, intelligence enables us to guide our societies towards sustainability. We reiterate here the essential need of focusing on human development to higher levels as a long-term or strategic goal of all types of our educational systems.

IDENTIFYING LIMITATIONS OF CURRENT LEARNING, EDUCATION, AND SOCIAL SYSTEMS WITH THE INTENTION OF OVERCOMING THEM

Some philosophers who have reflected deeply have gone to the extent of describing contemporary education systems as "brain damaging" (Houston 1999). Throughout this text, we have presented many limitations on contemporary learning, education, and social systems, providing justifications from the standpoint of educational neuroscience. Numerous current learning and education systems still have a lower-order learning focus. They mainly support left-cerebral-hemispheric-oriented auditory-sequential operations, instead of holistic brain operations that also support right-cerebral-hemispheric operations. Visual-spatial or gifted learners, who are inclined to use the right-cerebral hemispheres predominantly, face significant challenges, despite their highly useful characteristics.

Our education and social systems push every individual on the same path of narrow specialisations, trying to achieve higher speeds of operations, emulating machines devoid of emotions and creativity. By pressing everyone on the same path, we make them compete against each other vigorously (Clark 2016), disregarding the phenomenon of individuality in a neurodiverse society. Consequently, we see a significant increase in mental-health issues in the recent past, stigmatising individuals who struggle against a system that functions in a noncreative or nonhumanlike manner.

With a view on specialisations, higher speeds, and simple sequential operations, we have compartmentalised our learning into disintegrated disciplines, trying for quick returns instead of sustainable strategic goals. We tend to misprogram and misuse the human brain that has natural structural support for parallel and integrated operations, yielding creativity and wisdom. In the last few decades, we have seen the significance of the integrated operation in real life, albeit in the business world. Using advanced information and communication technologies, major businesses around the globe started focusing on the phenomenon of business processes that integrate operations across multiple organisational units or departments. It has become a highly successful endeavour over the years compared to previous silos-based functional operations of each organisational unit or department (Harmon 2014).

Sadly, we haven't seen that focus on integration penetrate into the human-development space. We want individuals to progress in human development, creating integrated neural networks of knowledge through learning, leading to consciousness and wisdom. We have seen revolutionary changes in the technology and business worlds in the recent past. The need of the moment is a similar revolutionary change in the social and human-development spaces to guide our world on a sustainable path. To achieve this elusive goal, we have to overcome the leadership dilemma (Houston 2004) that has caused leaders to pursue a speed-oriented, specialisation-based, short-term-goal-oriented, disintegrated, nonoptimised, and unsustainable path. We have a complex puzzle to disentangle. To start our journey, we first need to slow down to take a deep breath and reflect extensively to understand the natural human potential, before strategically targeting to unwrap it.

REFERENCES

• • •

Allman J. M., A. Hakeem, J. M. Erwin, E. Nimchinsky, and P. Hof. "The Anterior Cingulate Cortex: The Evolution of an Interface between Emotion and Cognition." *Proceedings of the New York Academy of Sciences* 935 (2001): 107–117.

Aminoff, M. and R. Daroff (eds.). *Encyclopaedia of the Neurological Sciences.* San Diego, CA: Academic Press, 2003.

Anderson, N. D., T. Iidaka, R. Cabeza, S. Kapur, A. R. McIntosh, and F. I. Craik. "The Effects of Divided Attention on Encoding- and Retrieval-Related Brain Activity: A PET Study of Younger and Older Adults. *Journal of Cognitive Neuroscience* 12(5) (2000): 775–792. doi:10.1162/089892900562598.

Anderson, L. W. (ed.), D. R. Krathwhol (ed.), P. W. Airasian, K. A. Cruikshank, R. E. Mayer, P. R. Pintrich, J. Raths, and M. C. Wittrock. *A Taxonomy for Learning, Teaching and Assessing: A Revision of Bloom's Taxonomy of Educational Objectives* (Complete edition). New York: Longman, 2001.

Armstrong, T. (2011). *The Power of Neurodiversity: Unleashing the Advantages of Your Differently Wired Brain.* Boston, MA: Da Capo Lifelong Books, 2011.

Baars, B. J. *A Cognitive Theory of Consciousness.* New York: Cambridge University Press, 1988.

———. "The Conscious Access Hypothesis: Origins and Recent Evidence. *Trends in Cognitive Sciences* 6(1) (2002): 47–52. doi:10.1016/S1364-6613(00)01819-2.

Baars, B. J., W. P. Banks, and J. B. Newman. *Essential Sources in the Scientific Study of Consciousness.* Cambridge, MA: MIT Press, 2003.

Baars, B. J. and N. M. Gage. *Cognition, Brain, and Consciousness—Introduction to Cognitive Neuroscience* (2nd ed.). Cambridge, MA: Elsevier, 2010.

Baddeley, A. D. "The Episodic Buffer: A New Component of Working Memory?" *Trends in Cognitive Sciences* 4(11) (2000): 417–423. doi:10.1016/S1364-6613(00)01538-2.

———. "Working Memory and Language: An Overview." *Journal of Communication Disorders* 36 (2003): 189–208.

Baddeley, A. D., and G. J. Hitch. "Working Memory." In G. A. Bower (ed.), *Recent Advances in Learning and Motivation: 8.* New York: Academic Press, 1974. doi:10.1016/s0079-7421(08)60452-1

Balduzzi, D., and G. Tononi. "Integrated Information in Discrete Dynamical Systems: Motivation and Theoretical Framework." *PLoS Computational Biology* 4(6) (2008). doi:10.1371/journal.pcbi.1000091

Banaji, M. R., and A. G. Greenwald. "Implicit Gender Stereo-Typing in Judgements of Fame." *Journal of Personality and Social Psychology* 68(2) (1995): 181–198. doi:10.1037/0022-3514.68.2.181.

Baron-Cohen, S. *Mindblindness: An Essay on Autism and Theory of Mind.* Boston: MIT Press/Bradford Books, 1995.

Battaglia, M. *A Hermeneutic Historical Study of Kazimierz Dabrowski and His Theory of Positive Disintegration.* PhD Thesis at Virginia Polytechnic Institute and State University, Blacksburg, 2002. Retrieved from http://scholar.lib.vt.edu/theses/available/etd-04082002-204054/unrestricted/Dissertation.pdf.

Beale, R., and T. Jackson. *Neural Computing—An Introduction.* Bristol, UK: Institute of Physics Publishing, 1990. doi:10.1887/0852742622

Beebe, J. "Psychological Types." In R. K. Papadopoulos (ed.), *The Handbook of Jungian Psychology—Theory, Practice and Applications.* Sussex, UK: Routledge, 2006.

Berry, D. C., and Z. Dienes. *Implicit Learning: Theoretical and Empirical Issues.* Hove, UK: Psychology Press, 1993.

Biggs, J. *Teaching for Quality Learning at University* (2nd ed.). Buckingham, UK: Society for Research into Higher Education and Open University Press, 2003.

Bloom, B. S. (ed.), M. D. Engelhart, E. J. Furst, W. H. Hill, and D. R. Krathwohl. *Taxonomy of Educational Objectives: The Classification of Educational Goals. Handbook 1: Cognitive Domain.* New York: David McKay, 1956.

Bor, D., J. Duncan, R. J. Wiseman, and A. M. Owen. "Encoding Strategies Dissociate Prefrontal Activity from Working Memory Demand." *Neuron 37* (2003): 361–367. doi:10.1016/S0896-6273(02)01171-6

Bowers, K. S., G. Regehr, C. Balthazard, and K. Parker. "Intuition in the Context of Discovery." *Cognitive Psychology* 22(1) (1990): 72–110. doi:10.1016/0010-0285(90)90004-N.

Brady, T. F., T. Konkle, and G. A. Alvarez. "Compression in Visual Working Memory: Using Statistical Regularities to Form More Efficient Memory Representations." *Journal of Experimental Psychology* (2009): 487–502. doi:10.1037/a0016797.

Brooks, J. G., and M. G. Brooks. *In Search of Understanding: The Case for Constructivist Classrooms* (2nd ed.). Alexandria, VA: Association for Supervision and Curriculum Development, 1999.

Buckner, R. L., W. M. Kelley, and S. E. Petersen. "Frontal Cortex Contribution to Human Memory Formation." *Nature Neuroscience 2* (1999): 311–314. doi:10.1038/7221.

Carpenter, S. K., H. Pashler, and N. J. Cepeda. (2009). "Using Tests to Enhance 8th Grade Students' Retention of U.S. History Facts." *Applied Cognitive Psychology* 23 (2009): 760–771. doi:10.1002/acp.1507.

Casement, A. "The Shadow." In R. K. Papadopoulos (ed.), *The Handbook of Jungian Psychology—Theory, Practice and Applications.* Sussex, UK: Routledge, 2006.

Chavez-Eakle, R. A., A. G. Graff-Guerrero, J. C. Garcia-Reyna, V. Vaugier, and C. Cruz-Fuentes. "Cerebral Blood Flow Associated with Creative Performance: A Comparative Study." *Neuroimage* 38 (2007): 519–528. doi:10.1016/j.neuroimage.2007.07.059.

Chein, J. M. and W. Schneider. "Neuroimaging Studies of Practice-Related Change: fMRI and Meta-analytic Evidence of a Domain-General

Control Network for Learning." *Brain Research. Cognitive Brain Research* 25(3), (2005): 607–623. doi:10.1016/j.cogbrainres.2005.08.013.

Clark, L. *Beautiful Failures: How the Quest for Success Is Harming Our Kids.* Sydney, Australia: Penguin Random House, 2016.

Claxton, G. "Wisdom: Advanced Creativity?" In A. Craft, H. Gardner, and G. Claxton (eds.). *Creativity, Wisdom and Trusteeship: Exploring the Role of Education.* Thousand Oaks, CA: Corwin Press, 2008.

Cleeremans, A. *Mechanisms of Implicit Learning: Connectionist Models of Sequence Learning.* Cambridge, MA: MIT Press, 1993.

Cohen, N. J., and L. R. Squire. "Preserved Learning and Retention of Pattern-Analysing Skill in Amnesia: Dissociation of Knowing How and Knowing That." *Science*, 210(4466) (1980): 207–210. doi:10.1126/science.7414331.

Cole, M. W., A. Bagic, R. Kass, and W. Schneider. "Prefrontal Dynamics Underlying Rapid Instructed Task Learning Reverse with Practice." *The Journal of Neuroscience* 30(42), (2010): 14245–14254. doi:10.1523/JNEUROSCI.1662-10. 2010.

Colman, W. "The Self." In R. K. Papadopoulos (ed.) *The Handbook of Jungian Psychology—Theory, Practice and Applications.* Sussex, UK: Routledge, 2006.

Coulthard, E. J., P. Nachev, and M. Husain. "Control Over Conflict During Movement Preparation: Role of Posterior Parietal Cortex." *Neuron* 58(1) (2008): 144–157. doi:10.1016/j.neuron.2008.02.009.

Cowan, N. "Sensory and Immediate Memory." In W. Banks (ed.), *Encyclopaedia of Consciousness.* New York: Academic Press, 2009.

Cowan, N., C. Izawa, and N. Ohta. "Working-Memory Capacity Limits in a Theoretical Context. Human Learning and Memory: Advances in Theory and Application." The 4th Tsukuba International Conference on Memory. Mahwah: Lawrence Erlbaum Associates, Publishers, 2005. doi:10.4324/9780203342398.

Curran, T. "Implicit Learning Revealed by the Method of Opposition." *Trends in Cognitive Sciences* 5(12) (2001): 503–504. doi:10.1016/S1364-6613(00)01791-5.

Dabrowski, K. (with A. Kawczak and M. M. Piechowski). *Mental Growth through Positive Disintegration*. London: Gryf Publications, 1970.

———. *Psychoneuroses Is Not an Illness*. London: Gryf Publications, 1972.

———. *Theory of Levels of Emotional Development (vol. 1)—Multilevelness and Positive Disintegration*. New York: Dabor Science Publications, 1977.

Damasio, A. *Descartes Error: Emotion, Reason, and the Human Brain*. London: Penguin Books, 2005.

Daniels, S., and M. M. Piechowski. *Living with Intensity: Understanding the Sensitivity, Excitability, and the Emotional Development of Gifted Children, Adolescents, and Adults*. Scottsdale, AZ: Great Potential, 2008.

den Ouden, H. E., K. J. Friston, N. D. Daw, A. R. McIntosh, and K. E. Stephan. "A Dual Role for Prediction Error in Associative Learning. *Cerebral Cortex* 19(5) (2009): 1175–1185.

Dewey, J. *Democracy and Education—An Introduction to the Philosophy of Education*. New York, USA: Macmillan Company, 1957.

———. *Experience and Education*. New York: Collier Books, 1963.

Diamond, M. C. "The Brain—Use it or Lose It." *New Horizons for Learning*: School of Education, Johns Hopkins University (1996). Retrieved from http://education.jhu.edu/newhorizons/Neurosciences/articles/.

———. (2000) "My Search for Love and Wisdom in the Brain." *New Horizons for Learning:* School of Education, Johns Hopkins University (2000). Retrieved from http://education.jhu.edu/PD/newhorizons/Neurosciences/articles/.

———. "Response of the Brain to Enrichment." *New Horizons for Learning*: School of Education, Johns Hopkins University (2001). Retrieved from http://education.jhu.edu/newhorizons/Neurosciences/articles/.

Diamond, M., and J. Hopson. *Magic Trees of the Mind: How to Nurture Your Child's Intelligence, Creativity and Healthy Emotions from Birth through Adolescence*. New York: Dutton, 1998.

Dudai, Y. "The Neurobiology of Consolidations, or How Stable Is the Engram?" *Annual Review of Psychology*, 55 (2004): 51–86. doi:10.1146/annurev.psych.55.090902.142050.

Edelman, G. M. *The Remembered Present: A Biological Theory of Consciousness*. New York: Basic Books Inc., 1989.

———. "Neural Darwinism: Selection and Re-entrant Signalling in Higher Brain Function." *Neuron* 10(2) (1993): 115–125. doi:10.1016/0896-6273(93)90304-A.

———. *Wider than the Sky: The Phenomenal Gift of Consciousness*. New Haven, CT: Yale University Press, 2005.

————. *Second Nature: Brain Science and Human Knowledge*. New Haven, CT: Yale University Press, 2007.

Edelman, G. M., and V. B. Mountcastle. *The Mindful Brain: Cortical Organisation and the Group-Selective Theory of Higher Brain Function*. Oxford: MIT Press, 1978.

Edelman, G. M., and G. Tononi. *A Universe of Consciousness: How Matter Becomes Imagination*. New York: Basic Books Inc., 2001.

Eide, B., and F. Eide. "Brains on Fire: The Multimodality of Gifted Thinkers." *New Horizons for Learning*: School of Education, Johns Hopkins University (2004). Retrieved from http://education.jhu.edu/PD/newhorizons/Neurosciences/articles/.

Ellsworth, J. A. "Adolescence and Gifted: Addressing Existential Dread. Supporting Emotional Needs of the Gifted (SENG)." (2012). Retrieved from http://www.sengifted.org/archives/articles/adolescence-and-gifted-addressing-existential-dread.

Entwistle, N. J. "Approaches to Learning and Forms of Understanding." In B. Dart and G. Boulton-Lewis (eds.), *Teaching and Learning in Higher Education*. Melbourne, Australia: Australian Council for Educational Research, 1998.

Feigenson, L., and J. Halberda. "Infants Chunk Object Arrays into Sets of Individuals." *Cognition*, 91 (2004): 173–190. doi:10.1016/j.cognition.2003.09.003.

Fink, A., M. Benedek, R. H. Grabner, B. Staudt, and A. C. Neubauer. "Creativity Meets Neuroscience: Experimental Tasks for the Neuroscientific Study of Creative Thinking." *Methods* 42, (2007): 68–76. doi:10.1016/j.ymeth.2006.12.001.

Fletcher, P. C., C. D. Frith, P. M. Grasby, T. Shallice, R. S. Frackowiak, and R. J. Dolan. "Brain Systems for Encoding and Retrieval of Auditory-Verbal Memory. An In Vivo Study in Humans." *Brain*, 118(Pt 2) (1995): 401–416. doi:10.1093/brain/118.2.401.

Fredrickson, B. L., and C. Branigan. Positive Emotions Broaden the Scope of Attention and Thought—Action Repertoires." *Cognition and Emotion*, 19 (2005): 313–332. doi:10.1080/02699930441000238.

Friederici, A. D. "Towards a Neural Basis of Auditory Sentence Processing." *Trends in Cognitive Sciences*, 6 (2002): 78–84.

Frith, C. D., and U. Frith. "Interacting Minds—A Biological Basis." *Science* 286(5445) (1999): 1692–1695. doi:10.1126/science.286.5445.1692.

Fuster, J. M. "Network Memory." *Trends in Neurosciences* 20(10) (1997): 451–459. doi:10.1016/S0166-2236(97)01128-4.

Gardner, H. *Multiple Intelligences: New Horizons*. New York: Basic Books, 2006.

Gates, N. *A Brain for Life: How to Optimise Your Brain's Health by Making Simple Lifestyle Changes Now*. Sydney, Australia: HarperCollins Publishers, 2016.

Gazzaniga, M. S. *The Mind's Past*. Berkeley: University of California Press, 1998a.

———. "The Split Brain Revisited." *Scientific American* 279 (1998b): 48–55. doi:10.1038/scientificamerican0798-50.

Gazzaniga, M. S., R. B. Ivry, and G. R. Mangun. *Cognitive Neuroscience: The Biology of the Mind* (2nd ed.). New York: Norton, 2002.

Geschwind, N. "Specialisations of the Human Brain." *Scientific American* 241(3) (1979): 180–199. doi:10.1038/scientificamerican0979-180.

Goldberg, E. *The Executive Brain: Frontal Lobes and the Civilised Mind* (Vol. XIX). New York: Oxford University Press, 2001.

Goleman, D. *Emotional Intelligence*. New York: Bantam Books, 2005.

Hatakenaka, M., I. Miyai, M. Mihara, S. Sakoda, and K. Kubota. "Frontal Regions Involved in Learning of Motor Skill—A Functional NIRS Study." *Neuroimage* 34 (2007): 109–116.

Harmon, P. *Business Process Change: A Business Process Management Guide for Managers and Process Professionals.* Burlington, MA, USA: Morgan Kaufmann-Elsevier, 2014.

Hauke, C. "The Unconscious—Personal and Collective." In R. K. Papadopoulos (ed.) *The Handbook of Jungian Psychology—Theory, Practice and Applications.* Sussex, UK: Routledge, 2006.

Hawkins, J., and S. Blakeslee. *On Intelligence.* New York: Times Books, 2004.

Hebb, D. O. *The Organisation of Behaviour: A Neuropsychological Theory.* Oxford, UK: Wiley, 1949.

Heilman, K. M., S. E. Nadeau, and D. O. Beversdorf. "Creative Innovation: Possible Brain Mechanisms." *Neurocase*, 9, (2003): 369–379. doi:10.1076/neur.9.5.369.16553.

Hickok, G. and D. Poeppel. "Opinion—The Cortical Organisation of Speech Processing." *Nature Reviews Neuroscience*, 8 (2007): 393–402.

Hobson, J. A., and R. Stickgold. "Sleep. Sleep the Beloved Teacher?" *Current Biology* 5(1), (1995): 35–36. doi:10.1016/S0960-9822(95)00011-X.

Houston, J. "Vision of the Future." *New Horizons for Learning*, School of Education, Johns Hopkins University (1999). Retrieved from http://education.jhu.edu/PD/newhorizons/Neurosciences/articles/.

———. "Social Artistry." *New Horizons for Learning*: School of Education, Johns Hopkins University (2004). Retrieved from http://education.jhu.edu/PD/newhorizons/Neurosciences/articles/.

Hunter, M. *Mastery Teaching.* Thousand Oaks, CA: Corwin, 2004.

Huttenlocher, P. R. "Synaptogenesis, Synapse Elimination, and Neural Plasticity in Human Cerebral Cortex: Threats to Optimal Development." In C. A. Nelson (ed.), *The Minnesota Symposia on Child Psychology*, 27. Hillsdale, NJ: Lawrence Erlbaum Associates, 1994.

Huttenlocher, P. R., C. De Courten, L. J. Garey, and H. Van der Loos. "Synaptic Development in Human Cerebral Cortex." *International Journal of Neurology* 16–17, (1982): 144–154.

Ingvar, D. H. "Memory of the Future: An Essay on the Temporal Organisation of Conscious Awareness." *Human Neurobiology* 4(3) (1985): 127–136.

Jackson, P. S. "Bright Star—Black Sky: A Phenomenological Study of Depression as a Window into the Psyche of the Gifted Adolescent." *Supporting Emotional Needs of the Gifted (SENG)*. Retrieved from http://www.sengifted.org/archives/articles/bright-star-black-sky-a-phenomenological-study-of-depression-as-a-window-into-the-psyche-of-the-gifted-adolescent, (1997).

Jackson, P. S., and J. Peterson. "Depressive Disorders in Highly Gifted Adolescents." *Supporting Emotional Needs of the Gifted (SENG).* Retrieved from http://www.sengifted.org/archives/articles/depressiv e-disorder-in-highly-gifted-adolescents, (2004).

James, W. *The Principles of Psychology* (Vol. I). New York: Henry Holt and Co., Inc., 1890. doi:10.1037/11059-000.

Jausovec, N., and K. Jausovec. "EEG Activity During the Performance of Complex Mental Problems." *International Journal of Psychophysiology,* 36 (2000): 73–88. doi:10.1016/S0167-8760(99)00113-0.

Kelly, A. M. C., R. Hester, J. J. Foxe, M. Shpaner, and H. Garavan. "Flexible Cognitive Control: Effects of Individual Differences and Brief Practice on a Complex Cognitive Task." *Neuroimage* 31 (2006): 866–886. doi:10.1016/j.neuroimage.2006.01.008.

Knoop, H. H. "Wise Creativity and Creative Wisdom." In A. Craft, H. Gardner, and G. Claxton (eds.), *Creativity, Wisdom and Trusteeship: Exploring the Role of Education.* Thousand Oaks, CA: Corwin, 2008.

Knowlton, B. J., J. A. Mangels, and L. R. Squire. "A Neostriatal Habit Learning System in Humans." *Science* 273(5280) (1996): 1399–1402. doi:10.1126/science.273.5280.1399.

Koch, C. "A Neural Correlates of Consciousness?" *Current Biology* 6(5) (1996): 492. doi:10.1016/S0960-9822(02)00519-5.

Koch, C., and G. Tononi. "Can Machines Be Conscious?" *IEEE Spectrum* 45(6) (2008): 55–59. doi:10.1109/MSPEC.2008.4531463.

Kolb, D. *Experiential Learning: Experience as the Source of Learning and Development.* Upper Saddle River, NJ: Prentice Hall, 1983.

Kuhlmann, S., C. Kirschbaum, and O. T. Woolf. "Effects of Oral Cortisol Treatment in Healthy Young Women on Memory Retrieval of Negative and Neutral Words." *Neurobiology of Learning and Memory* 83 (2005): 158–162. doi:10.1016/j.nlm.2004.09.001.

Kuhn, T. S. *The Structure of Scientific Revolutions.* Chicago: University of Chicago Press, 1962.

Langer, E. J., and L. G. Imber. "When Practice Makes Imperfect: Debilitating Effects of Overlearning." *Journal of Personality and Social Psychology* 37(11) (1979): 2014–2024. doi:10.1037/0022-3514.37.11.2014.

Larkin, K. "What to Say if Your Child Asks, 'What's the Point of Maths?'" *The Conversation*, Australia (2016). Retrieved from https://theconversation.com/what-to-say-if-your-child-asks-whats-the-point-of-maths-69628.

LeDoux, J. E. *The Emotional Brain.* New York: Simon and Schuster, 1996.

Lees, G. V., E. G. Jones, and E. R. Kandel. "Expressive Genes Record Memories." *Neurobiology of Disease* 7(5) (2000): 533–536. doi:10.1006/nbdi.2000.0348.

Limb, C. J., and A. R. Braun. "Neural Substrates of Spontaneous Musical Performance: An fMRI Study of Jazz Improvisation." *PLoS ONE*, 3(2) (2008): e1679.

Logothetis, N. K. "Single Units and Conscious Vision." *Philosophical Transactions of the Royal Society of London. Series B, Biological Sciences* 353(1377) (1998): 1801–1818. doi:10.1098/rstb.1998.0333.

Lovecky, D. V. "Identity Development in Gifted Children: Moral Sensitivity." *Supporting Emotional Needs of the Gifted (SENG).* Retrieved from http://

www.sengifted.org/archives/articles/identity-development-in-gifted-children-moral-sensitivity, 1997.

Luria, A. R. *Higher Cortical Functions in Man* (translated by B. Haigh). London: Tavistock, 1966.

———. *The Neuropsychology of Memory* (translated by Haigh). Oxford, UK: V. H. Winston and Sons, 1976.

MacLean, P. D. "The Brain in Relation to Empathy and Medical Education." *Journal of Nervous and Mental Disease* 144(5), (1967): 374–382. doi:10.1097/00005053-196705000-00005.

Maquire, E. A., C. D. Frith, and R. G. M. Morris. "The Functional Neuroanatomy of Comprehension and Memory: The Importance of Prior Knowledge." *Brain* 122 (1999): 1839–1850. doi:10.1093/brain/122.10.1839.

Maslow, A. *Toward a Psychology of Being.* New York: Van Nostrand Reinhold, 1968.

———. *Farther Reaches of Human Nature.* New York: Arkana, 1993.

McGaugh, J. L. "Memory—A Century of Consolidation." *Science* 287(5451) (2000): 248–251. doi:10.1126/science.287.5451.248.

Mestre, J. *Transfer of Learning: Issues and Research Agenda.* Arlington, VA: National Science Foundation, 2002.

Metcalfe, J. "Feeling of Knowing in Memory and Problem Solving." *Journal of Experimental Psychology. Learning, Memory, and Cognition* 12(2) (1986): 288–294. doi:10.1037/0278-7393.12.2.288.

Metcalfe, J., N. Kornell, and L. K. Son. "A Cognitive-Science Based Programme to Study Efficacy in a High- and Low-Risk Setting." *European Journal of Cognitive Psychology* 19 (2007): 743–768. doi:10.1080/09541440701326063.

Mihov, K. M., M. Denzler, and J. Forster. "Hemispheric Specialisation and Creative Thinking: A Meta Analytic Review of Lateralisation of Creativity." *Brain and Cognition* 72(3) (2010): 442–448. doi:10.1016/j.bandc. 2009.12.007.

Moore, K. D. *Effective Instructional Strategies: From Theory to Practice.* Thousand Oaks, CA: Sage, 2005.

Moyle, V. F. "Authentic Character Development—Beyond Nature and Nurture." *Supporting Emotional Needs of the Gifted (SENG).* Retrieved from http://www.sengifted.org/archives/articles/authentic-character-development- percentE2 percent80 percent93-beyond-nature-and-nurture, 2005.

Nauta, W. J. "Neural Association of the Frontal Cortex." *Acta Neurobiologiae Experimentalis* (Wars) 32(2) (1972): 125–140.

Neubauer, A. C., R. H. Grabner, H. H. Freudenthaler, J. F. Beckmann, and J. Guthke. "Intelligence and Individual Differences in Becoming Neutrally Efficient." *Acta Psychologica*, 116 (2004): 55–74.

Palmer, S. E. "Colour, Consciousness, and Isomorphism Constraint. Discussion 944–989." *The Behavioural and Brain Sciences*, 22(6) (1999): 923–943. doi:10.1017/S0140525X99002216.

Panksepp, J. *Affective Neuroscience: The Foundations of Human and Animal Emotions.* New York: Oxford University Press, 1998.

Parsons, L. M., and D. Osherson. "New Evidence for Distinct Right and Left Brain Systems for Deductive versus Probabilistic Reasoning." *Cerebral Cortex* 11 (2001): 954–965. doi:10.1093/cercor/11.10.954.

Paul, R., and L. Elder, L. *Critical Thinking: Tools for Taking Charge of Your Learning and Your Life.* Upper Saddle River, NJ: Pearson Education, 2000.

Penfield, W., and B. Milner. "Memory Deficit Produced by Bilateral Lesions in the Hippocampal Zone." *AMA Archives of Neurology and Psychiatry* 79(5)(1958): 475–497. doi:10.1001/archneurpsyc.1958.02340050003001.

Penhune, V. B., and J. Doyon. "Cerebellum and M1 Interaction During Early Learning of Timed Motor Sequences." *Neuroimage* 26 (2005): 801–812.

Perkins, D., and G. Salomon. "Teaching for Transfer." *Educational Leadership* 46 (1988): 22–32.

Peretz, I., and R. J. Zatorre. "Brain Organisation for Music Processing." *Annual Review of Psychology* 56 (2005): 89–114.

Phelps, E. A., and J. E. LeDoux. "Contributions of the Amygdale to Emotion Processing: From Animal Models to Human Behaviour." *Neuron* 48(2) (2005): 175–187. doi:10.1016/j.neuron.2005.09.025.

Piechowski, M. M. *Mellow Out, They Say. If I Only Could: Intensities and Sensitivities of the Young and Bright.* Madison, WI: Yunasa Books, 2006.

Piirto, J. *Understanding Creativity.* Scottsdale, AZ: Great Potential, 2004.

Poppenk, J., S. Kohler, and M. Moscovitch. "Revisiting the Novelty Effect: When Familiarity, Not Novelty, Enhances Memory. *Journal of Experimental Psychology: Learning, Memory and Cognition* 36 (2010): 1321–1330. doi:10.1037/a0019900.

Press, D. Z., M. D. Casement, A. Pascual-Leone, and E. M. Robertson. "The Time Course of Off-Line Motor Sequence Learning." *Cognitive Brain Research* 25 (2005): 375–378.

Raaijmakers, J. G., and R. M. Shiffrin. "Models for Recall and Recognition." *Annual Review of Psychology* 43 (1992): 205–234. doi:10.1146/annurev. ps.43.020192.001225.

Restak, R. M. *The New Brain: How the Modern Age Is Rewiring Your Mind.* New York: Rodale, 2003.

Rittle-Johnson, B., and A. O. Kmicikewycz. "When Generating Answers Benefits Arithmetic Skill: The Importance of Prior Knowledge." *Journal of Experimental Child Psychology*, 101 (2008): 75–81. doi:10.1016/j. jecp.2008.03.001.

Roediger, H. L., and K. B. McDermott. "Implicit Memory in Normal Human Subjects." *Handbook Neuropsychology*, 8 (1993): 63–131.

Rowe, M. B. "Wait-Time and Rewards as Instructional Variables: Their Influence on Language, Logic and Fate Control." *Journal of Research on Science Teaching* 2 (1974): 81–94. doi:10.1002/tea.3660110202.

Rozin, P. "The Evolution of Intelligence and Access to the Cognitive Unconscious." *Progress in Psychobiology and Physiological Psychology* 6 (1976): 245–280.

Ryle, G. *The Concept of Mind.* London: Hutchinson, 1949.

Schmarzo, B. *Big Data: Understanding How Data Powers Big Business.* Indianapolis, IN: Wiley, 2013.

Schneider, W. "Automaticity and Consciousness." In W. Banks (ed.), *Encyclopaedia of Consciousness* (1st ed.). Amsterdam: Academic Press, 2009. doi:10.1016/B978-012373873-8.00009-8.

Scholz, J., M. C. Klein, T. E. J. Behrens, and H. Johansen-Berg. "Training Induces Changes in White Matter Architecture." *Nature Neuroscience* 12 (2009): 1370–1371.

Seabrook, R., G. D. A. Brown, and J. E. Solity. "Distributed and Massed Practice: From Laboratory to Classroom." *Applied Cognitive Psychology* 19 (2005): 107–122. doi:10.1002/acp.1066.

Seitz, A., and T. Watanabe. "A Unified Model for Perceptual Learning." *Trends in Cognitive Science* 9(7) (2005): 329–334. doi:10.1016/j.tics.2005.05.010.

Semenza, C., M. Delazer, L. Bertella, A. Grana, I. Mori, F. M. Conti, and A. Mauro. "Is Math Lateralised on the Same Side as Language? Right Hemisphere Aphasia and Mathematical Abilities." *Neuroscience Letters* 406 (2006): 285–288. doi:10.1016/j.neulet.2006.07.063.

Shaw, P., D. Greenstein, and J. Lerch et al. "Intellectual Ability and Cortical Development in Children and Adolescents." *Nature* 440(7084) (2006): 676–679.

Shiffrin, R. M., and W. Schneider. "Controlled and Automatic Human Information Processing: II. Perceptual Learning, Automatic Attending and a General Theory." *Psychological Review* 84(2) (1977): 127. doi:10.1037/0033-295X.84.2.127.

Silverman, L. K. "Personality and Learning Styles of Gifted Children." In Van Tassel-Baska (ed.), *Excellence in Educating Gifted and Talented Learners* (3rd ed.). Denver, CO: Love Publishing Company, 1998.

———. *Upside-Down Brilliance: The Visual-Spatial Learner.* Denver, CO: DeLeon Publishing, 2002.

———. "The Moral Sensitivity of Gifted Children and the Evolution of Society." *Supporting Emotional Needs of the Gifted (SENG).* Retrieved from http://www.sengifted.org/archives/articles/the-moral-sensitivity-of-gifted-children-and-the-evolution-of-society, 2012.

Simonton, D. "Creative Wisdom." In A. Craft, H. Gardner, and G. Claxton (eds.), *Creativity, Wisdom and Trusteeship: Exploring the Role of Education.* Thousand Oaks, CA: Corwin, 2008.

Smyre, R. "On Searching for New Genes: A 21st Century DNA for Higher Education." *New Horizons for Learning:* School of Education, Johns Hopkins University. Retrieved from http://education.jhu.edu/PD/newhorizons/Neurosciences/articles/, 2006.

Sousa, D. A. *How the Brain Learns* (4th ed.), Thousand Oaks, CA: Corwin, 2011.

Sperry, R. "Brain Bisection and Consciousness." In J. Eccles (ed.), *How the Self Controls Its Brain.* New York: Springer-Verlag, 1966.

Squire, L. R. "Memory Systems of the Brain: A Brief History and Current Perspective." *Neurobiology of Learning and Memory 82* (2004): 171–177. doi:10.1016/j.nlm.2004.06.005.

———. "Memory and Brain Systems: 1969–2009." *Journal of Neuroscience* 29(41) (2009): 12711–12716. doi:10.1523/JNEUROSCI.3575-09.2009.

Squire, L. R., and E. R. Kandel. *Memory: From Mind to Molecules.* New York: W. H. Freeman, 1999.

Stevens, A. "The Archetypes." In R. K. Papadopoulos (ed.), *The Handbook of Jungian Psychology—Theory, Practice and Applications.* Sussex, UK: Routledge, 2006.

Sweeney, M. S. *Brain: The Complete Mind.* Washington, DC: National Geographic, 2009.

Sylwester, R. "The Downshifting Dilemma: A Commentary and Proposal." *New Horizons for Learning*: School of Education, Johns Hopkins University. Retrieved from http://education.jhu.edu/newhorizons/ Neurosciences/articles/, 1998.

Tolan, S. "Discovering the Gifted Ex-Child." *Supporting Emotional Needs of the Gifted (SENG).* Retrieved from *http://www.sengifted.org/archives/ articles/discovering-the-gifted-ex-child*, 2012.

Tollenaar, M. S., B. M. Elzinga, P. Spinhoven, and W. Everaerd. "Immediate and Prolonged Effects of Cortisol, but Not Propranolol, on Memory Retrieval in Healthy Young Men." *Neurobiology of Learning and Memory* 91 (2009): 23–31. doi:10.1016/j.nlm.2008.08.002.

Tong, F., K. Nakayama, J. T. Vaughan, and N. Kanwisher. "Binocular Rivalry and Visual Awareness in Human Extrastriate Cortex." *Neuron* 21(4) (1998): 753–759. doi:10.1016/S0896-6273(00)80592-9.

Tononi, G. "Consciousness as Integrated Information: A Provisional Manifesto." *Biological Bulletin* 215(3) (2008): 216–242. doi:10.2307/25470707.

Tononi, G., and G. M. Edelman. "Consciousness and Complexity." *Science* 282(5395) (1998): 1846–1851. doi:10.1126/science.282.5395.1846.

Tulving, E. "Episodic and Semantic Memory." In E. Tulving, W. Donaldson, and G. H. Bower (eds.), *Organisation of Memory*. New York: Academic Press, 1972.

———. *Elements of Episodic Memory*. New York: Oxford University Press, 1985.

———. "Episodic Memory: From Mind to Brain." *Annual Review of Psychology* 53 (2002): 1–25. doi:10.1146/annurev.psych.53.100901.135114.

Tytler, R. "Three Ways to Boost Science Performance in Australian Schools." *The Conversation*, Australia. Retrieved from https://the-conversation.com/three-ways-to-boost-science-performance-in-australian-schools-69770, 2016.

Wagner, A. D., D. L. Schacter, M. Rotte, W. Koutstaal, A. Maril, A. M. Dale, and R. L. Buckner. "Building Memories: Remembering and Forgetting of Verbal Experiences as Predicted by Brain Activity." *Science* 281 (1998): 1188–1191. doi:10.1126/science.281.5380.1188.

Walker, C. O., B. A. Greene, and R. A. Mansell. "Identification with Academics, Intrinsic/Extrinsic Motivation and Efficacy as Predictors of Cognitive Engagement." *Learning and Individual Differences* 16(1) (2006): 1–12. doi:10.1016/j.lindif.2005.06.004.

Walker, M. P., R. Stickgold, D. Alsop, N. Gaab, and G. Schlaug. "Sleep-Dependent Motor Memory Plasticity in the Human Brain." *Neuroscience* 133 (2005): 911–917.

Watagodakumbura, C. *Education from a Deeper and Multidisciplinary Perspective—To a Sustainable Development of a Neurodiverse Society—A Futuristic View*. Bloomington, IN, USA: Xlibris, 2013.

————. "Authentic Education, the Deeper and Multidisciplinary Perspective of Education, from the Viewpoint of Analytical Psychology." In *World Journal of Education, SCIEDU Press, Canada* 4(3) (2014) 19–28. Retrieved from http://www.sciedu.ca/journal/index. php/wje/article/view/4578, 2014a.

————. "Improvements to Student Learning through Multidisciplinary Perspectives Reviewed from the Dimensions of Analytical Psychology." *International Journal of Education.* Macrothink Institute 6(3) (2014) Retrieved from http://www.macrothink.org/journal/index.php/ije/ article/view/5696, 2014b.

Webb, J. T. (with E. R. Amend, N. E. Webb, J. Goerss, P. Beljan, and F. R. Olenchak). *Misdiagnosis and Dual Diagnoses of Gifted Children and Adults: ADHD, Bipolar, Ocd, Asperger's, Depression, and Other Disorders.* Tucson, AZ, USA: Great Potential Press, 2005.

————. "Dabrowski's Theory and Existential Depression in Gifted Children and Adults." Paper presented at the Eighth International Congress of the Institute for Positive Disintegration in Human Development, August 7–9, 2008, Canmore, Alberta, Canada.

Wigfield, A., and J. S. Eccles. "Students' Motivation During the Middle School Years." In J. Aronson (ed.), *Improving Academic Development: Impact of Psychological Factors in Education.* New York: Baywood, 2002. doi:10.1016/B978-012064455-1/50011-7.

Yero, J. "How Teacher Thinking Shapes Education." *New Horizons for Learning:* School of Education, Johns Hopkins University. Retrieved from *http://education.jhu.edu/PD/newhorizons/Neurosciences/articles/,* 2002.

Yzerbyt, V. Y., G. Lories, and B. Dardenne (eds.). *Metacognition: Cognitive and Social Dimensions.* Thousand Oaks, CA: Sage Publications, 1998. doi:10.4135/9781446279212.

Zenasni, F., and T. Lubart. "Pleasantness of Creative Tasks and Creative Performance." *Thinking Skills and Creativity* 6 (2011): 49–56. doi:10.1016/j.tsc. 2010.10.005.

Zull, J. E. *The Art of Changing the Brain: Enriching the Practice of Teaching by Exploring the Biology of Learning.* Sterling, Virginia, USA: Stylus Publishing, 2002.

———. *From Brain to Mind: Using Neuroscience to Guide Change in Education.* Sterling, Virginia, USA: Stylus Publishing, 2011.

INDEX

• • •

a, A

alcohol	alcohol use	21
Alzheimer's disease		200
ambiguous	ambiguous conditions	166, 168
ambiguous	ambiguous contents	195
ambiguous	ambiguous situations	70, 72, 74, 164, 166, 167, 168
ambiguous		70, 72, 74, 164, 166, 167, 168, 195
amygdala		9, 22, 36, 85, 86, 87
analytical processing		106,
analytical psychology		126, 127, 128, 132, 134, 232
anterior cingulate cortex		10, 42, 46, 211
anxiety	harmful anxiety	65, 152, 154
anxiety	helpful anxiety	31, 153
anxiety		31, 64, 65, 152, 153, 154, 185
asking questions		34, 51, 76, 139, 156, 158
assessment	coverage of assessment	179
assessment	timed assessment	179, 182

assessment	types of assessment	178
assessment	validity of assessment	155, 165
assessment		20, 21, 34, 60, 63, 66, 69, 109, 110, 112, 114, 153, 155, 156, 159, 160, 161, 162, 163, 165, 168, 169, 170, 171, 175, 178, 179, 188, 191
assessments		28, 35, 60, 67, 68, 98, 112, 119, 155, 158, 159, 160, 162, 163, 164, 167, 168, 169, 177, 178, 179, 182, 195
associative recall		25, 34, 35, 47, 68, 155, 156, 165, 170
attention	divided attention	38, 63, 152, 153, 211
attention	scope of attention	65, 219
attention	selective attention	37, 38
attention		3, 8, 9, 11, 19, 22, 25, 29, 30, 31, 33, 37, 38, 40, 45, 46, 51, 53, 62, 63, 65, 66, 76, 92, 103, 131, 134, 139, 142, 144, 149, 151, 152, 153, 154, 174, 181, 184, 186, 191, 200, 202, 204, 207, 211, 219
auditory cortex		6, 103
auditory-sequential		18, 82, 94, 95, 102, 103, 104, 107, 118, 129, 133, 142, 186, 187, 208
automaticity		19, 20, 25, 26, 29, 32, 33, 45, 47, 74, 75, 83, 157, 167, 180, 204, 228
axon		14, 15

b, B

basal ganglia		8, 18
basic needs		22, 122, 123, 124, 189
big data		206, 207, 228
binocular rivalry		38, 62, 152, 191, 230
Bloom's Taxonomy	analyse	105, 106, 109
Bloom's Taxonomy	apply	105, 106
Bloom's Taxonomy	complexity levels	111, 106
Bloom's Taxonomy	create	105, 106, 112, 157, 158, 178, 198
Bloom's Taxonomy	difficulty levels	111
Bloom's Taxonomy	evaluate	105, 106, 157, 158, 159, 178, 198
Bloom's Taxonomy	remember	105, 106
Bloom's Taxonomy	understand	105
Bloom's Taxonomy		89, 90, 93, 95, 96, 104, 105, 106,107, 108, 109, 110, 111, 112, 113, 115, 141, 142, 143, 146, 157, 158, 159, 176, 178, 198, 211
brain	brain damaging	85, 208
brain	brain lateralisation	11, 15, 80, 106
brain	brain localisation	11
brain	brain specialisation	11, 94
Broca's area		6
Brodmann areas		6
business processes		209, 220

c, C

career path		70, 129, 172, 201, 202, 203
cerebellum		6, 7, 8, 18, 19, 226
cerebral cortex		86, 121, 216, 221, 226

cerebral hemispheres		3,4, 12, 14, 23, 54, 118, 209
cerebral lateralisation		11, 94
cerebral specialisation		11
challenging content		149, 184
chunking		52, 53, 140, 154
civilisation		7, 8, 74, 97, 146, 166, 169
clarity		31, 45, 56, 59, 64, 130, 140, 144, 149, 150, 177, 185, 192, 195
cognitive	cognitive resources	19, 20, 23, 26, 27, 37
cognitive		4, 5, 7, 8, 9, 10, 17, 19, 20, 23, 26, 27, 36, 37, 38, 39, 41, 42, 43, 44, 45, 47, 58, 77, 84, 94, 101, 107, 119, 121, 124, 128, 190, 197, 205, 211, 212, 213, 214, 215, 216, 219, 222, 225, 227, 228, 231, 233
competition		102
computers		15, 20, 21, 37, 41, 70, 71, 73, 74, 75, 76, 84, 112, 131, 146, 163, 164, 188, 207
concepts	abstract concepts	12, 28, 40, 51, 56, 62, 67, 75, 143, 145, 159, 160, 165, 168, 169, 173, 180, 186, 192
concepts	high-level concepts	27, 52, 62, 67, 68, 118, 119, 139, 140, 141, 143, 144, 145, 153, 154, 159,

		160, 172, 174, 176, 177,
		181, 186, 192, 193,
conscious		17, 19, 26, 27, 29, 30, 31,
		32, 33, 35, 38, 40, 41,
		42, 68, 126, 127, 128,
		132, 134, 139, 142, 146,
		173, 188, 195, 197, 200,
		205, 212, 221, 223
consciousness		6,9, 25, 27, 32, 33, 39,
		40, 41, 42, 43, 44, 45,
		46, 47, 53, 60, 63, 64,
		67, 72, 76, 78, 79, 81,
		82, 83, 84, 86, 87, 88,
		90, 91, 94, 97, 101, 104,
		108, 109, 111, 112, 113,
		116, 117, 119, 120, 121,
		123, 126, 127, 128, 129.
		134, 142, 149, 150, 155,
		157, 168, 169, 170, 172,
		189, 195, 197, 198, 199,
		202, 204, 205, 206, 207,
		209, 212, 215, 217, 218,
		222, 225, 228, 229, 230
constructivism		54, 143, 162, 170
constructivist theory		69, 95, 99, 110, 114, 161,
of learning		192
continuous improvement		197, 205
corpus callosum		14
cortical control		19
cortisol		65, 86, 151, 223, 230
creativity	'little c' creativity	89, 91
creativity	Big C' creativity	89
creativity		4, 14, 15, 35, 39, 75, 77,

		88, 89, 90, 91, 92, 93,
		94, 97, 100, 101, 107,
		108, 117, 131, 158, 169,
		199, 209, 215, 217, 218,
		222, 225, 226, 229, 233
curriculum	curriculum construction	171, 173
curriculum		13,34, 35, 59, 162, 171,
		172, 173, 174, 175, 176,
		178, 179, 180, 181,182,
		188, 214

d, D

Dabrowski		79, 91, 100, 101, 120,
		121, 122, 123, 126, 128,
		133, 134, 163, 187, 213,
		216, 232
decision making	adaptive decision making	69, 74, 155, 157, 164,
		167, 169, 178, 187, 188
decision making	veridical decision-making	69, 73, 76, 155, 157, 158,
		164, 165, 166, 170, 178,
		187, 188
decision making		8, 42, 51, 69, 71, 72, 73,
		74, 75, 76, 85, 101, 116,
		117, 118, 119, 135, 155,
		157, 158, 164, 165, 166
		167, 169, 170, 178, 187, 188
deductive reasoning		106
dementia		200
dendrites		14, 15, 16, 20, 73
developmental psychology		120
Dewey		34, 132, 204, 216
dialectic		61, 100
didactic		61

disciplinary boundaries199, 203

disciplinary domains28

disengagement64, 65, 72, 142, 157

e, E

economic development91, 189, 195, 201, 203

educational neuroscience51, 77, 95, 108, 114, 116, 139, 145, 148, 149, 151, 155, 171, 183, 196, 197, 208

emotional brain4, 9, 36, 85, 223

emotional setbacks100, 103, 201, 204

emotions negative emotions62, 86, 151

emotions positive emotions44, 65, 84, 86, 94, 144, 151, 219

emotions4, 5, 9, 11, 12, 22, 23, 25, 35, 38, 39, 44, 47, 62, 65, 74, 77, 84, 85, 86, 87, 88, 93, 94, 100, 101, 104, 119, 121, 127, 144, 151, 205, 209, 208, 217, 219, 225

empathy44, 87, 88, 94, 121, 203, 206, 207, 224

employment120, 123, 124, 183, 185, 201, 203, 206

endorphins65, 86, 151

executive control8, 32, 33, 38, 47, 166

experience in education34

extroversion127

extroverts103

f, F

feeling   27, 35, 40, 46, 65, 86,
                                           87, 88, 124, 127, 128,
                                           151, 224

first person perspective   72, 157

frontal lobes   7, 17, 54, 59, 61, 65, 72,
                                           86, 91, 94, 95, 96, 97,
                                           99, 100, 114, 115, 127,
                                           134, 144, 145, 146, 147,
                                           151, 155, 156, 157, 166,
                                           167, 170, 179, 220

g, G

Gardner   79, 80, 129, 215, 219,
                                           222, 229

generalisations   27, 61, 62, 67

gifted   10, 15, 28, 36, 69, 87,
                                           88, 95, 100, 101, 102,
                                           103, 114, 121, 122, 125,
                                           128, 131, 133, 163, 187,
                                           205, 206, 209, 216, 218,
                                           221, 222, 223, 224, 225,
                                           229, 230, 232

global workspace theory   41

goals of education   75, 116, 134

grey matter   14, 83

h, H

healthy lifestyle   197, 202

healthy society   125, 126

Hebb   36, 81, 220

hierarchical needs   23

hierarchical response   22

higher order responses   61

higher-order processing   6, 87, 93, 146

hippocampus   8, 9, 36, 87

holistic   5, 12, 11, 44, 45, 47, 81, 82, 86, 94, 104, 118, 129, 133, 197, 201, 202, 209

human development   3, 20, 21, 25, 40, 44, 45, 63, 71, 79, 81, 82, 88, 91, 94, 104, 111, 113, 114, 115, 116, 119, 121, 122, 123, 124, 126, 128, 129, 132, 134, 135, 142, 150, 155, 168, 169, 170, 172, 175, 178, 179, 180, 181, 183, 185, 184, 186, 189, 195, 197, 201, 202, 203, 204, 205, 206, 208, 209, 210, 232

human evolution   3, 8, 9, 47, 134, 169

human potential   120, 210

humble   208

hypothalamus   9

i, I

idealistic   101

idiosyncratic   58, 108, 125, 157, 199

incidental learning   33, 35, 51, 68, 69, 101, 163, 163, 170, 204

incidental education   34

inclusive   69, 162, 163, 206

individualised   23, 35, 60, 98, 125, 133, 134, 142, 143,156, 157, 162, 165, 166, 167, 170

individuation		126, 128, 132
inductive reasoning		106
inference		12, 14, 57, 58, 68, 94, 103, 108, 109, 112, 157, 169, 179, 191, 195, 207
inhibition		92, 94, 143, 150
instructionist		20, 37, 73, 76, 131, 163
integrated theory of consciousness		40, 41, 81, 117
integrative body-mind training		46
intelligence		39, 44, 77, 78, 79, 81, 82, 83, 88, 93, 94, 100, 101, 114, 129, 208, 217, 219, 220, 225, 227
intelligence quotient		83
intentional education		34, 116, 204
interdisciplinary		204
introversion		127
introverts		103, 186, 187
intuition		89, 127, 128, 214

j, J

Jung		120, 126, 127, 128, 132, 213, 214, 215, 220, 230
Jungian psychology		126, 213, 214, 215, 220, 230

k, K

Kolb's experiential learning cycle	abstract conceptualisation	95, 96, 97, 114, 147, 153, 160
Kolb's experiential learning cycle	active experimentation	95, 98, 114
Kolb's experiential learning cycle	concrete experience	95, 96, 98, 114

| Kolb's experiential learning cycle | reflective observation | 95, 96, 98, 114 |
| Kolb's experiential learning cycle | | 95, 98, 114, 147, 160 |

I, L

leadership		210, 226
learning	explicit learning	30, 69, 116, 129, 131, 134, 161
learning	Hebbian learning	25, 36, 47
learning	higher-order learning	55, 73, 86, 89, 95, 96, 97 102, 104, 105, 107, 109, 110, 112, 113, 115, 133, 135, 147, 155, 159, 162, 163, 164, 169, 178, 179, 182, 183, 184, 195, 198, 199, 206, 207
learning	implicit learning	30, 33, 35, 68, 102, 116, 132, 146, 161, 162, 163, 170, 213, 215, 216
learning	incidental learning	25, 35, 51, 68, 69, 101, 162, 204
learning	learning theories	95, 99, 114
learning	lifelong learning	20, 33, 37, 44, 47, 115, 120, 123, 129, 143, 170, 183, 185, 186, 190, 197, 200
learning	lower-order learning	97, 115, 198, 208
learning	phases of learning	30
learning	strategic learning	55, 57, 95, 97, 98, 109, 114, 177
learning	surface learning	97, 98, 99, 114, 195
left hemisphere		6, 11, 12, 13, 14, 80, 82, 142

Leonardo da Vinci		189
limbic system		4, 5, 9, 22, 36, 43, 85, 86, 101

m, M

machines		51, 70, 74, 75, 76, 84, 90, 112, 131, 146, 187, 188, 209, 222
mammalian brain		4, 5
Maslow		23, 78, 91, 120, 122, 123, 124, 125, 126, 134, 202, 203, 224
meditation		45, 46, 203
memory	autobiographical memory	27, 67
memory	declarative memory	26, 27
memory	episodic memory	27, 140, 160, 231
memory	explicit memory	26, 65
memory	immediate memory	17, 58, 215
memory	implicit memory	26, 65, 227
memory	long-term memory	17, 18, 19, 29, 51, 52, 53, 54, 55, 56, 57, 58, 59, 63, 87, 100, 103, 105, 108, 130, 148, 163, 193, 194, 200
memory	memory consolidation	19, 194
memory	nondeclarative memory	26
memory	procedural memory	19, 20, 26, 32
memory	semantic memory	6, 27, 62, 68, 140, 157, 160, 178, 181, 231
memory	short-term memory	9, 17, 29, 36, 53, 55, 57, 58, 59, 68, 98, 99, 103, 105, 109, 119, 147, 162, 177, 178, 193

memory	working memory	7, 17, 18, 28, 29, 46, 51, 52, 53, 54, 57, 58, 59, 63, 67, 75, 130, 140, 148, 149, 152, 176, 177, 212, 213, 214, 216
metacognition		9, 11, 25, 42, 43, 44, 45, 46, 60, 84. 92, 101, 119, 197, 202, 205, 206, 208, 233
metacognitive practices		10, 45, 46, 60, 101, 103, 119, 121, 190, 205
mind		31, 42, 43, 45, 46, 72, 74, 87, 89, 92, 99, 125. 126, 140, 145, 151, 175, 184, 186, 192, 194, 195, 201, 203, 204, 205, 207, 208, 213, 217, 219, 220, 227, 228, 230, 231, 233
mindfulness		45, 46
mirror neurones		88, 94
misdiagnosed		206
motivation	extrinsic motivation	63, 231
motivation	intrinsic motivation	55, 63, 76, 148, 150, 231
motivation		5, 31, 32, 38, 51, 53, 55, 62, 63, 65. 76, 81, 148, 150, 172, 174, 191, 192, 200, 202, 212, 231, 232
motor cortex		6, 78, 88, 95, 96, 97
multidimensional		6, 119, 120, 135, 208
multidimensional perspectives		6, 119, 120
multidisciplinary		231, 232
multiple choice questions		165, 166, 170
multiple disciplines		44, 198

multiple domains		67, 94, 118, 132, 135, 141, 142, 157, 168
multiple intelligence		79, 80, 88, 129, 219
multiple intelligences	bodily-kinaesthetic intelligence	78, 79
multiple intelligences	interpersonal intelligence	79, 88
multiple intelligences	intrapersonal intelligence	79, 208
multiple intelligences	logical-mathematical intelligence	79
multiple intelligences	musical intelligence	79
multiple intelligences	verbal-linguistic intelligence	78, 79
multiple intelligences	visual-spatial intelligence	79

n, N

neocortex		86, 100, 101, 108, 127, 152
neural complexity		41
neural Darwinism		3, 20, 23, 37, 217
neural efficiency		45, 82, 83, 94, 130, 134, 150
neural networks	existing neural networks	54, 55, 66, 70, 72, 99, 110, 113, 140, 161
neural networks		8, 16, 19, 21, 27, 31, 36, 41, 44, 45, 47, 54, 55, 64, 66, 67, 70, 71, 72, 73, 75, 78, 82, 84, 86, 90, 91, 92, 94, 97, 99, 100, 101, 107, 108, 109, 110, 112, 113, 117, 119, 121, 124, 129,130, 131, 132, 134, 140, 141, 144, 146, 150, 153, 161, 163,

		167, 168, 171, 172, 175,
		177, 178, 179, 180, 184,
		188, 189, 190, 195, 197,
		200, 204, 209, 208
neurodiversity		102, 133, 187, 195, 211
neurone		10, 11, 14, 15, 16, 18, 19,
		20, 22, 36, 41, 43, 81,
		83, 88, 94, 161
neuroplasticity		20, 37, 46, 131, 150, 202
neuroscience		1, 25, 34, 37, 38, 45, 46,
		49, 51, 77, 80, 81, 85, 97,
		90, 95, 103, 105, 106,
		108, 111, 114, 116, 117,
		121, 126, 127, 134, 137,
		139, 141, 145, 146, 148,
		149, 151, 155, 160, 161,
		171, 172, 183, 184, 196,
		197, 208, 211, 212, 214,
		215, 217, 218, 219, 220,
		221, 225, 228, 229,
		230,231, 233
novelty-seeking		3, 21, 23, 31, 150, 195,
		198, 200

o, O

one-sided development		82, 202, 203, 206
open-ended questions		68, 69, 110, 153, 157,
		165, 168, 169, 199
open-minded thinking		21, 93
overexcitabilities	emotional overexcitabilities	100, 101, 128, 206
overexcitabilities	imaginational overexcitabilities	100, 101, 206

overexcitabilities	intellectual overexcitabilities	100, 101, 128, 206
overexcitabilities	psychomotor overexcitabilities	100
overexcitabilities	sensual overexcitabilities	100
overexcitabilities		100, 101, 128, 206

p, P

pace of presentation	145, 148
patterns	12, 15, 21, 23, 51, 52, 78, 97, 154
pedagogical practices	32, 110, 111, 137, 139, 155, 171, 198
personality	13, 186, 187, 212, 223, 229
PFC	6, 7, 8, 39, 40, 59, 71, 74
Phineas Gage	85
phonological loop	17, 152
physiological changes	121
prefrontal cortex	6, 18, 39, 59, 71, 74, 96
premeditated	83, 157, 158, 159, 167, 179, 188, 203
priming	21, 26, 36, 68, 69, 130, 132, 165
problem solving	10, 11, 29, 41, 44, 51, 55, 69, 72, 75, 101, 109, 116, 117, 118, 119, 135, 224
protein synthesis	19, 194
psyche	126, 221
psychologists	78, 89, 103, 107
psychoneurotics	187

r, R

real-life		13, 27, 30, 34, 130, 143, 172, 204, 209
recognition test		25, 34, 35, 47, 68, 155, 165
rehearsal	distributed rehearsal	58, 150, 194
rehearsal	elaborate rehearsal	19, 75, 98, 105, 114, 115, 130, 143, 148, 149, 150, 153, 156, 157, 179, 191, 196
rehearsal	initial rehearsal	57, 146, 152
rehearsal	massed rehearsal	58
rehearsal	rote rehearsal	59, 60, 66, 68, 69, 97, 98, 99, 104, 105, 109, 110, 112, 113, 114, 145, 147, 153, 155, 156, 165, 170, 177, 178, 191
rehearsal	secondary rehearsal	57, 58, 60
religious leaders		202, 208
reptilian brain		4
resilience		44, 206
retention		18, 30, 36, 54, 58, 59, 63, 143, 145, 191, 193, 194, 214, 215
retrieval		30, 119, 211, 219, 223, 230
revolutionary		91, 210
right hemisphere		11, 12, 13, 14, 80, 82, 142, 228
robots		10, 35
rote memorisation		60, 61, 63, 93, 103, 133

s, S

satellite organs	8, 18
science education	34, 72, 73, 157, 158, 169
selectionist	20, 37, 73, 76, 94, 131, 163
self-actualisation	23, 44, 91, 94, 104, 115, 123, 124, 125, 126, 129, 134, 184, 189, 195, 197, 202
self-awareness	42, 45, 46, 60, 93, 101, 103, 119, 120, 124, 128, 134, 144, 175, 190, 191
self-expression	92, 94, 143, 198
self-regulation	21, 46, 47, 89, 92, 94, 119, 143, 150, 198
sense and meaning	29, 51, 53, 54, 56, 57, 59, 63, 66, 67, 75, 90, 96, 98, 99, 105, 114, 192
sensing	40, 97, 127, 128
sensory cortex	6, 95
sequencing	13, 106
sequential	11, 12, 18, 73, 82, 94, 95, 103, 104, 107, 112, 113, 118, 127, 129, 133, 142, 146, 186, 187, 208, 209
shadow	128, 129, 132, 214
sick societies	125, 126
somatosensory cortex	6
status quo	124, 189
stigmatised	206
stimuli	11, 12, 21, 31, 35, 36, 38, 66, 87, 103
strategic goal	104, 120, 183, 208, 209

subcortical control		19
subjective answers		158, 166, 167
subjective knowledge		114, 161, 162
subjective response		162, 163
sustainable social development		203
synapses		15, 16, 18, 22, 37
synaptic connections		18, 36, 37, 73, 82
synaptogenesis		37, 221

t, T

teaching-learning		28, 31, 34, 35, 38, 60, 61, 62, 64, 73, 75, 76, 86, 90, 99, 102, 104, 105, 107, 115, 129, 131, 132, 139, 140, 141, 142, 143, 144, 145, 148, 151, 152, 153, 154, 161, 162, 169, 171, 176, 177, 179, 180, 181, 191, 192, 193, 196
temporal cortex		18
thalamus		8
thematic units		56
theory of mind		87, 213
theory of positive disintegration		121, 134, 213
thinking	convergent thinking	93, 107, 110, 141, 147, 151
thinking	critical thinking	65, 109, 151, 226
thinking	divergent thinking	61, 79, 141, 142, 150, 158, 162, 178
thinking	higher-order thinking	107, 109, 141, 147, 158
third person perspective		72, 157
timed tests		158

tolerance		121, 203, 206
TPD		121
transfer	negative transfer	56
transfer	positive transfer	56
transfer	transfer during learning	56, 145
transfer	transfer of learning	56, 114, 115, 118, 119, 130, 133, 149, 158
transfer		30, 51, 53, 55, 56, 57, 58, 66, 76, 97, 105, 114, 115, 118, 119, 130, 133, 141, 145, 148, 149, 158, 161, 172, 178, 224, 226

u, U

unconscious		27, 29, 30, 35, 68, 126, 130, 132, 162, 163, 202, 220, 227

v, V

visual cortex		6
visual-spatial		15, 18, 28, 36, 79, 80, 81, 82, 94, 95, 102, 103, 104, 107, 118, 127, 129, 133, 142, 148, 152, 186, 187, 205, 209, 229
visuospatial sketchpad		17, 152
vulnerable		18, 19, 27, 115, 186, 187, 206

w, W

wait times		51, 61, 76, 139, 147
wellbeing	mental wellbeing	200
Wernicke's area		6, 78

white matter   14, 228
wisdom   6, 20, 27, 63, 76, 79, 82,
                                84, 88, 90, 91, 92, 93,
                                94, 97, 101, 104, 108,
                                111, 112, 113, 117, 120,
                                141, 149, 150, 155, 158,
                                169, 170, 172, 184, 189,
                                195, 197, 198, 199, 202,
                                204, 206, 207, 209, 215,
                                217, 222, 229

www.ingramcontent.com/pod-product-compliance
Lightning Source LLC
Chambersburg PA
CBHW030423290526
45786CB00001B/103